Coffee and Colonialism in Angola, 1820–1960

Coffee and Colonialism in Angola
1820–1960

Jelmer Vos

JAMES CURREY

First published 2025
James Currey

ISBN 978 1 84701 356 9

James Currey
is an imprint of
Boydell & Brewer Ltd
PO Box 9, Woodbridge
Suffolk IP12 3DF (GB)
www.jamescurrey.com
and of
Boydell & Brewer Inc.
668 Mt Hope Avenue
Rochester, NY 14620-2731 (US)
www.boydellandbrewer.com

Our Authorised Representative for product safety in the EU is Easy Access System Europe – Mustamäe tee 50, 10621 Tallinn, Estonia, gpsr.requests@easproject.com

British Library Cataloguing in Publication Data
A CIP record for this book is available from the British Library

Contents

Illustrations

Maps

Plates

Graphs

Full credit details are provided in the captions to the images in the text. The author and publisher are grateful to all the institutions and individuals for permission to reproduce the materials in which they hold copyright. Every effort has been made to trace the copyright holders; apologies are offered for any omission, and the publisher will be pleased to add any necessary acknowledgement in subsequent editions.

Acknowledgements

RESEARCH FOR this monograph was supported by a Leverhulme Research Fellowship (RF-2019-194), a research fellowship at the Biblioteca Nacional de Portugal funded by the Luso-American Development Foundation, a summer research grant from Old Dominion University, and research funding from the University of Glasgow. I thank these institutions for their generosity. Thanks also go to the archivists and librarians in Angola, Portugal, the Netherlands, France, Brazil, the USA, and Great Britain without whom no research would have been possible. I am furthermore indebted to the following people for providing materials, advice, or feedback on parts of the manuscript: Keith Allen, Jeremy Ball, Florentina Bondo, Cláudia Castelo, Oli Charbonneau, William Clarence-Smith, Samuël Coghe, Aaron Davis, Henry Dee, David Eltis, Roquinaldo Ferreira, Helga Johnson, Alex Marshall, Mariana Dias Paes, Esteban Salas, David Thompson, and Christine Whyte. Their help has been invaluable. Aharon deGrassi not only supplied sources, but also designed the maps for the book. A shoutout, finally, to my former colleagues at Old Dominion University, Anna Mirkova, Brett Bebber, Erin Jordan, John Weber, Liz Zanoni, Megan Nutzman, Michael Carhart, Nick Abbott, and Tim Orr, who were there when the project started and read a first exploratory paper.

The same paper was read by the Commodities of Empire international workshop 'Global Commodity Frontiers in Comparative Context'. More developed parts of the manuscript were discussed at the 'Across Colonial Lines' conference at the University of Leeds; the 'Global Coffeescapes' international winter school, University of Pavia; the 'Hidden Economies of Slavery' workshop at the German Historical Institute London; the international conference 'Diversity and Empires' at the University of Leiden; the African Economic History seminar at the University of Cambridge; and the 'Extraction, Sovereignty and Markets' conference at the University of Bern. I am grateful to all participants and discussants for their comments and suggestions. Ideas for chapters were also presented at the 'Marcas do Império' seminar at the Institute of Contemporary History, Nova University, Lisbon; the African History seminar at the University of Lisbon; the Afrikakolloquium at the Humboldt University Berlin; the Economic and Social History seminar at the University of Glasgow; the history research seminar at the University of Lancaster; and the Wilberforce Institute, University of Hull. I thank the organizers for inviting me and the participants for their helpful feedback.

Abbreviations

AEH	*African Economic History*
AHD	Arquivo Histórico Diplomático
AHM	Arquivo Histórico Militar
AHU	Arquivo Histórico Ultramarino
ALA	Angus Library and Archive
ANA	Arquivo Nacional de Angola
BAA	*Boletim de Agricultura da Província de Angola*
BGC	*Boletim da Agência Geral das Colónias*
BGU	*Boletim Geral do Ultramar*
BOA	*Boletim oficial do Governo Geral da Provincia de Angola*
FO	Foreign Office
GG	Governador-geral
ILO	International Labour Organization
ISAU	Inspecção Superior da Administração Ultramarina
JAH	*Journal of African History*
JGH	*Journal of Global History*
MSENMU	Ministro e secretário de Estado dos Negócios da Marinha e Ultramar
MU	Ministério do Ultramar
NA	Nationaal Archief
NAHV	Nieuwe Afrikaansche Handels-Vennootschap
RCP	*Revista do Café Português*
SG	Secretário-geral
TCTJ	*Tea and Coffee Trade Journal*
TNA	The National Archives

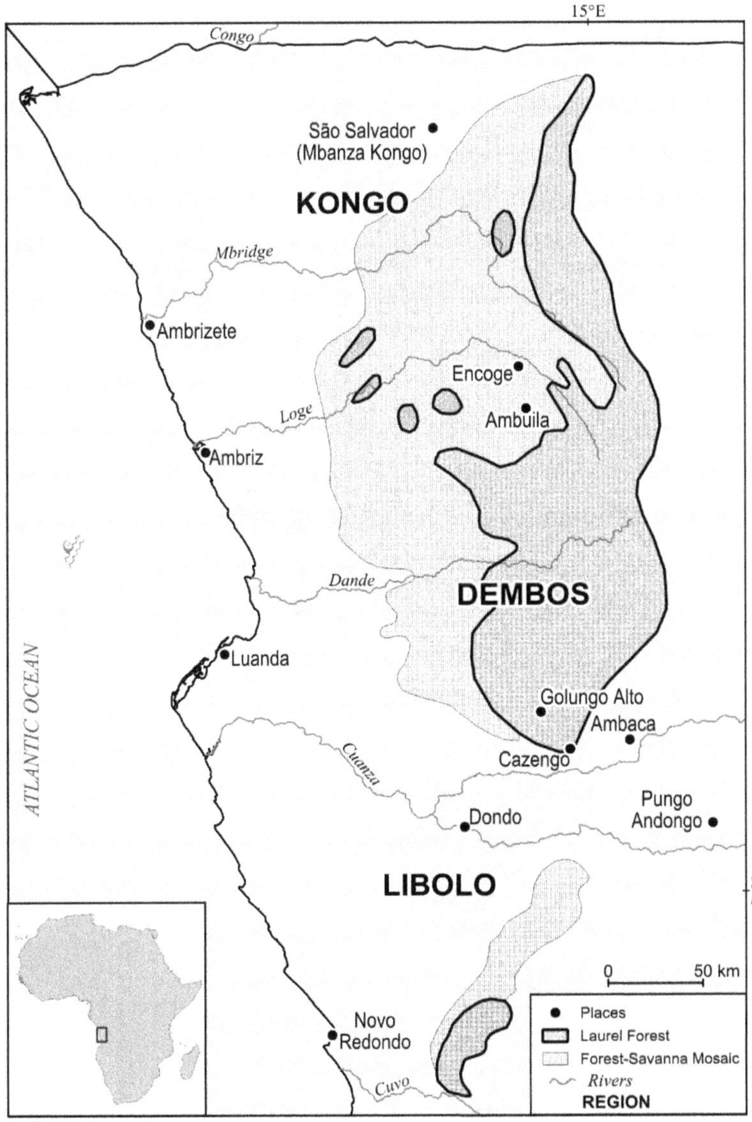

Map 1 Northern Angola, c.1885.

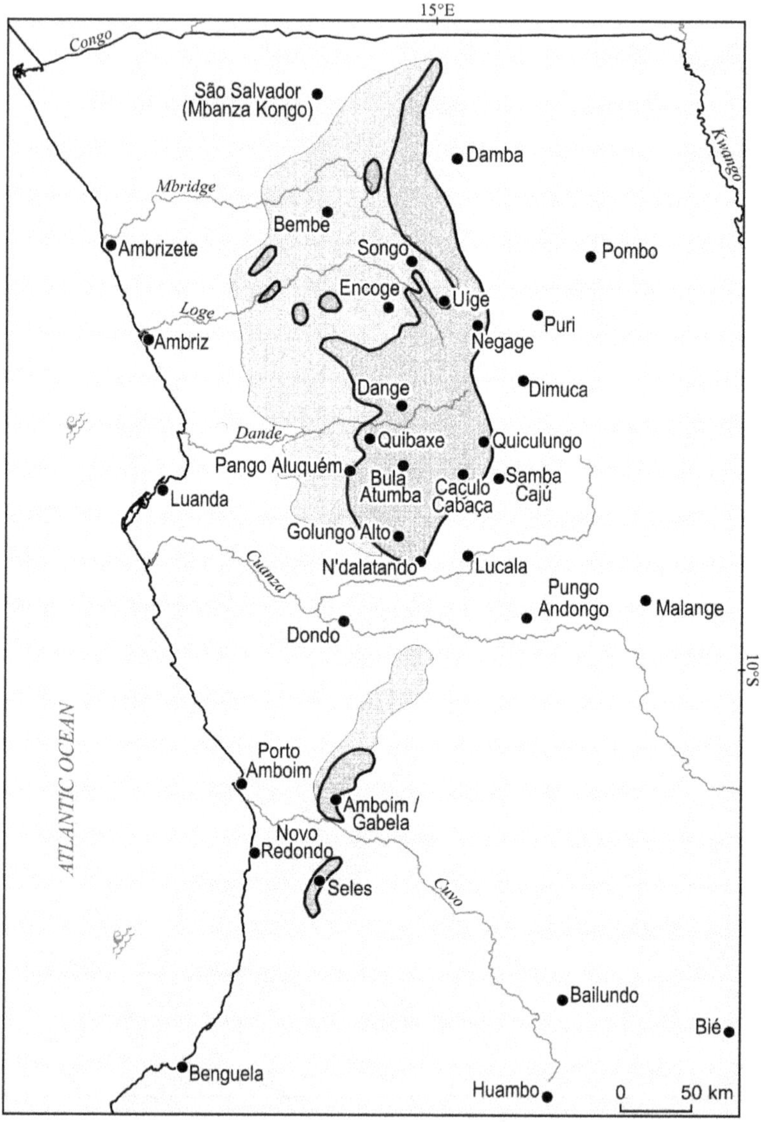

Map 2 Northern and central Angola, c.1950.

Introduction

When the transatlantic slave trade ended in 1865, the business of selling people had dominated economic life in Angola for almost three hundred years, creating trade routes, shaping social relations, and stimulating some commercial activities while stifling others. From the early nineteenth century, however, coffee plantations, large and small, had begun to change the land in this corner of Atlantic Africa, where they steadily became crucial sites for wealth creation and labour exploitation. While the coffee crop transformed Angola, local producers transformed the global coffee trade as they pioneered the commercialization of *Coffea canephora,* also known as robusta, a species that grew in several native and naturalized varieties in the montane forests of northern and central Angola. Step by step, these new coffees found their way through international trade networks into the blends that grocers and manufacturers in Europe and North America prepared for their customers. Cheaper than most commercial varieties of the better-known *Coffea arabica,* African robustas became increasingly popular during the twentieth century. By the time of the Angolan war of independence (1961–74), global dependence on robusta had encouraged the creation of more than a thousand large and medium-sized white-owned coffee plantations in Angola, which competed for space and labour with the farms of some thirty thousand African coffee growers. Supported by the Portuguese colonial state, European planters employed approximately 90,000 workers annually on short- and long-term contracts, plus an unknown number of informally and often randomly recruited men, women, and children.[1] These workers came from far and wide, often under threat of force. As Angola's most important cash crop in the modern era, coffee therefore not only redefined Angola's place in the Atlantic world, but also marked the lives of countless families involved in its production.

In Angolan popular memory, coffee has an ambivalent position. For some people it brings up memories of colonial forced labour, as conveyed by the poem and popular song 'Monangamba', which expresses the suffering of contract workers on the estates: 'The coffee will be roasted / ground, tortured / it will turn black, black as the colour of the *contratado*'.[2] Anyone speaking

1 Angola, Repartição Central de Estatística Geral, *Anuário estatístico de Angola, ano de 1956* (Luanda: Imprensa Nacional, 1958); René Coste, *Les caféiers et les cafés dans le monde* (2 vols, Paris: Éditions Larose, 1955–61), vol. 2, pp. 452, 689–90, 717–18.

2 'O café vai ser torrado / pisado, torturado / vai ficar negro, negro da cor do contratado'. António Jacinto, 'Monangamba', in Mário de Andrade, *Antologia da poesia*

with Angolans old enough to remember the last phase of Portuguese rule in Africa will more than likely hear stories of colonial abuse. But they may just as easily hear people reminisce about successful family farms, which many only abandoned when the country's civil war (1975–2002) forced them to relocate. These contrasting memories reflect the entangled realities of estate and small-scale coffee production that are the subject of this book. Focusing on northern Angola, where competing modes of cultivation existed from the early nineteenth century, the book investigates how African smallholders and colonial settlers, alongside Portuguese administrators, agronomists, foreign traders, and overseas industries, created one of the largest coffee economies in sub-Saharan Africa. This was an old commodity frontier, forged in the wake of abolition, when Angola experienced a series of socioeconomic changes, some intended, others more spontaneous, ushering in what the British called 'legitimate' commerce, essentially meaning cash-crop agriculture.[3] Colonial slavery, forced labour, and dispossession played a key role in the making of this frontier, but African entrepreneurship was just as vital.

The book brings different dimensions of commodity production into view, connecting historical developments that are often seen as contradictory, geographically opposed, or temporally divided and therefore treated separately from one another in studies of empire and colonialism. Tracing Angola's modern history, this study demonstrates that integration into global commodity markets could both disadvantage African populations and provide them with opportunities to prosper. It shows that plantation building under colonial rule sometimes involved deforestation, but that growers' understanding of coffee as naturally shade-grown often led them to cultivate the crop under native canopy. It shows that places of production were at the same time places of consumption, eliminating the spatial separation between the two spheres that defines the standard image of the commodity chain. Finally, it shows how ideologies and practices in Angola's proto-colonial settler economy created repertoires for exploiting African land and labour, but also how the modern colonial state modified models of resource extraction.

---

negra de expressão portuguesa (Paris: P. J. Oswald, 1958). *Monangamba* was a Kimbundu term for 'carrier', the most common job Africans performed for Europeans before the rise of plantation labour.

3 Robin Law (ed.), *From Slave Trade to 'Legitimate' Commerce: The Commercial Transition in Nineteenth-Century West Africa* (Cambridge: Cambridge University Press, 1995). In this book, 'commodity frontier' is defined as a concrete site or 'advancing boundary' of primary production and trade, and not as an analytical device to study global capitalist expansion. For these contrasting uses, compare Corey Ross, 'The Tin Frontier: Mining, Empire, and Environment in Southeast Asia, 1870s–1930s', *Environmental History*, 19 (2014), 454–79, at p. 456; Ulbe Bosma and Eric Vanhaute, 'Commodity Frontiers: Linking Global Capitalism and Local Resilience', in Jonathan Curry-Machado *et al.* (eds), *The Oxford Handbook of Commodity History* (Oxford: Oxford University Press, 2024), pp. 85–101.

The story is told largely chronologically, starting around 1820, with different thematic threads transecting this linear narrative. These threads reveal a pattern of three interconnected transitions in the history of Angola: the reorientation of the export economy from Global South to Global North, the conversion from peasant economy into settler colony, and the shift from slavery to new ways of organizing plantation labour. The analysis stops before the start of the liberation war in 1961, because then a different era with its own peculiar dynamics began. As other historians have shown, during the Portuguese counterinsurgency, northern populations fled across the border with Congo while others were resettled by the colonial administration, all deeply affecting the coffee economy.[4]

The first broad theme is Angola's changing role in the global economy following the closure of the Atlantic slave trade. From labour supplier to Brazil and Cuba, where enslaved people from Angola grew coffee and sugar for North American and European markets, the region itself became a major commodity producer during the nineteenth century. This was in line with a wider reordering of the Atlantic world caused by abolition and the unfolding industrial revolution, which generally reoriented Africa's Hesperian pivot from the New World towards the European core and from slave trading to 'raw-material' production.[5] Chapter 1 examines why this transition occurred so late in Angola compared to other parts of western Africa, especially where agricultural production was concerned – coffee being a good example. Despite growing global consumption, an abundance of indigenous coffee reserves, and low opportunity costs for cultivators, production only flourished more than forty years after the crop's initial 'discovery'. Exports of palm oil, palm kernels, and peanuts took equally long to develop, although wild products like ivory and wax were successful early on. An explanation for this slow change can be found in the shipping patterns of the South Atlantic slave trade, which tied Angola to the Brazilian economy and dis-

4 Diogo Ramada Curto and Bernardo Pinto da Cruz, 'Cidades coloniais: Fomento ou controlo?', in Nuno Domingos and Else Peralta (eds), *Cidade e Império: Dinâmicas coloniais e reconfigurações pós-coloniais* (Lisbon: Edições 70, 2013), pp. 113–65; Miguel Bandeira Jerónimo, 'A Robust Operation: Resettling, Security, and Development in Late Colonial Angola (1960s–1970s)', *Itinerario*, 44:1 (2020), 55–79.

5 J. Forbes Munro, *Africa and the International Economy, 1800–1960* (London: J. M. Dent, 1976), p. 13; José C. Moya, 'Modernization, Modernity, and the Trans/formation of the Atlantic World in the Nineteenth Century', in Jorge Canizares-Esguerra and Erik R. Seeman (eds), *The Atlantic in Global History, 1500–2000*, 2nd edn (New York: Routledge, 2018), pp. 187–207. For a longer view of African commodity production, see Stephen D. Behrendt *et al.*, *The Diary of Antera Duke, an Eighteenth-Century African Slave Trader* (Oxford: Oxford University Press, 2010), pp. 81–101; Robin Law *et al.* (eds), *Commercial Agriculture, the Slave Trade and Slavery in Atlantic Africa* (Woodbridge: James Currey, 2013); Angus Dalrymple-Smith, *Commercial Transitions and Abolition in West Africa 1630–1860* (Boston: Brill, 2020).

advantaged local cash-crop producers.[6] The chapter shows that the progression of commodity trading in Angola depended on the replacement of Brazilian and Cuban slavers, who had little interest in buying vegetable oils, coffee, or rubber from African producers, by a new group of merchants from ports like Liverpool, Salem, and Rotterdam.

The effective suppression of the slave trade in the 1860s brought Angola into the orbit of the world economy's industrial core.[7] As coffee prices rose around the same time, African farmers took over from the handful of slave-owning settlers who had dominated coffee cultivation in previous decades. Thanks largely to the efforts of these smallholders, by the 1870s green, unroasted coffee had become Angola's most valuable product and Angola their largest exporter in Africa.

The reorganization of the Angolan economy around coffee – initially concentrated in the montane forest north of the river Cuanza – continued during the twentieth century, when not just Angolan, but a range of African robustas conquered the world coffee market. As Chapter 3 explains, Angola nurtured particularly strong connections with coffee traders in the Netherlands and the United States. This relationship deepened when outputs from the world's leading robusta producer, Indonesia, collapsed during the Second World War. Demand from Dutch and North American coffee brokers kept 'Angolans' – as they called the product – at the vanguard of the global robusta trade, given that the market for coffee in Portugal, the colonial metropole, was only small. The American axis is especially significant from an Atlantic perspective. Until 1850, enslaved people from Angola had populated the Brazilian plantations from which the United States sourced the bulk of its coffee imports. Now, American demand for robusta created a direct link between Angola and the United States, with steamers of the American West African Line, the Mississippi Shipping Company, and Farrell Lines providing regular connections from Angolan harbours to New York and New Orleans, the main coffee-handling ports on the Atlantic coast of North America.[8]

6 For the concept of the South Atlantic, see David Richardson and Filipa Ribeiro da Silva (eds), *Networks and Trans-Cultural Exchange: Slave Trading in the South Atlantic, 1590–1867* (Leiden: Brill, 2015).

7 The United States was itself moving from periphery to centre. See Stefan Link and Noam Maggor, 'The United States as a Developing Nation: Revisiting the Peculiarities of American History', *Past and Present*, 246 (2020), 269–306. Brazil also industrialized, but did so relatively late, while Angola had little to contribute. See Mauricio A. Font, *Coffee and Transformation in São Paulo, Brazil* (Lanham: Lexington Books, 2010).

8 See sailing and shipping news and advertisements in the *Tea and Coffee Trade Journal* (1949–50). For the coffee trade between Brazil and the United States during slavery, see Daniel Rood, *The Reinvention of Atlantic Slavery: Technology, Labor, Race, and Capitalism in the Greater Caribbean* (New York: Oxford University Press, 2017), pp. 121–47.

The linkage of the Angolan coffee sector to non-metropolitan markets was managed by Portugal through import, export, and exchange controls, with the Coffee Export Board becoming important from 1940 onwards. Political economists have long criticized colonial marketing boards for effectively taxing agricultural producers by paying them less than going market rates.[9] Less emphasis has been placed on the vital role these organizations played in connecting small growers to global traders.[10] In Angola, the Coffee Export Board took on the burden of standardizing dried robusta beans for sale in international markets, an operation that otherwise only highly capitalized estates could manage on their own. Coffee manufacturers generally insisted on uniformity in bean appearance, which was achieved through grading, but some roasters also demanded stability in taste. This required another kind of intervention, increasing the involvement, across imperial lines, of American and Dutch agents in coffee sourcing and processing in Angola.[11]

Angola's capture of Dutch and American coffee markets enabled a gradual expansion of exports in the interwar period and rapid growth during the postwar commodity boom, placing Angola among the world's top producers. In the meantime, however, the colonial state had made the momentous decision to intervene in the organization of land and labour, which ensured that white colonists, rather than African farmers, benefited most from Angola's growing coffee sales.

The development of a settler economy in Angola, particularly in the coffee sector, is the book's second theme, and is analysed in Chapters 2 and 4. Settler expansion depended on the creation of a colonial state with the power to control indigenous populations militarily and place European law above existing legal customs. In Angola, this state uniquely emerged from a system of proto-colonial rule. This older regime was based on a limited number of coastal and inland enclaves where European and African 'residents' (*moradores*) engaged in military, commercial, and agricultural activities – including coffee production – for which they used labour extracted from enslaved people and from the subjects of allied African chiefs.[12] Colonialism in Angola entailed the expansion of the worst

9 Robert H. Bates, *Markets and States in Tropical Africa* (Berkeley: University of California Press, 2014); Douglas Rimmer, *Staying Poor: Ghana's Political Economy, 1950–1990* (Oxford: Pergamon Press, 1992).

10 Benoit Daviron, 'Small Farm Production and the Standardization of Tropical Products', *Journal of Agrarian Change*, 2:2 (2002), 162–84.

11 Maria Gago, 'Moving Coffee from the Forests of Colonial Angola to the Breakfast Tables of Main Street America, 1940–1961', in John Krige (ed.), *Knowledge Flows in a Global Age: A Transnational Approach* (Chicago: Chicago University Press, 2022), pp. 231–52, at pp. 242–4.

12 Mariana Pinho Candido, *Wealth, Land, and Property in Angola: A History of Dispossession, Slavery, and Inequality* (Cambridge: Cambridge University Press, 2022), defines early Portuguese settlement in Angola as colonial, but this overstates the

features of proto-colonial rule, which were a combination of settler enterprise and forced labour, although this outcome was by no means inevitable.

When colonial states were constructed in Africa around 1900, European rulers, including the Portuguese, were faced with the problem of how to extract resources from indigenous lands and peoples. Historically, three different economic regimes developed: settler-elite colonies, where individual colonists appropriated a large part of the cultivable land; concession colonies, where large mining or plantation companies gained monopoly access to land; and peasant colonies, where Africans retained ownership of most of the land and used it for cash-crop production, mainly in small units.[13] To explain how colonial governments shaped these different trajectories, some economic historians invoke the idea of path dependency. Their argument is that early evidence of a productive peasant economy led governments to endorse the smallholder model, which involved the least interference in African societies; whereas early settler success was a reason to support further expansion, which typically required radical intervention in African land and labour markets to ensure they worked to the advantage of settlers.[14] In Angola, however, a scenario unfolded that defied the logic of economic theory.

At the start of the twentieth century, Angola was fundamentally a peasant colony with a few pockets of settler enterprise. Rubber and coffee were the main export goods, the first extracted from the roots of latex-bearing shrubs that grew in the savannas of the deep interior, the second from trees cultivated in the forest hinterland of Angola's northern coast, mainly in areas outside Portuguese colonial control. Europeans played no part in the production of rubber, while in coffee cultivation their role was peripheral, although coffee had created the most advanced plantation sector in proto-colonial Angola.[15] Applying simple

power of Portuguese colonizers and understates the hybridity of the legal and political structures of Portuguese proto-colonial rule in Africa. On this point, see Toby Green, 'Baculamento or Encomienda?', *Journal of Global Slavery*, 2:3 (2017), 310–36; Cátia Antunes and Jelmer Vos, 'Port Cities and Commodities: Luanda in the Early-Modern Period', in Curry-Machado *et al.*, *Oxford Handbook*, pp. 127–43.

13 In Africa, settlers generally remained a minority population that relied on indigenous populations for labour, rather than promoting their eradication, as suggested by Patrick Wolfe, 'Settler Colonialism and the Elimination of the Native', *Journal of Genocide Research*, 8:4 (2006), 387–409.

14 Gareth Austin, 'Capitalism and the Colonies', in Larry Neal and Jeffrey G. Williamson (eds), *The Cambridge History of Capitalism*, vol. 2 (Cambridge: Cambridge University Press, 2014), pp. 301–47, at pp. 315–23, 338–9; Ewout Frankema *et al.*, 'Endogenous Processes of Colonial Settlement: The Success and Failure of European Settler Farming in Sub-Saharan Africa', *Revista de Historia Económica*, 34:2 (2016), 237–65.

15 By the 1870s, the coffee districts of Cazengo and Golungo Alto had the highest value of rural commercial property and the largest concentrations of enslaved

but well-honed propagation techniques and relying largely on family labour, from the 1860s, African smallholders had transformed the northern montane forest into a highly productive coffee frontier. Economic reason dictated that Portugal would follow the 'peasant' model in Angola. But this was not the path taken.[16] The colonial state predominantly supported individual colonists (and some large concession companies, such as Diamang in the far northeast) at the expense of African producers. Helped by land grants, bank loans, and relatively cheap labour supplies, settlers over the course of the twentieth century managed to shed their economic marginality and dominate the production of coffee and other valuable export crops, like sugar and sisal.

Various hypotheses help explain this unexpected outcome. First, policy-makers in Lisbon and Luanda might have been impressed by the dire state of the Angolan coffee economy around 1900 – which nonetheless affected settler plantations far more than it did African farms – and the collapse of the mighty rubber trade around 1910, concluding that peasant production had run its course. But these were partly cyclical issues, and while some officials certainly used poor growth numbers to argue for new directions in colonial policy, there was enough institutional memory to look beyond a negative business cycle. Ideological trends in European thinking about African economies were a more important cause. Early colonial regimes fostered a belief in the superiority of large-scale, capital-intensive agriculture based on what was considered scientific learning, as opposed to the supposedly primitive farming techniques of African smallholders. Plantations, historian Corey Ross has argued, were 'incarnations of European agronomic knowledge and symbols of European power'.[17] In Angola, such convictions were embedded in century-old imperial dreams of colonization by white settlement. There was a brief period during the 1870s when colonial officials nurtured the prospect of Angola as a peasant colony, but many soon

---

people in Angola. Arquivo Histórico Ultramarino (Lisbon, henceforth AHU), Secretaria de Estado da Marinha e Ultramar, Direcção Geral do Ultramar, Angola, no. 645/2, 'Mapa estatístico dos prédios registrados e seus valores e do respectivo movimento hypotecário, 1874', enclosed in GG interino to MSENMU, no. 18, 19 Jan. 1875; *BOA*, 42 (15 Oct. 1870), 596–7.

16 This is a variation on Lowell Gudmundson's argument that smallholders in Costa Rica survived against the odds during the twentieth century. Lowell W. Gudmundson, 'On Paths Not Taken: Commercial Capital and Coffee Production in Costa Rica', in William Gervase Clarence-Smith and Steven Topik (eds), *The Global Coffee Economy in Africa, Asia, and Latin America, 1500–1989* (Cambridge: Cambridge University Press, 2003), pp. 335–59.

17 Corey Ross, 'The Plantation Paradigm: Colonial Agronomy, African Farmers, and the Global Cocoa Boom, 1870s–1940s', *JGH*, 9:1 (2014), 49–71, at p. 51. See also William Gervase Clarence-Smith, *Cocoa and Chocolate, 1765–1914* (London: Routledge, 2000), 146–94.

reversed course.[18] They did so, not coincidentally, when states in different parts of the world began to view settler colonialism as the most effective strategy to conquer internal or external frontiers and extract riches from indigenous lands.[19]

Nevertheless, ideological trends alone cannot explain why settler initiative was allowed to continue in some regions, while it was aborted in others. In sub-Saharan Africa, most colonial administrations soon learned from experience that the option of leaving production in African hands, while skimming part of the profits by levying export duties, was less costly and carried fewer political risks. Businesses and governments generally encountered resistance to the introduction of large-scale plantation agriculture, creating economic trajectories in the sub-continent very different from simultaneous developments in Southeast Asia.[20]

In addition to ideology, habit and improvisation played a role in settler expansion. First, a unique tradition of state-backed settler enterprise, starting in the wake of slave trade abolition, set the Portuguese in Angola apart from other colonizers in Africa. Although this experience was characterized by economic failure more than success, it implanted a model of rule in the minds of colonial officials that proved hard to dislodge.[21] Portugal was therefore always likely to continue, with some adjustments, the land and labour policies it had developed after 1850 to support a budding planter class. Second, settler colonialism almost never worked according to government dictates, as Chapter 4 will demonstrate. While favourable political structures helped, the twentieth-century plantation economy was fundamentally created by the colonists themselves, a point not sufficiently acknowledged in Portuguese imperial history. As Lorenzo Veracini has argued, 'settlers typically act on their own behalf, not as agents of distant

18 Gervase Clarence-Smith, *The Third Portuguese Empire, 1825–1975: A Study in Economic Imperialism* (Manchester: Manchester University Press, 1985), pp. 76–7.

19 Sven Beckert, 'American Danger: United States Empire, Eurafrica, and the Territorialization of Industrial Capitalism, 1870–1950', *American Historical Review*, 122:4 (2017), 1137–70, at pp. 1151–5; Sidney Xu Lu, 'A Great Convergence: The American Frontier and the Origins of Japanese Migration to Brazil', *JGH*, 17:1 (2022), 109–27.

20 Gareth Austin, 'The Economics of Colonialism in Africa', in Célestin Monga and Justin Yifu Lin (eds), *The Oxford Handbook of Africa and Economics*, vol. 1 (Oxford: Oxford University Press, 2015), pp. 522–35, at pp. 525–7; Valeria Giacomin, 'The Transformation of the Global Palm Oil Cluster: Dynamics of Cluster Competition between Africa and Southeast Asia (c.1900–1970)', *JGH* 13:3 (2018), 374–98.

21 Roquinaldo Ferreira, 'Agricultural Enterprise and Unfree Labour in Nineteenth-Century Angola', in Law *et al.*, *Commercial Agriculture*, pp. 225–42; Mariana Pinho Candido, 'Conquest, Occupation, Colonialism and Exclusion: Land Disputes in Angola', in João Vicente Serrão *et al.* (eds), *Property Rights, Lands and Territory in the European Overseas Empires* (Lisbon: Imprensa de Ciências Sociais, 2014), pp. 223–33, at p. 227.

metropoles'.[22] Despite an age-old, seemingly endless discourse in Portuguese political circles about the economic and civilizational benefits of white settlement to Angola, the emergence of the largest settler-dominated coffee sector in Africa was quite unexpected and occurred without much planning from above. But once in place, its sheer size and apparent success legitimized further support by the colonial state.

Angola still retained elements of a peasant colony. Unlike British policy in Kenya – another coffee-producing settler colony – the Portuguese government did not deprive Africans of the right to produce for export. In fact, colonial administrators had a legal duty to protect African land use, and through the creation of export boards the state even tried to improve smallholder yields. African producers concentrated on food crops like maize and cassava, which settlers largely stayed away from, and they continued to grow coffee.[23] They did this quite effectively, giving rise to a substantial class of relatively well-off farmers, as Chapter 7 explains. Typical of peasant colonies, however, Africans lost their position as crucial intermediaries in coastal and long-distance trade to foreign firms, essentially reducing them to the role of agrarian producers. Like the Lebanese merchant community in West Africa, Portuguese immigrants also occupied the retail trade, taking the coffee harvest off African growers for onward sale.[24] Although coffee purchasing by merchants could be considered a 'vital service' to smallholders, as Steven Topik and William Clarence-Smith have argued, when shopkeepers became planters with their own land and labour needs, they became competitors.[25] Again, politics intervened. African growers who could

22 Lorenzo Veracini, 'Introduction: Settler Colonialism as a Distinct Mode of Domination', in Edward Cavanagh and Lorenzo Veracini (eds), *The Routledge Handbook of the History of Settler Colonialism* (Abingdon: Routledge, 2017), pp. 1–8, at p. 2.

23 AHU, Ministério do Ultramar, Direcção-Geral de Economia, Repartição Administrativa, no. 1637, 'Estimativa dos quinhões procedentes da produção indígena na exportação de alguns produtos', Luanda, 15 Oct. 1951. On maize, see Maria da Conceição Neto, 'In Town and Out of Town: A Social History of Huambo (Angola), 1902–1961' (Unpublished PhD dissertation, University of London, 2012), <http://eprints.soas.ac.uk/13822>, pp. 99–102, 166–8.

24 Ralph Austen, *African Economic History: Internal Development and External Dependency* (Oxford: James Currey, 1987), pp. 122–39. For a contrary view on African middlemen, see A. G. Hopkins, *Capitalism in the Colonies: African Merchants in Lagos, 1851–1931* (Princeton: Princeton University Press, 2024). On the Lebanese, see Andrew Arsan, *Interlopers of Empire: The Lebanese Diaspora in Colonial French West Africa* (New York: Oxford University Press, 2014). Smallholder marginality in the supply chain was typical for coffee economies with mixed production systems. For example, see Julie A. Charlip, 'Small Farmers and Coffee in Nicaragua', in Clarence-Smith and Topik, *Global Coffee Economy*, pp. 236–53.

25 Steven Topik and William Gervase Clarence-Smith, 'Conclusion: New Propositions and a Research Agenda', in Clarence-Smith and Topik, *Global Coffee Economy*, pp. 385–410, at p. 399.

not prove their 'independent' or 'self-employed' status – for which there existed various arbitrary criteria such as having a yield of 1,000kg of dried coffee or cultivating three thousand stands – were eligible for compulsory labour service. In the eyes of the state, after all, Angolan peasants were never just producers; they also represented a potential labour pool.

The third thematic strand in the book is the transition from slavery to contract labour, a theme still poorly studied in the historiography of Angola, which has focused more on the Atlantic dimensions of unfree labour than on its role in internal migrations.[26] Proto-colonial coffee plantations depended fundamentally on slave labour and, to a lesser extent, on workers requisitioned from African allies of the Portuguese administration. This organization remained in place until the early twentieth century, although from 1875 the enslaved were put on token contracts and renamed *serviçais* to conform to new ideologies of free labour. The military occupation of Angola, largely completed by 1920, allowed the colonial government to impose the contract system on wider segments of the black population and intervene directly in recruitment. As a result, settlers were able to abandon their reliance on slavery, which by now was not only a legally but also a morally bankrupt model of labour coercion. To date, historians have mainly debated the colonial legacy of nineteenth-century slavery. But, as Chapter 5 shows, while the contract system inherited notions of white mastery and African servitude from slavery, in legal terms it was modelled on Portugal's proto-colonial regime of tributary labour.

26 Recent studies of the Angolan slave trade include Roquinaldo Ferreira, *Cross-Cultural Exchange in the Atlantic World: Angola and Brazil during the Era of the Slave Trade* (Cambridge: Cambridge University Press, 2012); Mariana P. Candido, *An African Slaving Port and the Atlantic World: Benguela and Its Hinterland* (Cambridge: Cambridge University Press, 2013); Catherine Higgs, *Chocolate Islands: Cocoa, Slavery, and Colonial Africa* (Athens: Ohio University Press, 2013); Daniel B. Domingues da Silva, *The Atlantic Slave Trade from West Central Africa, 1780–1867* (Cambridge: Cambridge University Press, 2017). On coerced internal migrations, see Jeremy Ball, *Angola's Colossal Lie: Forced Labor on a Sugar Plantation, 1913–1977* (Boston: Brill, 2015); Todd Cleveland, *Diamonds in the Rough: Corporate Paternalism and African Professionalism on the Mines of Colonial Angola, 1917–1975* (Athens: Ohio University Press, 2015). Generally, contract labour has been studied mainly in the context of overseas migration. A classic example is David Northrup, *Indentured Labor in the Age of Imperialism, 1834–1922* (Cambridge: Cambridge University Press, 1995). The historiography of Lusophone Africa has helped change this. For examples beyond Angola, see Allen F. Isaacman, *Cotton is the Mother of Poverty: Peasants, Work, and Rural Struggle in Colonial Mozambique, 1938–1961* (Cape Town: Heinemann, 1996); Eric Allina, *Slavery by Any Other Name: African Life Under Company Rule in Colonial Mozambique* (Charlottesville: University of Virginia Press, 2012); Zachary Kagan Guthrie, *Bound for Work: Labor, Mobility, and Colonial Rule in Central Mozambique, 1940–1965* (Charlottesville: University of Virginia Press, 2018).

Twentieth-century contract labour, Chapter 6 argues, was more complex in its operation and effects than the commonly used concept of 'forced labour' suggests. Recruitment for the coffee plantations after 1920 involved a range of methods, from police raids and kidnapping to humdrum requisitioning and informal negotiations. Some workers were day labourers and had their homes nearby, while others served on long-term contracts and hailed from regions hundreds of kilometres away. Some came alone, others brought families. Some were housed in barracks, others built their own homes and had access to gardens. Officially, they were all wage workers. A census taken around 1960 suggests that there were 780,436 people in Angola who 'worked for others' on a salaried basis – remarkably all men – of whom more than 10 per cent were in the coffee sector.[27] But in reality, if you had to apply a taxonomy of labour relations to the coffee estates, this was wage labour intersected by forms of slavery, tribute, and indenture.[28] Generally, Africans tried to avoid plantation labour, but taxation, financial debts, physical threats, or a simple 'call of the government' forced them to accept a contract. Government coercion allowed settlers to pay workers below the reservation wage (the lowest wage rate at which a worker would be willing to work for someone else), although structural labour shortages led to wage increases over time as well as wage competition between planters.

In terms of labour, too, the Angolan plantation economy followed global patterns as much as local precedent. The Portuguese used repertoires of coercion developed in plantation societies across the world's tropical and sub-tropical zones after 1800, including slavery, compulsory apprenticeship, indenture, requisition, and forced conscription.[29] In coffee production, there were clear parallels between forced labour recruitment in twentieth-century Angola and institutionalized labour drafts and obligatory 'free' labour in Central America.[30]

27 Angola, Direcção dos Serviços de Estatística, *3º Recenseamento geral da população, 1960*, vol. 4, *População residente segundo as condições perante o trabalho* (Luanda: Direcção dos Serviços de Estatística, 1964).

28 Jan Lucassen, *The Story of Work: A New History of Humankind* (New Haven: Yale University Press, 2021), pp. 4–13, 292–3, 356–61.

29 For an overview, see David Eltis and Stanley Engerman (eds), *The Cambridge World History of Slavery*, vol. 4, *ad 1804–ad 2016* (Cambridge: Cambridge University Press, 2017). For a study of knowledge exchange between colonial states, see Benoit Daviron, 'Mobilizing Labour in African Agriculture: The Role of the International Colonial Institute in the Elaboration of a Standard of Colonial Administration, 1895–1930', *JGH*, 5:3 (2010), 479–501.

30 David McCreery, 'Wage Labor, Free Labor, and Vagrancy Laws: The Transition to Capitalism in Guatemala, 1920–1945', in William Roseberry *et al.* (eds), *Coffee, Society, and Power in Latin America* (Baltimore: Johns Hopkins University Press, 1995), pp. 206–31; 'Coffee and Indigenous Labor in Guatemala, 1871–1980', in Clarence-Smith and Topik, *Global Coffee Economy*, pp. 191–208; Elizabeth Dore, 'Patriarchy from Above, Patriarchy from Below: Debt Peonage on Nicaraguan Coffee

Within Africa, the Portuguese contract system resembled the French regime in Côte d'Ivoire, not least in the way its implementation made a mockery of legal provisions that prohibited administrators from recruiting for private enterprise.[31] Moreover, the racialized discourse underpinning the organization of plantation labour utilized the same old tropes about non-white people one could hear around the Global South.[32]

What distinguished Angola from other settler-elite colonies was a profound inability to change, or to visualize alternative paths, even when the pressures to do so increased after the Second World War. While there had always been discord within Portuguese imperial ranks about rampant settler expansion and accompanying labour abuses, especially in northern Angola, few officials dared to question the legitimacy of the system.[33] The result was the continuation of wasteful agricultural practices, as planters were not only less efficient coffee producers than smallholders, but also left large parts of their estates unused because of chronic labour shortages. Parcelling up unused land and leasing it to small farmers, a strategy successfully used in South America from the late 1800s, was never seriously contemplated.[34] Instead, planters managed to offset their inefficiencies by purchasing coffee from African growers and through state subsidies, for which Africans paid the price in coerced, low-wage labour. Meanwhile, by allowing the expansion of settler agriculture, Portugal narrowed the path of smallholder-led growth that had so invitingly opened during the nineteenth century. From the perspective of African farmers, as this book aims to show, colonialism became an often-dreadful story of closing opportunities.

Estates, 1870–1930', *ibid.*, pp. 209–35; Jan Rus, 'Coffee and the Recolonization of Highland Chiapas, Mexico: Indian Communities and Plantation Labor, 1892–1912', *ibid.*, pp. 257–85.

31 Frederick Cooper, *Decolonization and African Society: The Labor Question in French and British Africa* (Cambridge: Cambridge University Press, 1996), pp. 31–43, 77–92, 150–3.

32 Augustine Sedgewick, *Coffeeland: A History* (Dublin: Penguin Books, 2020), pp. 69–72, 128–31.

33 Douglas L. Wheeler, 'The Galvão Report on Forced Labor (1947) in Historical Context and Perspective: The Trouble-Shooter Who was "Trouble"', *Portuguese Studies Review*, 16:1 (2008), 115–52; Alexander Keese, 'The Constraints of Late Colonial Reform Policy: Forced Labour Scandals in the Portuguese Congo (Angola) and the Limits of Reform under Authoritarian Colonial Rule, 1955–61', *Portuguese Studies*, 28:2 (2012), 186–200; Miguel Bandeira Jerónimo and José Pedro Monteiro, 'Colonial Labour Internationalized: Portugal and the Decolonization Momentum (1945–1975)', *International History Review*, 42:3 (2020), 485–504.

34 Marco Palacios, *Coffee in Colombia: An Economic, Social and Political History* (Cambridge: Cambridge University Press, 1980), pp. 78–83, 101–4; Verena Stolcke, 'The Labors of Coffee in Latin America: The Hidden Charm of Family Labor and Self-Provisioning', in Roseberry *et al.*, *Coffee, Society, and Power*, pp. 65–93.

1

Out of the Slave Trade

When David Livingstone, famed Scottish missionary and devout abolitionist, travelled through northern Angola in 1854, he could not help but notice the many enslaved people in the country's inland towns, the way their Luso-African masters employed them, and how some were trafficked to the coast to fill the holds of Cuban slave ships. While this culture of slavery clearly worried him, something else impressed him positively. Livingstone found a land lush with wild coffee, which some colonial settlers had begun to cultivate. To him, this budding coffee economy seemed a model for the future development of a colony going through the final throes of the Atlantic slave trade. 'The fact of other avenues of wealth opening up so readily seems like a providential invitation to forsake the slave-trade and engage in lawful commerce', he wrote in his travel memoir.[1]

Commercial exploitation of natural forest coffees in Angola had started on a small scale in the 1820s near São José de Encoge, a Portuguese settlement more than 300km inland by caravan track from the colonial capital, Luanda. Contemporaries claimed the taste of this product was 'as good as that of Mocha', referring to the arabica cultivars introduced in the colonies of Brazil and São Tomé decades earlier.[2] Banking on rising coffee prices, dozens of adventurous settlers had since bought captives to transform indigenous coffee forests into plantations, giving abolitionists hope that a new export economy based on agriculture

1 David Livingstone, *Missionary Travels and Researches in South Africa* (New York: Harper and Brothers, 1858), pp. 383–488, quote at p. 442.

2 Arquivo Histórico Ultramarino (Lisbon, henceforth AHU), Secretaria de Estado da Marinha e Ultramar (SEMU), Direcção Geral do Ultramar (DGU), Angola, no. 825, Perguntas do Bernardo de Sá Nogueira a que responde Luis José da Silva, Angra, 8 Jan. 1831. See also José Joaquim Lopes de Lima, *Ensaios sobre a statística das possessões portuguezas* (3 vols, Lisbon: Imprensa Nacional, 1844–46), vol. 3, pt 1, pp. 11–12, citing Fortunato de Melo, 'Memória', in *Periódico dos Pobres de Lisboa*, 193 (17 Aug. 1838); Joaquim António de Carvalho e Menezes, *Demonstração geográfica e politica do território portuguez na Guiné inferior* (Rio de Janeiro: Typ. Classica de F. A. de Almeida, 1848), pp. 131–2.

could replace the unlawful slave trade.[3] In reality, however, the transition to 'legitimate' commerce was notoriously slow in Angola, especially when based on agricultural production. In the year Livingstone was there, merchants in Luanda only sold about fifty metric tons of green coffee, an underwhelming result given the size of both the Angolan economy and the global coffee trade. Other crops hardly fared better. Meanwhile, American slave ships still carried thousands of captives from nearby shores.[4] Instead of undermining this 'odious' commerce by offering merchants and producers an attractive alternative, commercial agriculture in Angola seemed to suffer from the slave trade's remarkable longevity.[5]

Only after the last transatlantic slavers were driven from the coast during the 1860s did Angola's agrarian transition take off. Until then, coffee remained a trivial item on local export registers, although world trade in coffee was growing rapidly and opportunity costs for smallholders were low because of coffee's natural abundance in Angola and the crop's compatibility with subsistence farming.[6] The slave trade in Angola thus appeared to conflict with commodity production, apart from the exchange of wild goods like ivory, beeswax, and orchil lichen. This incompatibility was in large part due to long-term shipping patterns in the South Atlantic, where wind and ocean currents gave Brazilian traders an advantage over European rivals in Angola. Contemporary observers hinted at this problem, blaming the sluggish growth of legitimate commerce on the power of Brazilian slaving interests in the Portuguese colony. In contrast to West Africa, where British and French commercial dominance created continuity between old and new trades during the nineteenth century, the growth of commodity trading in Angola became dependent on the replacement of traffickers from Brazil and Cuba by a new group of merchants from the world's industrial core.[7]

As this chapter will show, three simultaneous developments in global commerce allowed European commodity traders to puncture the South Atlantic

3 On abolitionist toleration of slavery in Africa, see Bronwen Everill, *Not Made by Slaves: Ethical Capitalism in the Age of Abolition* (Cambridge: Harvard University Press, 2020), pp. 190–5.

4 The National Archives (Kew, henceforth TNA), FO84/1013, Gabriel to Clarendon, no. 11, Luanda, 11 Feb. 1857. Estimates (2019), SlaveVoyages, <www.slavevoyages.org/estimates/LzTWxWA9>, accessed 6 Dec. 2023.

5 David R. Murray, *Odious Commerce: Britain, Spain and the Abolition of the Cuban Slave Trade* (Cambridge: Cambridge University Press, 1981).

6 Mario Samper and Radin Fernando, 'Appendix: Historical Statistics of Coffee Production and Trade from 1700 to 1960', in William Gervase Clarence-Smith and Steven Topik (eds), *The Global Coffee Economy in Africa, Asia, and Latin America, 1500–1989* (Cambridge: Cambridge University Press, 2003), pp. 411–62, at pp. 417–19.

7 For another case in coffee history where barriers to entry delayed development, see William C. Van Norman, Jr, *Shade-Grown Slavery: The Lives of Slaves on Coffee Plantations in Cuba* (Nashville: Vanderbilt University Press, 2013), pp. 11–16.

slave trade system and reorient Angolan export production towards the Global North. The first was the effective suppression of the slave trade in the 1860s. The second was the steamship revolution, which pulled Angola more strongly in the orbit of Liverpool, the maritime capital of the nineteenth century, and other European ports.[8] The third was increased demand in the industrializing West for tropical commodities, including coffee. Rising commodity prices not only drove steam-powered merchants from Western Europe and North America to explore Angolan resources, but also enticed African smallholders, so far absent from the export economy, to start growing coffee for the world market. These small-scale, price-sensitive producers ensured that Angola, long the largest supplier of captive labour in the Atlantic world, in the 1870s became Africa's leading coffee exporter.

Angola and Brazil

The nineteenth-century expansion of the world coffee trade was a mixed blessing for Angolan producers. On the hand, it created opportunities for new growing regions, including Angola; on the other, it led to increased demand for enslaved labour in southeast Brazil, the new centre of global coffee production, which complicated efforts to reshape the Angolan export economy. Coffee was part of a larger expansion of global trade, generated by industrialization in the West and some of its well-known side effects: innovations in transportation and communication, rising living standards, and growing demand for imported food and drink in Western Europe and North America.[9] Against this background, world coffee exports tripled to almost a million metric tons between 1850 and 1900, satisfying a growing appetite for caffeinated beverages in the industrial centres of the Global North. One producing country had an especially strong hand in shaping this trade. A relative newcomer on the global coffee scene, Brazil was both instigator and beneficiary of the boom in consumer demand. Exploiting ample supplies of slave labour and cheap virgin lands from the 1820s, Brazilian producers pumped out ever larger amounts of inexpensive arabica coffees. As Brazilian coffees flooded the market, prices dropped, which in combination with relatively inexpensive sugar supplies stimulated consumption among urban populations in Europe and America. From luxury item, coffee became a drink for the urban lower and middle classes. By producing large amounts of coffee relatively cheaply, Brazil thus helped create a mass market for the beverage in

8 Paul Butel, *The Atlantic* (London: Routledge, 1999), pp. 223–41.

9 Michael F. Jiménez, '"From Plantation to Cup": Coffee and Capitalism in the United States, 1830–1930', in William Roseberry *et al.* (eds), *Coffee, Society, and Power in Latin America* (Baltimore: Johns Hopkins University Press, 1995), pp. 38–64, at pp. 40–1; Steven C. Topik and Allen Wells, 'Commodity Chains in a Global Economy', in Emily Rosenberg (ed.), *A World Connecting, 1870–1945* (Cambridge: Belknap Press of Harvard University Press, 2012), pp. 591–812, at p. 613.

the Global North. This in turn created niches for other latecomers, especially in Latin America and Africa, which farmers and traders were quick to exploit.[10]

Angola differed from other newly emerging coffee economies in two ways. First, while the global coffee market was built on a few strains of arabica extracted from Ethiopia and Yemen, the Angolan trade consisted of indigenous robusta varieties. This was partly because natural robusta stands were available to planters, but also because ecological conditions restricted the possibility of growing arabica in much of the colonized hinterland.[11] Robusta added little to the world coffee market in terms of quality, making it impossible for Angola to follow the trajectory of Latin American latecomers, who avoided competition with Brazil by growing higher-quality arabica coffees, so-called Milds.[12] Entry into the world coffee trade was ultimately guaranteed because demand outpaced supply, and Angola provided a product that was generally cheaper than what others had to offer.

Second, the transatlantic slave trade had forged a peculiar relationship between Angola and Brazil, transforming Portugal's main colony in Africa into the periphery of a large American plantation economy. Until 1850, Brazilian agriculture strongly relied on Angolan labour supplies, and this was particularly true for its coffee sector. The vast majority of the 1.3 million enslaved Africans shipped to southeast Brazil, the country's main coffee-growing region, during the nineteenth century came from Angola.[13] This relationship survived Brazilian independence from Portugal in 1822 and hampered the production of agricultural exports in Angola, including coffee. On numerous occasions, Portuguese officials designed plans to make Angola a producer of raw materials for nascent metropolitan industries and claw back power in the region from Brazil. These efforts persistently failed because of the continuing hold of Brazilian slavers over the Angolan economy and the lack of Portuguese

10 Topik and Wells, 'Commodity Chains', pp. 776–82; Samper and Fernando, 'Appendix', pp. 418, 432–3.

11 Stuart McCook, *Coffee Is Not Forever: A Global History of the Coffee Leaf Rust* (Athens: Ohio University Pres), pp. 22–5, 108–24; Alan de Carvalho Souza, 'Do Brasil para África: O café na viragem do império português (1807–1850)', PhD dissertation, University of Lisbon (2020). For plans to introduce arabica, see Arquivo do Instituto Histórico e Geográfico Brasileiro (Rio de Janeiro), DL32.04, Joaquim José da Silva to Miguel Antônio de Melo, Ambaca, 30 Oct. 1797.

12 William Roseberry, 'Introduction', in Roseberry *et al.*, *Coffee, Society, and Power*, pp. 1–37, at p. 12. For figures of the coffee trade in Latin America, see Samper and Fernando, 'Appendix', pp. 424–33. While better than Brazilian and Indonesian coffees, the quality of Latin American arabicas at the time should not be overstated. See Augustine Sedgewick, *Coffeeland: A History* (Dublin: Penguin Books, 2020), pp. 62, 77, 113.

13 Estimates (2019), *SlaveVoyages*, <www.slavevoyages.org/estimates/ruB06H50>, accessed 30 June 2021.

investments in local agricultural or mining activities. As Gabriel Paquette has argued, so long as the slave trade to Brazil continued, all capital invested in Angola 'gravitated toward it', foreclosing alternative commercial opportunities.[14] Commodity production in Angola therefore depended on two things: the suppression of the slave trade and the arrival on Angolan shores of a new generation of well-capitalized foreign merchants interested in buying forest and agricultural products instead of captives.[15]

Ideas about diversifying Angola's export economy had circulated among Liberal politicians in Portugal from the late eighteenth century, but the British-led campaign to abolish the Atlantic slave trade pushed the issue up the Portuguese colonial agenda.[16] Portugal's 1815 treaty with the United Kingdom to ban the slave trade north of the equator raised widespread concerns about the viability of alternative forms of commerce in Africa, although in Angola, located south of the equator, the treaty had the unintended effect of temporarily boosting the slave trade. When newly independent Brazil promised the British government, in 1826, to ban slaving within five years in exchange for recognition of its sovereignty, the end of the trade appeared in sight. Since the slave trade was the lifeblood of the Angolan export economy, Portuguese officials feared its collapse would be catastrophic for government revenue.[17] The overseas ministry in Lisbon urged colonial administrators in Luanda to do everything they could to ensure a smooth transition to an export trade in products, which the ministry believed was possible. In Portugal, so the colonial secretary António Manoel de Noronha argued in 1827, 'there is great demand for indigo, coffee, cotton and sugar, the production of which, if they could be sold in Lisbon at a suitable price, merits your kind consideration.'[18] Echoing the excitement of British abolition-

14 Gabriel Paquette, *Imperial Portugal in the Age of Revolutions: The Luso-Brazilian World, c.1770–1850* (Cambridge: Cambridge University Press, 2013), p. 323. See also Gervase Clarence-Smith, *The Third Portuguese Empire, 1825–1975: A Study in Economic Imperialism* (Manchester: Manchester University Press, 1985), p. 6; Joseph C. Miller, *Way of Death: Merchant Capitalism and the Angolan Slave Trade, 1730–1830* (Madison: University of Wisconsin Press, 1988), pp. 634–5.

15 For a similar process in Portuguese Guinea, see Joyce L. Bowman, '"Legitimate" Commerce and Peanut Production in Portuguese Guinea, 1840s–1880s', *JAH*, 28:1 (1987), 87–106.

16 Paquette, *Imperial Portugal*, pp. 52–3, 58–60. For a different view on Liberal interest in Africa, see João Pedro Marques, *Os sons do silêncio: O Portugal de Oitocentos e a abolição do tráfico de escravos* (Lisbon: Imprensa de Ciência Sociais, 1999), pp. 357–451.

17 Valentim Alexandre, *Origens do colonialismo português moderno (1822–1891)* (Lisbon: Sá da Costa Editora, 1979), p. 77; *Velho Brasil, novas Áfricas: Portugal e o Império (1808–1975)* (Porto: Edições Afrontamento, 2000), pp. 84–5.

18 AHU, SEMU-DGU, Angola, no. 588, António Manoel de Noronha to Nicolau de Abreu Castelo Branco, Ajuda, 5 May 1827, enclosed in Noronha to Visconde de Sá

ists about the possibilities of legitimate commerce in Africa, policymakers in Lisbon began to portray Angola as a 'new Brazil', a land rich in soils and natural resources, which could replace the increasingly indefensible trade in human beings, although they rarely matched their enthusiasm for new commerce with a consistent effort to suppress the old.[19]

Coffee was part of Portuguese colonial planning in Africa from the early nineteenth century. Politicians in Lisbon usually mentioned it in one breath with cotton, sugar, and tobacco, archetypal colonial crops that also grew in Angola and that, in their view, merited special attention if the colony was to reduce its dependency on slaving. These plants long remained niche crops in Angola, except coffee, which became an important export product in the late 1860s. Africans cultivated tobacco and foraged wild cotton, but more for their own use than for export. Africans had little interest in growing cotton because of its low value-to-bulk and seasonal incompatibility with food cropping, while early Portuguese attempts to increase cultivation by settlers failed because of recurring low prices, labour shortages on estates, and natural causes. Moreover, as the Swiss botanist Friedrich Welwitsch reported in 1858, dependence on head transport posed a significant problem for cotton traders in the interior, because the product deteriorated before it reached the coast. Colonial initiatives to develop large sugar plantations in Angola failed until the early twentieth century as high capital requirements kept investors away, although production of sugarcane for the internal rum trade happened on small estates.[20]

---

da Bandeira, Luanda, 22 Feb. 1839. See also Mariana Pinho Candido, *Wealth, Land, and Property in Angola: A History of Dispossession, Slavery, and Inequality* (Cambridge: Cambridge University Press, 2022), pp. 72–3.

19 Alexandre, *Origens do colonialismo*, p. 34; *Velho Brasil*, p. 91; Clarence-Smith, *Third Portuguese Empire*, p. 2; Roquinaldo Ferreira, 'Agricultural Enterprise and Unfree Labour in Nineteenth-Century Angola', in Robin Law *et al.* (eds), *Commercial Agriculture, the Slave Trade and Slavery in Atlantic Africa* (Woodbridge: James Currey, 2013), pp. 225–42; Paquette, *Imperial Portugal*, pp. 316–71. For British enthusiasm about the economic potential of abolitionism, see Colin W. Newbury, *British Policy towards West Africa: Select Documents, 1786–1874* (Oxford: Clarendon Press, 1965), pp. 103–6; Christopher Leslie Brown, *Moral Capital: Foundations of British Abolitionism* (Chapel Hill: University of North Carolina Press, 2006), pp. 259–330; Suzanne Schwarz, 'A Just and Honourable Commerce: Abolitionist Experimentation in Sierra Leone in the Late Eighteenth and Early Nineteenth Centuries', *AEH*, 45:1 (2017), 1–45; Everill, *Not Made by Slaves*, pp. 142–7.

20 TNA, FO84/1043, Welwitsch to Gabriel, Luanda, 15 March 1858; Jill R. Dias, 'Changing Patterns of Power in the Luanda Hinterland: The Impact of Trade and Colonisation on the Mbundu ca. 1845–1920', *Paideuma: Mitteilungen zur Kulturkunde*, 32 (1986), 285–318, at pp. 297, 300; 'Angola', in Valentim Alexandre and Jill Dias (eds), *O império africano, 1825–1890* (Lisbon: Editorial Estampa, 1998), pp. 319–556, at pp. 447–57; Ferreira, 'Agricultural Enterprise'; Anne Pitcher, 'Sowing

Coffee proved successful because it was an indigenous tree crop, which African smallholders could exploit without major capital outlays or adjustments to their system of mixed cropping. The crop demanded significant labour inputs only during the harvest season, in the dry months from July to September, when growers needed extra hands to pick ripe cherries, process them for sale, and plant new trees. As the dry season was usually a period of low agricultural activity, the opportunity cost of labour was low. Moreover, because the tree was indigenous to Angola, cultivators were able to profit immediately from favourable market conditions, in contrast to regions where coffee was introduced and planters had to wait four to six years for the first harvest.[21] However, a depressed world coffee market from the 1820s to the early 1850s gave African smallholders little incentive to cultivate wild stands, as prices barely compensated the costs of transportation (Graph 1.1). During this period, coffee was a marginal export crop grown mainly by a handful of ambitious Portuguese and Brazilian settlers in the hinterland of Luanda. For them, coffee was attractive because the initial capital outlays were lower than for sugar. For labour, they relied on slavery and forced porterage, which meant they could only establish plantations in areas under effective Portuguese rule.[22]

The enthusiasm in Lisbon about Angola's untapped riches stood in stark contrast to the sobering observations of officials and merchants on the ground. For them, the issue was not the effect low prices had on agricultural exports, but the stifling influence of the transatlantic slave trade on the Angolan economy. In 1827, the governor of Angola, Nicolau de Abreu Castelo Branco, predicted that neither cultivators nor merchants in Africa would show much interest in developing new export products so long as the slave trade continued. After a government-sponsored project to establish a cotton mill in the inland district of Golungo ended in failure, he noted in despair: 'It seems only necessity will move the inhabitants to new initiatives, considering that so far the slave trade gives them

---

the Seeds of Failure: Early Portuguese Cotton Cultivation in Angola and Mozambique, 1820–1926', *JAH*, 17:1 (1991), 43–70.

21 John Tosh, 'The Cash-Crop Revolution in Tropical Africa: An Agricultural Reappraisal', *African Affairs*, 79:314 (1980), 79–94, at p. 85; Ralph Austen, *African Economic History: Internal Development and External Dependency* (Oxford: James Currey, 1987), p. 139; Gareth Austin, 'Explaining and Evaluating the Cash Crop Revolution in the "Peasant" Colonies of Tropical Africa, ca. 1890–ca. 1930: Beyond "Vent for Surplus"', in Emmanuel Akyeampong *et al.* (eds), *Africa's Development in Historical Perspective* (Cambridge: Cambridge University Press, 2014), pp. 295–320, at p. 310.

22 For export figures, see TNA, FO84/1013, Gabriel to Clarendon, no. 11, Luanda, 11 Feb. 1857, covering 1854–7; Portugal, *Relatórios do Ministro e Secretário d'Estado dos Negócios da Marinha e Ultramar* (Lisbon: Imprensa Nacional, 1875), p. 56, covering 1870–2.

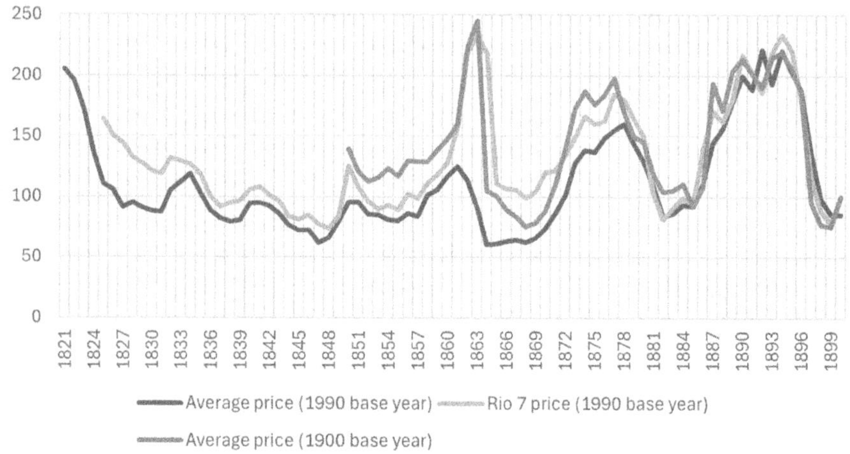

Graph 1.1 Real coffee prices, 1821–1900. Source: Samper and Fernando, 'Appendix', pp. 455–8; Jacks, 'From Boom to Bust'.

more profits for the same work than any other trade.'[23] Castelo Branco ignored that some industries failed because they were unrewarding on their own. But he was not alone in believing that slaving posed an obstacle to economic change.

Feeding a growing demand for African slave labour in Brazil and Cuba, merchants in Angola found ways to thwart the growing international campaign to suppress the transatlantic slave trade (Graph 1.2). Supported by corrupt officials on both sides of the Atlantic, human traffickers increasingly moved their operations to the coasts north and south of Luanda to avoid detection by the British navy. The main flow of traffic ended when Brazil effectively banned the importation of enslaved Africans in 1850, two decades after its official abolition. With financial and logistical support from North American and Brazilian business partners, Cuban slavers continued trading in the Congo River for another seventeen years. This last phase of the transatlantic slave trade ended in 1867 as the pursuit of illegal Spanish and North American slave ships by the United States and British navies and the looming end of slavery in the Americas raised the costs of trafficking to unsustainable levels.[24]

23 AHU, Conselho Ultramarino (CU), Angola, caixa 156, doc. 28, Nicolao de Abreu Castelo Branco to António Manoel de Noronha, no. 269, Luanda, 28 June 1827.

24 Alexandre, *Velho Brasil*, pp. 89–100, 117–18; Dias, 'Angola', 370–6; David Eltis, *Economic Growth and the Ending of the Transatlantic Slave Trade* (Oxford: Oxford University Press, 1987), pp. 207–22; Roquinaldo Ferreira, 'The Suppression of the Slave Trade and Slave Departures from Angola, 1830s–1860s', in David Eltis and David Richardson (eds), *Extending the Frontiers: Essays on the New Transatlantic Slave Trade Database* (New Haven: Yale University Press, 2008), pp. 313–34; John Harris, *The Last Slave Ships: New York and the End of the Middle Passage* (New Haven: Yale

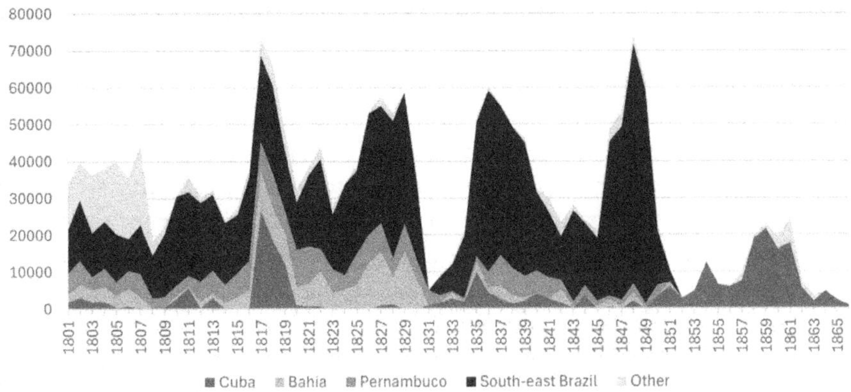

Graph 1.2 Enslaved people shipped from west-central Africa, 1801–66, by destination. Source: Estimates (2019), *SlaveVoyages*, www.slavevoyages.org/estimates/cCJ9g7Vo, accessed 23 June 2024.

The elongated lifespan of the Angolan slave trade, many local observers agreed, was hampering the growth of an embryonic commodity trade. Even after Portugal unilaterally abolished the slave trade in 1836, these visitors doubted that an export economy based on commodities could flourish while Brazil and Cuba kept importing large numbers of enslaved people from the region. As the later governor of Angola, Pedro Alexandrino da Cunha, noted in 1841, 'while there remains even a glimmer of hope to smuggle slaves, all efforts and measures taken in this colony to develop agriculture and trade will come to nothing'.[25] A French captain echoed these sentiments after visiting Ambriz, a prominent slaving port north of Luanda, in 1846. Although some European and American merchants had established factories there to purchase ivory, gum copal, and copper ore, he said the place 'offers no advantage except to the slave trader'.[26]

It was not for want of natural resources that Angola's export economy struggled to diversify. 'The whole of this coast produces ivory and palm oil', a British naval officer noted in 1831, 'the northern parts, woods for dying and the southern, wax, hides and gum copal but I doubt much if any increase of the British traffic could be pushed with the slightest success, as the trade appears (with the single

University Press, 2020); Herbert S. Klein, *African Slavery in Latin America and the Caribbean* (Oxford: Oxford University Press, 1986), pp. 92–5; Herbert S. Klein and Francisco Vidal Luna, *Slavery in Brazil* (Cambridge: Cambridge University Press, 2010), pp. 74–114, 253–4.

25 AHU, SEMU-DGU, Angola, no. 827, P. A. da Cunha to Sá da Bandeira, Luanda, 7 Feb. 1841.

26 Archives Nationales d'Outre-Mer, Fonds Ministériel, Série Géographique, Afrique IV, Dossier 23A, Rapport du navire Antilope (1846–7). The owners of this vessel were former slave traders.

exception of slaves) to be quite trifling.'[27] Early forms of legitimate commerce in Angola consisted mainly of ivory, orchil lichen, and beeswax, trades that were logistically compatible with slaving and controlled by merchant groups with access to specialized technologies, trade routes, and labour supplies.[28] Exports of oleaginous products like peanuts and palm oil, which were developing fast in other parts of western Africa, remained notoriously weak. This was partly because a shortage of navigable rivers in Angola made transport of these products through the coastal hinterland relatively expensive. Additionally, Brazilian and Cuban traders and their local Portuguese and Luso-African business partners showed little interest in any industry other than slaving.[29]

Some officials believed that by abolishing the slave trade, cash-crop production would automatically increase as, one argued, 'the capital employed in [slaving] will be directed to [agriculture]'.[30] The idea that legal pressure would force slavers to invest their profits in alternative trades was nonetheless misguided. As Commodore Arthur Wilmot of the British West Africa Squadron noted in 1864, few Brazilian and Cuban slave traders had a stake in the fledgling commodity trade, which mainly supplied the world's industrial heartlands. 'Capital is wanting at St. Paul's [Luanda] and everywhere else, for the development of African productions. Money made by the Slave Trade is rarely used, as in the days of old, for the improvement of this country, and hence we cannot be surprised at the want of even common progress.'[31] After abolition, Brazilian traffickers withdrew their capital from Africa to speculate in urban real estate. Some notable slave dealers in Luanda, like Arsénio de Carpo, António Francisco Flores, and Ana Joaquina dos Santos Silva, invested in agricultural ventures and commodity trades while continuing their illegal slaving operations. Generally, however, Angola was a place where slavers 'barely knew how to invest their capital differently', as the colonial chronicler José Joaquim Lopes de Lima put it.[32]

27 TNA, FO84/126, Harrison to Haynes, 23 Sep. 1831, enclosed in Haynes to Admiralty, no. 102, 4 Oct. 1831, enclosed in Admiralty to FO, 12 Dec. 1831.

28 TNA, FO84/792, Gabriel to Palmerston, London, 5 Aug. 1850; TNA, FO84/1043, Gabriel to Clarendon, no. 18, Luanda, 25 Feb. 1858. On 'predatory' production, see Austen, *African Economic History*, pp. 68–71; Jean-Luc Vellut, 'Diversification de l'économie de cueilllette: Miel et cire dans les sociétés de la forêt claire d'Afrique centrale (c.1750–1950)', *AEH*, 7 (1979), 93–112; Dias, 'Changing Patterns', 294–9.

29 Alexandre, *Origens do colonialismo*, pp. 49–52.

30 AHU, SEMU-DGU, Angola, no. 590, Luiz Antonio de Miranda, Exposição do estado da província, Luanda, 27 March 1840.

31 TNA, FO541/8, no. 220, Wilmot to Admiralty, Annual report on slave trade on west coast, Ascension, 1 Dec. 1864.

32 Lopes de Lima, *Ensaios*, vol. 3, pt 1, p. xxxviii; Manolo Florentino, *Em costas negras: uma história do tráfico de escravos entre a África e o Rio de Janeiro (séculos XVIII e XIX)* (São Paulo: Companhia das Letras, 1997); Dias, 'Angola', pp. 386–7. On slave dealers engaged in licit business, see João Pedro Marques, 'Arsénio Pompílio Pompeu de

The sluggishness of commodity trading in Angola was different from the situation in the bights of Benin and Biafra, the two largest slaving zones in West Africa. There, British and African merchants increased their investments in the palm oil trade in response to abolition, although the slave trade to the French Caribbean, Cuba, and Brazil continued as if little had changed. Places like Bonny and Calabar, in the Niger Delta, were the first to develop 'legitimate' commerce after Britain abolished its slave trade in 1807, followed in the 1830s by Little Popo on the western Slave Coast. These ports benefited from good water links with their hinterlands and established palm oil trades. During the 1840s and 1850s, merchants in the trafficking bastions of Ouidah and Lagos also entered the palm oil business. Some Brazilian traders in these ports became commercial intermediaries and palm-plantation owners, but these activities were generally supplementary to their slaving operations. The transition from slave to commodity trading went more swiftly in some West African ports than in others, but the two trades seemed compatible in most of them.[33]

Angola did not have the continuity in merchants that characterized the early palm oil trade in West Africa.[34] The big leap in the export of vegetable oils and coffee came only in the 1860s, when the contraband slave trade ended and local traffickers either closed shop or offered their services to legal business ventures.[35] While the volumes remained small compared to West Africa, between 1858 and

---

Carpo: um percurso negreiro no século XIX', *Análise Social*, 36:160 (2001), 609–38; Susan J. Herlin, 'Brazil and the Commercialization of Kongo, 1840–1870', in José C. Curto and Paul E. Lovejoy (eds), *Enslaving Connections: Changing Cultures of Africa and Brazil during the Era of Slavery* (Amherst: Humanity Books, 2004), pp. 265–87, at pp. 265–7, 272; Roquinaldo Ferreira, *Dos sertões ao Atlântico: Tráfico ilegal de escravos e comércio lícito em Angola, 1830–1860* (Luanda: Kilombelombe, 2012); Vanessa Oliveira, *Slave Trade and Abolition: Gender, Commerce, and Economic Transition in Luanda* (Madison: University of Wisconsin Press, 2021).

33 David Northrup, 'The Compatibility of the Slave and Palm Oil Trades in the Bight of Biafra', *JAH*, 17:3 (1976), 353–64; Elisée Soumonni, 'The Compatibility of the Slave and Palm Oil Trades in Dahomey, 1818–1858', in Robin Law (ed.), *From Slave Trade to 'Legitimate' Commerce: The Commercial Transition in Nineteenth-Century West Africa* (Cambridge: Cambridge University Press, 1995), pp. 78–92; Martin Lynn, *Commerce and Economic Change in West Africa: The Palm Oil Trade in the Nineteenth Century* (Cambridge: Cambridge University Press, 1997), pp. 11–33; Robin Law, *Ouidah: The Social History of a West African Slaving 'Port', 1727–1892* (Athens: Ohio University Press, 2004), pp. 189–230; Kristin Mann, *Slavery and the Birth of an African City: Lagos, 1760–1900* (Bloomington: Indiana University Press, 2007), pp. 117–59; Silke Strickrodt, *Afro-European Trade in the Atlantic World: The Western Slave Coast, c.1550–c.1885* (Woodbridge: James Currey, 2015), pp. 210–24.

34 Lynn, *Commerce and Economic Change*, pp. 60–101.

35 TNA, FO84/1214, Vredenburg, Annual report on the slave trade, Luanda, 25 Oct. 1864, encl. in Vredenburg to Russell, no. 33, Luanda, 25 Oct. 1864.

1867, peanut exports from Luanda increased from 261 tons to 1,879 tons, palm oil from 119 tons to 1,311 tons, and coffee from 73 tons to 913 tons.[36] These trades benefited greatly from the opening of the Cuanza steamship line in 1866, connecting the inland market of Dondo to Luanda.[37] At the same time, the arrival of new traders from Western Europe and North America looking to open the commodity markets of the so-called South Coast contributed to a fundamental shift in the mercantile networks structuring the Angolan export economy.

Commodity trades

Major changes in the Atlantic economy during the middle of the nineteenth century gave coffee cultivation in Angola a sudden boost. First, the effective suppression of the transatlantic slave trade released the Angolan economy from the stranglehold of American slavers and their local suppliers. Second, the arrival of a new group of produce traders on the Angolan coast, along with a general expansion of the trade in tropical commodities, created opportunities for small producers to participate in export production. The first of these new firms arrived in the 1830s and settled in the northern port of Ambriz, an important outlet for captives and commodities from regions north of Portuguese Angola.[38] When Portugal occupied Ambriz in 1855, many traders moved further north to evade Portuguese customs.[39] They included several palm oil traders from Liverpool, like Thomas Tobin and Sons, Horsfall and Son, and Hatton and Cookson, as well as a few North American and French firms, such as peanut traders Brookhouse and Hunt from Salem and Louis and Victor Régis from Marseille, later succeeded by Marius Daumas from Le Havre.[40] In 1857, Kerdijk and Pincoffs, Dutch merchants from Rotterdam, joined this predominantly Anglophone community after they took over the African business of Leopold Samson, a Manchester-based trader with roots in Hannover and Rotterdam. Using a small fleet of coastal and ocean-going vessels, within a decade they became one of the

36 João Mesquita, *Dados estatísticos para o estudo das pautas de Angola: Exportação pelas alfândegas do Círculo e do Congo nos anos de 1888 a 1913* (Luanda: Imprensa Nacional, 1918), p. 12. For West Africa, see George E. Brooks, 'Peanuts and Colonialism: Consequences of the Commercialization of Peanuts in West Africa, 1830–70', *JAH*, 16:1 (1975), 29–54, at pp. 34, 45, 52; Bowman, 'Legitimate Commerce', 95; Lynn, *Commerce and Economic Change*, p. 21.

37 Dias, 'Changing Patterns', 300–1.

38 Phillips Library, Peabody Essex Museum (Salem), Log 970, Glear (Brig) Journal, 1835–36.

39 Dias, 'Changing Patterns', 293.

40 TNA, FO84/569, Gabriel to FO, 2 Nov. 1845. On peanut traders, see Brooks, 'Peanuts and Colonialism', 36–40. On Salem merchants, see Alexandra Celia Kelly, *Consuming Ivory: Mercantile Legacies of East Africa and New England* (Seattle: University of Washington Press, 2021), pp. 45–50.

leading companies in the region. In 1869, they became a public company, the Afrikaansche Handelsvereeniging, later reformed into the Nieuwe Afrikaansche Handels-Vennootschap (NAHV), the most dominant trade house north of Luanda, whose supremacy was based on efficient sourcing of textiles, alcohol, guns, and other merchandise in Britain, the Netherlands, and Belgium.[41] Because trading in Luanda, still the main outlet for African produce in the region, required a Portuguese licence, most foreign commodity traders settled on the northern coast. To gain access to the Luanda market, they formed partnerships with local Portuguese traders, like Alberto Schut, or with British and American businessmen such as John Carnegie and Augustus Archer Silva, who had their own connections in the city.[42]

These early commodity traders came to Angola in search of wild products like orchil, ivory, gum copal, and beeswax and to locate new sources of vegetable oils outside the busier West African markets. Despite their interest in purchasing products, they could not easily distance themselves from the ongoing traffic in human captives. Many supplied merchandise to slave dealers in exchange for money payments, which was sometimes the only way to keep business afloat in this part of Africa given the paucity of the produce trade. For instance, in the 1840s, Robert Brookhouse, the bothers Régis, and other 'legitimate' traders transported goods like gunpowder, rum, and textiles to Angola on behalf of Francisco Barbosa Rodrigues, a known slave trader.[43] A decade later, the coastal agent of Kerdijk and Pincoffs admitted privately that cash sales to Cuban slavers were his most profitable line of trade.[44] Moreover, to purchase commodities,

41 A. F. Schepel (ed.), *Reisjournaal van Lodewijk Kerdijk: West-Afrika 1857/1858* (Schiedam: Interbook International, 1978), pp. 7–39; Nationaal Archief (The Hague, henceforth NA), Nieuwe Afrikaansche Handels-Vennootschap (NAHV) (2.18.10.09), 145/364, Letters from Lodewijk Kerdijk to Kerdijk and Pincoffs, 1857–58; *ibid.*, 72/167, 1st annual report (1880), 3 June 1881; *ibid.*, 145/364, Schalwijk and De Bloeme to Foreign Affairs, Rotterdam, 18 Jan. 1889; NA, Ministerie van Buitenlandse Zaken: A-Dossiers, 1815–1940 (2.05.03), 217, Gericke to Foreign Affairs, no. 114, Lisbon, 8 June 1885; Maritiem Museum Rotterdam, Library, H753, Reis naar Afrika (1858); Stadsarchief Rotterdam, Fa. R. Mees en Zonen (305), 624, Memo, Rotterdam, 24 Oct. 1868.

42 Dias, 'Angola', p. 388. On Schut, see Schepel, *Reisjournaal*, p. 136. On Archer Silva, see Frederico Antonio Ferreira, 'Augustus Archer, entre o passado e o future das relações entre o império do Brasil e a África portuguesa', *Transversos*, 15 (2019), 213–29.

43 AHU, SEMU-DGU, no. 769, Miscelânea, São Tomé, 2ª Repartição, Mapa dos navios portuguezes entrados no porto de Loanda, durante o primeiro semestre de 1849.

44 NA, NAHV, 145/364, L. P. Kerdijk to H. Kerdijk and L. Pincoffs, no. 7bis, Luanda, 29 March 1858; AHU, SEMU-DGU, Angola, no. 824, Arthur P. Eardley-Wilmot to Palmerston, Congo, 19 Jan. 1853 (printed London, 1853). On wider British involve-

many traders employed Portuguese agents whose commercial know-how and networks stemmed from their previous role as brokers for Brazilian and Cuban merchants. As the Commander-in-Chief of the British West Africa Squadron William Dowell observed in 1868, almost 'all the old slave dealers [have] given up their barracoons and turned their attention to legitimate trade, acting principally as "middlemen" between the licit traders and the natives'.[45] Within a decade, however, most of these old intermediaries had retired, making way for a new cohort of small Portuguese traders. Like their predecessors, these young arrivals from Portugal remained dependent for supplies on better-capitalized firms from Western Europe.[46]

Coffee was not what initially attracted commodity traders to Angola. While locally grown coffee had been sold to consumers in Luanda from the 1820s, it long remained a marginal export. In 1857, for example, Portuguese and foreign merchants shipped a meagre seventy-six tons of coffee from Luanda, which, valued at 3,600 pounds sterling, accounted for only 1.5 per cent of local exports.[47] Meanwhile, there were few if any signs of coffee trading on the coast north of Luanda. In fact, the main coffee-related business of Kerdijk and Pincoffs in Angola that year consisted of importing roasters, mills, and jugs for local coffee consumption.[48] The slow development of the Angolan coffee economy was partly due to Brazil's fast-growing *fazendas*, which pushed world coffee prices down and thereby discouraged African smallholders from investing family and neighbourhood labour in coffee cultivation. Local coffee production was still largely concentrated in the plantations of a dozen entrepreneurial settlers in the Luanda hinterland, who used the Portuguese colonial system to gain access to land and labour.[49]

---

ment in the slave trade, see TNA, FO84/792, Gabriel to Palmerston, London, 5 Aug. 1850; John A. E. Harris, 'Circuits of Wealth, Circuits of Sorrow: Financing the Illegal Transatlantic Slave Trade in the Age of Suppression, 1850–66', *JGH*, 11:3 (2016), 409–29, at p. 424, and literature there cited.

45 TNA, FO84/1295, Dowell to Admiralty, no. 139, Lagos, 4 July 1868. On Brazilian intermediaries in the legal trade, see Herlin, 'Brazil and the Commercialization of Kongo', pp. 265–7. See also TNA, FO541, no. 167, Wilmot to Admiralty, Sierra Leone, 19 Dec. 1865, Report on slave and legitimate trade on West Coast; FO84/1268, Hornby to Admiralty, no. 103, River Congo, 15 May 1866, enclosed in Admiralty to FO, 11 July 1866; FO84/1286, Annual report on slave trade, Luanda, 30 Sep. 1867; FO84/1299, Annual report on the slave trade, enclosed in Vredenburg to Stanley, no. 20, Luanda, 30 Sep. 1868; FO541/12, no. 57, Hornby to Admiralty, Ascension, 1 Dec. 1868, Report on slave and legal trade.

46 Francisco Teixeira da Silva, 'Relatório da Estação Naval d'Angola acerca da questão do norte da província, especialmente Ambriz, Quicombo e rio Zaire, em 1880', *Arquivo das Colónias*, 5 (1930), 183–99.

47 TNA, FO84/1043, Gabriel to Clarendon, no. 18, Luanda, 25 Feb. 1858.

48 NA, NAHV, 145/364, L. P. Kerdijk to H. Kerdijk and L. Pincoffs, no. 1, 6 Dec. 1857.

49 David Birmingham, 'The Coffee Barons of Cazengo', *JAH*, 19:4 (1978), 523–38.

In the late 1850s, global coffee prices began to recover, while Brazil's ban on the import of enslaved Africans caused slave prices in Angola to fall.[50] This enticed a growing number of local farmers and colonial settlers to invest in coffee cultivation. The fruits of their labour became visible in a record shipment of more than fourteen hundred tons of coffee from Luanda in 1863, with unknown quantities sold to traders on the northern coast.[51] As coastal merchants picked up small batches of coffee during routine negotiations with traders from the interior, knowledge about Angolan coffee began to spread around the Atlantic world. One British intelligence officer noted that same year that Luanda supplied 'coffee of good quality', while the coast to the north produced 'excellent coffee ... which, though the berry is small, is of exceedingly good flavour'.[52] Angolan coffees began to appear at auctions in major European coffee ports, such as Le Havre and Rotterdam. They usually sold at the low end of the market because, while generally acceptable, in terms of flavour they did not compare to most Latin American coffees.[53] Meantime, grocers across Europe welcomed Angolan coffee as a comparatively cheap addition to the blends of roasted and ground beans they prepared for their customers.[54]

Sustained price increases in the 1870s and 1880s, declining freight rates in oceanic transport, and Angola's growing reputation for producing 'coffee of very good quality', as a German correspondent in Luanda put it, ushered in a period of significant expansion.[55] Shipments from Luanda surpassed two thousand

50 Alexandre, *Origens do colonialismo*, p. 53; Dias, 'Angola', pp. 405, 453; Ferreira, 'Agricultural Enterprise', p. 239.

51 Aida Freudenthal, *Arimos e fazendas: a transição agrária em Angola* (Luanda: Chá de Caxinde, 2005), p. 178; Stadsarchief Rotterdam, Fa. R. Mees en Zonen (305), 624, Staat van bezittingen en voorraden aan de Zuidwestkust van Afrika, 31 Dec. 1867; Charles de Rouvre, 'La Guinée Méridionale Indépendante: Congo, Kacongo, N'Goyo, Loango, 1870–1877', *Bulletin de la Société de Géographie*, 20 (1880), 289–327, 401–34, at p. 420; Charles Jeannest, *Quatre années au Congo* (Paris: G. Charpentier, 1883), pp. 33, 47.

52 TNA, FO541/8, no. 176, Wilmot to Walker, Report on slave trade on West Coast, Sierra Leone, 31 Dec. 1863.

53 *The Economist*, 10 Dec. 1864, p. 1522; NA, Koninklijke Nederlandse Vereniging voor de Koffiehandel (2.19.012), no. 245, sales advertisements of coffee supplied by the NAHV in 1887 (nos 50, 52, 64).

54 Robert Hewitt, Jr, *Coffee: Its History, Cultivation, and Uses* (New York: D. Appleton & Co., 1872), p. 73; B. B. Keable, *Coffee: from Grower to Consumer* (London: Isaac Pitman and Sons, 1933 [1910]), pp. 91–2; Francis B. Thurber, *Coffee: From the Plantation to the Cup* (New York: American Grocer Publishing Association, 1881), p. 31; Joseph M. Walsh, *Coffee: Its History, Classification, and Description* (Philadelphia: Henry T. Coates & Company, 1894), pp. 223–7.

55 NA, Ministerie van Buitenlandse Zaken: A-Dossiers, 1815–1940 (2.05.03), 203, *Weser Zeitung* (Bremen), 12 Nov. 1876, letter from Eduard Mohr, Luanda, 11 Sep. 1876; Topik and Wells, 'Commodity Chains', pp. 630–3.

tons in the early 1870s, when coffee became Angola's most valuable export good.[56] Shipped alongside rubber, wax, and vegetable oils, Angolan coffees landed in ports across the North Atlantic, including in the United States, where experts added tentative descriptions of them to a growing catalogue of exotic coffee varieties.[57]

Enthusiasm about the coffee business manifested in correspondence from John Carnegie, who traded on commission for several British companies, including John Holt of Liverpool. 'Last year was a grand year for us Luanda coffee men', Carnegie told Holt in 1874. He had taken advantage of price lags between Africa and Europe, as rapidly rising world coffee prices made it possible to buy low and sell high. Illustrating the fortunes of brokers like himself, Carnegie mentioned the agent of Isaac Zagury, one of Angola's most successful coffee merchants, who in one year had earned three thousand pounds sterling from his purchases. Profit margins narrowed, however, when local coffee prices caught up with global trends. In March of 1874, Carnegie informed Holt that the trade was still 'splendid', but that he had 'not a bag of coffee in store right now and cannot buy', as he refused to pay producers the prices they were asking. To gain greater control of the supply chain and capture more of the value-added, Carnegie and his business partner in Luanda, Francisco Newton, bought the 600-hectare Monte Bello plantation in the coffee district of Cazengo when prices picked up during the late 1880s. They had to sell the estate when the market collapsed a decade later.[58]

Commercial expansion was not driven by white-owned estates such as Monte Bello, however, but by small-scale farmers, most of whom lived and worked out of sight of the colonial authorities. While during the early 1880s, Angola's two main coffee ports, Luanda and Ambriz, had a combined annual export of about five thousand tons, this was only part of what the country produced.[59] Smallholder production developed most rapidly in the hinterland of the coast north of Ambriz. Portugal had no jurisdiction over this coast before the Berlin Conference of 1885, and in the absence of customs records it is difficult to

56 Freudenthal, *Arimos*, p. 178; Mesquita, *Dados*, p. 13.

57 AHU, SEMU-DGU, no. 837, Angola, 2ª Repartição, Província de Angola, Alfândega de Luanda, importação, exportação, 1880–4; Walsh, *Coffee*, pp. 104–5.

58 Rhodes House Library (Oxford), John Holt & Company, MSS Afr. S1525, Box 12/6, Carnegie to Holt, 3 March 1874, 22 May 1874, and 5 Aug. 1874; Cadbury Research Library, University of Birmingham, Cadbury/308, Visit to West Africa (1908–09), journal entry 28 Nov. 1908; *ibid.*, Letter 4 Dec. 1908; David Birmingham, *A Short History of Modern Angola* (Oxford: Oxford University Press, 2015), pp. 29, 131–2; Alberto de Souza Maia Leitão, *Relatório da visita sanitária aos concelhos de leste de Loanda mais victimados pela doença de somno* (Porto: Typ. a vapor da Empreza Litteraria e Typographica, 1901), p. 65.

59 António José Valente, *Novo projeto da pauta aduaneira da alfândega do Ambriz* (Lisbon: Typgraphia Franco-Portugueza, 1889), p. 28; Tito Augusto de Carvalho, *Les colonies portugaises* (Paris: Aillaud, 1900), pp. 55–7.

assess the volume of regional coffee exports. Several years earlier, the governor of Angola, José Baptista de Andrade, informed the colonial ministry that the trade there probably rivalled that of Luanda, which strengthened Portuguese resolve to claim this region during the colonial partition of Africa.[60] Andrade's guess was corroborated by estimates of the coffee trade of the NAHV obtained by Dutch coffee historian Carel Frederik van Delden Laerne, showing that this firm alone imported 1,411 tons from the northern coast in 1884. Hendrik Muller, the company director, added that this number only included coffee shipped directly to Rotterdam; any bags dispatched via Liverpool and Lisbon, using British and Portuguese steamers, were not counted.[61] Figures became more reliable when Portuguese customs became effective on the northern coast after the Berlin Conference. In 1890, total exports from Angola had reached 8,300 tons. Half passed through Luanda, and this was mainly the product of settler estates and African smallholder farms in the colonial districts of Cazengo and Golungo Alto. The other half passed through customs in Ambriz and Ambrizete (modern-day N'Zeto), ports mainly supplied by farmers in the unoccupied Kongo and Dembos regions of northern Angola.[62]

A first taste

At the Great Exhibition in London in 1851, Portugal gave the world a first taste of Angolan coffee. Farmers in Angola had been growing coffee for decades, but their limited outputs had mainly reached consumers in Luanda and Portugal. This coffee enjoyed a decent reputation in Portuguese colonial circles, where

60 AHU, SEMU-DGU, Angola, 2ª Repartição, no. 828, GG interino, José Baptista de Andrade, to MSENMU, 'Relatório com relação ao ano de 1873', Luanda, 28 Oct. 1873, enclosed in GG interino to MSENMU, no. 282, Luanda, 29 Oct. 1873. On the partition, see Françoise Latour de Veiga Pinto, *Le Portugal et le Congo au XIXe siècle* (Paris: Presses Universitaires de France, 1972).

61 Stadsarchief Rotterdam, Familie Muller (41), 268a, Hendrik Muller to Van Delden Laerne, 6 Jan. 1885. See also Cornelis Frederik van Delden Laerne, *Brazil and Java: Report on Coffee Culture in America, Asia and Africa* (The Hague: Martinus Nijhoff, 1885), pp. 458–61. Because Portugal levied differential duties on goods entering and leaving the colonies, most coffee from Luanda travelled to Lisbon first, from where shippers re-exported the larger part to markets in Western Europe. Portugal, *Relatório do ministério e secretário d'estado dos negócios da marinha e ultramar* (Lisbon: Imprensa Nacional, 1898), pp. 243–4. The policy was ended by the *Estado Novo*, which used exchange controls, quotas, and price fixing to profit from the African commodity trade. See Clarence-Smith, *Third Portuguese Empire*, pp. 146–91.

62 António José Valente, *Novo projeto da pauta aduaneira da alfândega do Ambriz* (Lisbon: Typgraphia Franco-Portugueza, 1889), p. 25; Tito Augusto de Carvalho, *Les colonies portugaises* (Paris: Aillaud, 1900), pp. 55–7; Mesquita, *Dados*, pp. 18, 46–7.

those who dreamed of a new Eldorado in southwest Africa believed it equalled the product of Brazil. To boost colonial trade, Portugal used the London exhibition to display a range of commodities from across the empire, including coffee samples from Madeira, Cabo Verde, São Tomé, Mozambique, Timor, and Angola. The exhibition catalogue classified Angolan coffee as neither 'excellent' nor 'bad', but as 'good', which in retrospect was surprising given that this was robusta coffee, arabica's poor cousin often despised for its coarse taste, although no expert knew the biological difference between the species at the time.[63] The exhibition signalled the arrival of Angola in the world coffee market. While hardly exchanged internationally before 1850, during the next hundred years Angolan robusta came to dominate the global trade in low-grade coffees feeding the manufacture of blended and soluble coffee products.

Although high transportation costs, droughts, and epidemics (especially smallpox and sleeping sickness) hampered Angolan coffee production during the nineteenth century, the general trend was strongly upward, in line with global patterns.[64] Coffee exports from Angola reached a peak of eleven thousand tons in 1895, when the world coffee market entered a long depression.[65] While this was less than 2 per cent of the global coffee trade, it placed Angola in the same league as Central American newcomers such as Costa Rica and El Salvador and consolidated the country's position as the leading coffee producer in Africa.[66] This chapter has shown how the rise of coffee production in Angola was part of a larger transition to commodity trading in the region. It has particularly emphasized the ambivalent role of Brazil, the world's largest coffee producer, in this process. On the one hand, Brazilian outputs of cheap arabicas helped create a mass demand for coffee among urban populations in the industrializing Global North, of which other young producing countries like Angola could take advantage. On the other, the dependence of Brazilian and Cuban agriculture on unfree labour supplies from Africa kept the Angolan export economy under the sway of American slave traders, slowing the development of Angola's own cash-crop economy. Brazilian and Cuban slavers did not actively impede legitimate commerce, but the economies they served had no stake in Africa's burgeoning produce trade, while for British and French merchants Angola was a distant market ever since

63 P. L. Simmonds, *The Commercial Products of the Vegetable Kingdom* (London: T. F. A. Day, 1854), p. 78; *Tropical Agriculture* (London: E. and F. N. Spon, 1889), pp. 44–6.

64 Jill R. Dias, 'Famine and Disease in the History of Angola, c. 1830–1930', *JAH*, 22:3 (1981), 349–78; 'Angola', pp. 454, 472–3; Yonah Seleti, 'Finance Capital and the Coffee Industry of Angola, 1865–1895', *Transafrican Journal of History*, 16 (1987), 63–77, at pp. 68–9; Pedro Avelino Joyce, *O café nas nossas colonias* (Lisbon: Ilustração Portugueza, 1915), p. 92.

65 Mesquita, *Dados*, pp. 21, 46.

66 Samper and Fernando, 'Appendix', pp. 424, 440.

their governments abolished the slave trade in the early nineteenth century. The landscape changed dramatically during the 1860s, as the illegal slave trade came to an end and commodity traders began to offer growers favourable terms of trade based on a surge in world coffee prices. African smallholders were best equipped to respond, as the next chapter will demonstrate.

2

Coffee Frontier

DENSE WOODLANDS graced the rolling hills and mountain slopes connecting the coastal plains of northern and central Angola to the interior highlands. Botanically known as laurel forest, they formed a natural habitat for several varieties of robusta coffee (*Coffea canephora*). This forest landscape stretched from Mbanza Kongo (São Salvador) in the north to Seles in the south, at altitudes between 350 and 1,200 meters, with coffee growing best in areas between 800 and 1,000 meters above sea level. The river Cuanza divided this distinctive ecosystem into a northern and a southern zone. Because the transition from coast to plateau was more gradual in the north than in the south, woodlands were more extensive in the northern zone, where dense laurel forest changed into a forest-savanna mosaic towards the west. This area contained the oldest coffee-producing regions in Angola, which during the twentieth century were incorporated in the Cuanza-Norte and Congo administrative districts.

Botanists knew these rugged woodlands also as the 'cloud forest', as the hills attracted condensation building up in the lower areas, while they shielded vegetation from dry winds blowing from the east. As a Scottish visitor to the region noted in 1854, 'every evening clouds come rolling in great masses from the mountains in the west [and] generally remain on the hills till the morning is well spent'.[1] Vegetation depended for water more on clouds than on rainfall, which was relatively modest in the region. There was an upper stratum of trees growing up to forty metres in height that shielded a lower storey of shrubs including natural coffee stands, which thrived in the humid and relatively mild climate of the montane forest. The forest canopy provided shade that kept soils moist and depressed weed growth, it reduced variations in temperature between day and night, and it protected coffee trees and soils from sun, wind, and occasional heavy rain. In the nineteenth century, coffee growers carved plantations out of the forest by cutting away the bush around wild coffee stands. From the 1920s, however, European settlers increasingly removed both the upper and the lower strata for new coffee planting.[2]

1 David Livingstone, *Missionary Travels and Researches in South Africa* (New York: Harper and Brothers, 1858), p. 418.

2 John Gossweiler and Francisco de Ascensão Mendonça, *Carta fitogeográfica de Angola* (Lisbon: Ministério das Colónias, Governo Geral de Angola, 1939), pp.

This chapter examines the exploitation of Angola's natural coffee reserves by local and foreign planters from the 1820s through the early twentieth century. It shows that small farms rather than large estates drove the expansion of coffee production discussed in Chapter 1. The first section discusses early settler initiatives in the colonial districts of Cazengo and Golungo Alto, revealing several important natural conditions the forest environment imposed on coffee planting in Angola. The second section analyses the cultivation methods of small farming units. From the 1850s, independent smallholders, mainly in the unoccupied territories north of Portuguese Angola, pushed the Angolan coffee frontier to the boundaries it retained throughout the twentieth century. Their history shows that the woodlands of northern Angola were not a 'pristine' natural environment used by Africans to 'gather' wild produce, as the historical literature has long suggested.[3] Like most African landscapes, the montane forest was 'anthropogenic', that is, 'the product of human action', as environmental historian James McCann explains.[4] The final two sections examine why smallholder production was generally more efficient than estate production, suggesting that the colonial government's endorsement of settler expansion after the First World War was a political choice based on ideology and habit rather than economic evidence.

In the absence of detailed reports on coffee cultivation before the twentieth century, fragmented data from colonial archives and printed primary sources constitute the bulk of the evidence for this early period. In 1904, Augusto Eduardo Neuparth, a former engineer of the Cazengo Agricultural Company (Companhia Agrícola de Cazengo), lamented that despite the long presence of foreign coffee farmers in Cazengo, none of them had cared to write down what they knew about soils, vegetation, and cultivation practices in the region.[5] The colonial government

---

74–103; Royal Botanic Gardens Library (Kew), Herbert Kenneth Airy Shaw, 'The Vegetation of Angola' (1947), unpublished manuscript; L. A. Grandvaux Barbosa, *Carta fitogeográfica de Angola* (Luanda: Instituto de Investigação Científica de Angola, 1970), pp. 60–71, 92–7; Jeffery M. Paige, *Agrarian Revolution: Social Movements and Export Agriculture in the Underdeveloped World* (New York: Free Press, 1975), pp. 213–14. On the forest habitat of robusta, see Paul Janssens, *Le café robusta dans l'Angola* (Brussels: Imprimerie Industrielle et Financière, 1930), pp. 24, 29; Alec Ernest Haarer, *Modern Coffee Production* (London: Leonard Hill, 1958), pp. 47–62, 79; Gordon Wrigley, *Coffee* (Harlow: Longman, 1988), pp. 135–6.

3 Francisco António Pinto, *Angola e Congo: Conferências* (Lisbon: Livraria Ferreira, Editora, 1888), p. 53; Henrique Augusto Dias de Carvalho, *Descripção da viagem á Mussumba do Muatiânvua* (4 vols, Lisbon: Imprensa Nacional, 1890–94), vol. 1, p. 114; Manuel José Martins Contreiras, *A província de Angola* (Lisbon: La Bécarre, 1894), p. 54; Jill Dias, 'Angola', in Valentim Alexandre and Jill Dias (eds), *O império africano, 1825–1890* (Lisbon: Editorial Estampa, 1998), pp. 319–556, at pp. 402, 475.

4 James C. McCann, *Green Land, Brown Land, Black Land: An Environmental History of Africa, 1800–1990* (Oxford: James Currey, 1999), p. 2.

5 Augusto Eduardo Neuparth, *Apontamentos para a história da Companhia Agrícola de Cazengo* (Lisbon: Typographia do Commercio, 1904), p. 10. A lack of written

occasionally published snippets of intelligence collected from these settlers. The settlers themselves may have been influenced by plantation guides printed around 1800, notably the work of Pierre Joseph Laborie, *The Coffee Planters of Santo Domingo*, which was translated into Portuguese.[6] In building their plantations, they sometimes followed Caribbean patterns. Using a few dozen enslaved workers to open the forest, creating a nursery for coffee plants, provision grounds for the workforce, the drying terrains, the 'big house' at the centre, the majestic avenues: this was all by the book.[7] But since the Angolan coffee landscape was significantly different from the American environment, planters also had to improvise, leaning on knowledge produced and exchanged locally by African, European, and Brazilian farmers.

Documentation improved in the early twentieth century, when colonial scientists in Angola began to gather information about local agricultural practices.[8] In 1908, the Angolan Department of Agriculture established an experimental station on the site of an abandoned coffee plantation in Cazengo, where plant scientists and agronomists focused on breeding cash crops for scientific and commercial use. At the same time, it started the publication of the *Boletim de agricultura, pecuária e fomento*, a periodical that among other things contained articles on coffee growing. Ten years later, John Gossweiler, botanist to the colonial state and head of the experimental station, produced a study of African cultivation techniques based on his observations in the Uíge district north of Cazengo. In 1930, a Belgian agronomist, Paul Janssens, published the first manual, in French, for coffee planters in Angola, applying general knowledge of coffee production to the peculiarities of the Angolan landscape. These publications provide a record of best practices as farmers and agronomists understood them before the 1920s, adding useful information to the fragmented data from the nineteenth century.

Settler initiatives

News of spontaneously growing coffees in the Angolan hinterland first reached the colonial government in Luanda around 1820. Considering Portugal's interest

knowledge also existed in Brazil. See Howard Dean, 'The Green Wave of Coffee: Beginnings of Tropical Agricultural Research in Brazil (1885–1900)', *Hispanic American Historical Review*, 69:1 (1989), 91–115, at p. 95.

6 Pierre Joseph Laborie, *The Coffee Planter of Santo Domingo* (London: T. Cadell & W. Davies, 1798); José Mariano da Conceição Velloso, *O fazendeiro do Brasil, cultivador* (Lisbon: Officina de Simão Thaddeo Ferreira, 1799).

7 William C. Van Norman, Jr, *Shade-Grown Slavery: The Lives of Slaves on Coffee Plantations in Cuba* (Nashville: Vanderbilt University Press, 2013), pp. 16–33.

8 Helen Tilley, *Africa as a Living Laboratory: Empire, Development, and the Problem of Scientific Knowledge, 1870–1950* (Chicago: University of Chicago Press, 2011), pp. 115–68.

in developing alternative forms of commerce to the slave trade, the discovery of coffee trees near São José de Encoge, a proto-colonial settlement about 350km inland from Luanda, created hopes in imperial ranks that coffee was a viable new export crop. Early production focused on a few thousand natural stands, which some African *moradores* (residents of Portuguese jurisdictions, typically slave-owning and engaged in trade or agriculture) had begun to ameliorate by bush clearing. The local administrator collected the berries as a tax in kind and dispatched them to Luanda, probably unhusked and sometimes not even properly dried.[9] Because this production system was principally a private trade of colonial officers using their power to collect tribute and requisition porters from chiefs to carry produce to Luanda, outputs from Encoge long remained comparatively small. In the 1850s, they barely surpassed fifteen metric tons per year.[10]

The discovery of coffee in Encoge motivated the colonial government to promote cultivation in other colonized areas of Angola. Its first strategy was to promulgate coffee through plant transfers. In 1827, government agents distributed coffee seeds to planters in the coastal district of Dande, a lowland region that proved unsuitable to coffee growing. The government also transferred a thousand seedlings from Encoge to Pungo-Andongo, a colonial station near the Cuanza River. The seedlings took root, but the young trees wilted after their caretaker, a convict from Portugal, found himself imprisoned in the early 1830s. The Pungo-Andongo area contained few wild coffees and never became a significant growing region, despite renewed attempts by settlers in the 1870s to introduce coffees from other Angolan districts and abroad.[11] Plant material was

9 Alan de Carvalho Souza, 'Do Brasil para África: O café na viragem do império português (1807–1850)' (Unpublished PhD dissertation, University of Lisbon, 2020), <http://hdl.handle.net/10451/45282> [accessed 10 May 2023], p. 50; José Acúrsio das Neves, *Considerações políticas e comerciais sobre os descobrimentos e possessões portuguezes na África e na Ásia* (Lisbon: Impressão Regia, 1830), p. 221; José Joaquim Lopes de Lima, *Ensaios sobre a statística das possessões portuguezas na África occidental e oriental, na Ásia occidental, na China e na Oceania* (3 vols, Lisbon: Imprensa Nacional, 1844–46), vol. 3, pt 1, pp. 11–12; Portugal, *Relatórios do Ministro e Secretário de Estado dos Negócios da Marinha e do Ultramar apresentados às Cortes na sessão legislativa de 1870* (Lisbon: Ministério do Ultramar, 1969), p. 159.

10 Joaquim António de Carvalho e Menezes, *Demonstração geográfica e politica do território portuguez na Guiné inferior* (Rio de Janeiro: Typ. Classica de F. A. de Almeida, 1848), pp. 131–2; Francisco de Salles Ferreira, 'Diário da viagem para S. José de Encoge, feita em dezembro de 1854', *Annaes do Conselho Ultramarino*, parte não official, ser. 2 (1859), 51–4; Gonçalo de Oliveira Beça, 'Presídio de Encoge', *Annaes do Conselho Ultramarino*, parte não official, ser. 2 (1860), 90–3; Arquivo Nacional de Angola (Luanda, henceforth ANA), caixa 4998, doc. 396, Ordem de remessa de café de Encoge para Bembe, 1 Dec. 1862.

11 Arquivo Histórico Ultramarino (Lisbon, henceforth AHU), Conselho Ultramarino (CU), Angola, caixa 156, doc. 28, Nicolao d'Abreu Castelo Branco to António Manoel de Noronha, no. 269, Luanda, 28 June 1827; AHU, Secretaria de Estado da

also sent to southern Angola. Early colonial experiments with plant transfers were often unsuccessful because of insufficient knowledge of suitable growing conditions. Failures were most apparent when settler farmers planted coffee outside its natural forest habitat.[12]

Apart from distributing seeds and seedlings to colonial settlers, administrators tried to involve African farmers in improving natural coffee stands. In 1831, district officers received official instructions to create inventories of plants in their areas that local populations could exploit for commercial use. Manoel Pedro Gomes Teixeira, the Luso-African commander of Cazengo, responded that coffee grew spontaneously on the hills around his station, about 200km east of Luanda. He had directed local chiefs to clear bush and plant imported seedlings.[13] It is unclear whether Teixeira's proto-colonial coffee development scheme sorted any effect. Across the montane forest, *moradores* and independent African farmers were reluctant to invest time and labour in the cultivation of cash crops before prices and marketing opportunities increased in the 1850s.[14]

As efforts to stimulate smallholder farming faltered, the government began to support adventurous settler farmers with land grants and supplies of coerced labour to boost coffee production. Until the early twentieth century, limited colonial control and high transportation costs restricted this strategy to the Cazengo and Golungo Alto districts in the Luanda hinterland. But the policy of land concessions and labour coercion laid the foundation for a more extensive settler regime thereafter. The most famous of the early settlers was an immigrant from Brazil, João Guilherme Pereira Barboza, later heralded as Angola's 'pioneer' coffee planter. Barboza arrived in Luanda in 1832 with a capital of 500 *milréis*, the equivalent of about 2,500 pounds sterling, gained from unknown commercial activities in South America. After watching coffee cultivation expand in the Paraiba Valley of Brazil, Barboza saw an increase in world coffee prices as an

---

Marinha e Ultramar (SEMU), Direcção Geral do Ultramar (DGU), Angola, no. 825, 'Presídio de Pungo Andongo, vulgarmente chamado Pedras Negras' [1838]; *ibid.*, Angola, no. 644-1, Chefe António Mathias Portugal, Pungo-Andongo, 30 April 1874, enclosed in GG, no. 152, 28 May 1874; John Gossweiler, 'Informação sobre cafeicultura na fazenda "Monte Belo" – Cazengo', *BAA*, ser. 6, 5:16–19 (1932), 73–85, at p. 82.

12 Yonah Ngalaba Seleti, 'Portuguese Colonialism, Capitalism and the Angolan Coffee Industry: 1850–1950' (Unpublished PhD dissertation, Dalhousie University, 1987), p. 79; Aida Freudenthal, *Arimos e fazendas: A transição agrária em Angola* (Luanda: Chá de Caxinde, 2005), p. 334.

13 AHU, CU, Angola, caixa 156, doc. 106, Manoel Pedro Gomes Teixeira, 'Instruções do café', Cazengo, 15 April 1832.

14 AHU, SEMU-DGU, Angola, no. 590, Capitão José da Silva Carmo to GG, Ambaca, 3 Jan. 1840, enclosed in Manoel Eleutério Malheiro to Francisco de Paula d'Aguiar Ottolini, no. 32, Luanda, 29 Jan. 1840; *ibid.*, Chefe do districto do Golungo Alto to Boaventura de Lemos Simeão, 3 Jan. 1840; Freudenthal, *Arimos*, p. 340.

opportunity to develop the crop in Angola. He acquired a piece of forest from the colonial government in Cazengo and bought twenty-five enslaved people in the nearby Dondo market to turn the land into a plantation. By 1838, Colónia São João, as he called the estate, had around sixty thousand young and fully grown coffee trees (Plate 2.1). Six years later, he owned 250 enslaved workers, who cultivated seventy thousand mature coffee stands with an annual yield of more than ten tons. A Brazilian slave trader, José de Carvalho Bastos, helped Barboza market his coffee in Luanda. Until Barboza's death in 1847, his estate supplied the bulk of the Angolan coffee trade.[15]

Colónia São João was no smaller than many American coffee plantations. However, compared to the Paraiba Valley, where enslaved labourers (mostly originating from Angola) produced average yields of almost four tons per year by 1850, the productivity of workers and coffee bushes in Colónia São João was extremely low. These were early days, and median outputs of settler estates in Angola increased later in the century. But the challenging geography of the coffee plantations in northern Angola meant that, even in good years, average yields rarely exceeded 1,000kg per worker, comparable to the *haciendas* built on the Andean slopes of Colombia.[16]

Barboza might have gained some knowledge about coffee growing in Brazil, but he quickly learned that what counted as best practice in the Americas did not necessarily work well in Angola. From an American perspective, Angola was peculiar, first because coffee was indigenous, making planting supplementary. In addition, natural stands and steep hills made it very difficult to align trees in an orderly manner. Barboza's cultivation methods struck contemporary observers as innovative and have been the subject of some scholarly speculation.[17] Rather

15 AHU, SEMU-DGU, Angola, no. 590, Manoel Eleutério Malheiro to Francisco de Paula de Aguiar Ottolini, no. 27, Luanda, 28 Jan. 1840; José de Almeida Santos, 'João Guilherme Pereira Barboza – O Grande Pioneiro do Cazengo', *Boletim Cultural da Câmara Municipal de Luanda*, 36 (1972), 27–32; António Carreira, *Angola – da escravatura ao trabalho livre: Subsidios para a história demográfica do século XVI até à independência* (Lisbon: Arcadia 1977), p. 130, citing *Arquivos de Angola*, 2:15 (1936), governo de Angola, ofício no. 1, 24 Feb. 1838.

16 Rafael de Bivar Marquese, 'African Diaspora, Slavery, and the Paraiba Valley Coffee Plantation Landscape: Nineteenth-Century Brazil', *Review (Fernand Braudel Center)*, 31:2 (2008), 195–216, at p. 203; Freudenthal, *Arimos*, pp. 169, 234; Armando Castro, *O sistema colonial português em África (meados do século XX)*, 2nd edn (Lisbon: Editorial Caminho, 1980), p. 129; Marco Palacios, *Coffee in Colombia: An Economic, Social and Political History* (Cambridge: Cambridge University Press, 1980), p. 100.

17 Freudenthal, *Arimos*, p. 176; Roquinaldo Ferreira, 'Agricultural Enterprise and Unfree Labour in Nineteenth-Century Angola', in Robin Law *et al.* (eds), *Commercial Agriculture, the Slave Trade and Slavery in Atlantic Africa* (Woodbridge: James Currey, 2013), pp. 225–42; Souza, 'Brasil para África', pp. 259, 264.

Plate 2.1 Colónia S. João, Cazengo, c.1880. Source: José Augusto da Cunha Morais, *Africa occidental: Album photographico e descriptivo* (4 vols, Lisbon: David Corazzi, 1885–8), vol. 2, PT/AHM/FE/010/B02/PQ/06. Image provided by Arquivo Histórico Militar.

than felling or burning forest before planting, as was common in Brazil and later also in Colombia, Barboza created his plantation by ordering his enslaved workers to cut away all underbrush that was not coffee. They then pruned the remaining coffee bush and filled gaps with new stands, which minimized the need for weeding. The native forest canopy protected trees and soils from exposure to sun, wind, and heavy rain.[18] The landscape had forced Barboza to adapt. 'The sight of woods located on such mountainous terrain', he confided to a colonial officer in 1840, 'frightens any planter.' However, growing coffee in its natural habitat seemed to pay off in better yields. 'I don't believe that one could obtain good fruits from this plant without improving it and planting it in places where it is already naturally growing', Barboza added.[19] Much to his credit, twentieth-century field scientists held the same belief.

18 On Brazilian techniques, see Warren Dean, *With Broadax and Firebrand: The Destruction of the Brazilian Atlantic Forest* (Berkeley: University of California Press, 1997), pp. 168–91; Marquese, 'African Diaspora', 199–200. For Colombia, see Palacios, *Coffee*, p. 92.

19 AHU, SEMU-DGU, Angola, no. 591, João Guilherme Pereira Barboza to Joaquim Filippe d'Andrade, Cazengo, 24 March 1840, enclosed in Manoel Eleutério Malheiro to MSENMU, no. 87, Luanda, 11 April 1840.

In 1846, Manoel Alves de Castro Francina, an Angolan government official, travelled from Luanda to Colónia São João to deliver a dozen male and female captives taken from a captured slave ship.[20] Francina found a plantation extending over several hills. At the bottom of each hill was an open space for drying harvested berries and a store to keep dried coffee. After hulling the coffee, workers sorted the green beans in different categories, an early form of product standardization to expedite sales in Portuguese and Brazilian markets. The enslaved kept their own provisioning grounds, where they grew manioc, beans, and maize as well as some tobacco, cotton, and rice. In this regard, Colónia São João operated very much like an American coffee plantation. What struck Francina most, however, was the random distribution of coffee trees within the estate, which gave a disorderly impression compared to Brazil's neatly aligned plantations.

> It is impossible to count the number of stands, not only because some are surrounded by bush, but also because during planting the method of alignment used in Brazil was not followed; the reason is undoubtedly that, since most stands in the district are natural or spontaneous, [new] stands were only planted in spaces in-between, although [Barboza] has worked hard to improve [the natural stands]'.[21]

The improvement Francina alluded to consisted of pruning or thinning (*descobrir café*) and planting seedlings or cuttings of healthy trees.

In later years, Barboza waxed lyrical about Cazengo's montane forest, saying that coffee trees were in some places 'so abundant that all you need to do is to clean and thin them out', momentarily ignoring the amount of labour plantation building required.[22] Carving plantations out of natural coffee forests long remained standard practice in Angola. Portuguese settlers in the 1950s called this planting method the 'indigenous way', as opposed to the newer method of aligning stands and concentrating them in cleared, semi-shaded terrain.[23] The prac-

20 The ship was the Brazilian schooner Flor de Campos, captured in 1846. See Margarida Seixas, 'Escravos e libertos no Boletim Oficial de Angola (1845–1875), II parte', *E-Revista de Estudos Interculturais do CEI-ISCAP*, 3 (2015), <https://doi.org/10.34630/erei.vi3.3917>, 4. See also Mariana Pinho Candido, *Wealth, Land, and Property in Angola: A History of Dispossession, Slavery, and Inequality* (Cambridge: Cambridge University Press, 2022), pp. 174, 179–80. For context, see Samuël Coghe, 'The Problem of Freedom in a Mid Nineteenth-Century Atlantic Slave Society: The Liberated Africans of the Anglo-Portuguese Mixed Commission in Luanda (1844–1870)', *Slavery & Abolition*, 33:3 (2012), 479–500.

21 Manuel Alves de Castro Francina, 'Viagem a Cazengo pelo Quanza, e regresso por terra', *Annaes do Conselho Ultramarino*, parte não official, ser. 1 (1858), 452–64, at p. 460.

22 João Guilherme Pereira Barbosa, 'Cazengo: Descripção d'este districto', *Annaes do Conselho Ultramarino*, parte não official, serie 1 (1858), 470–4, at p. 470.

23 Arquivo Nacional de Angola (Luanda, henceforth ANA), caixa 2170, Administrador de Ambaca to Chefe de C. Cabaça, no. 2387, Camabatela, 23 Oct. 1956;

tice drew the attention of several foreign observers. For example, in 1854, David Livingstone met a Portuguese colonist in Golungo Alto who, after purchasing forestland from the colonial government, followed the procedures suggested by Barboza to create an estate.[24] Travel writer Mary Kingsley, visiting Angola in 1893, noted that Africans and Europeans shared the practice of thinning and adding new stands. 'The greater part of these plantations consist of clearing and taking care of the wild coffee, but in addition regularly planting and cultivating young trees, as it is found that the yield per tree is immensely increased by cultivation.'[25]

A United States consular report from 1914 mentioned another common practice, which was stumping. 'In the Cazengo valley the wild trees are so thick that thinning out is the only operation necessary to the plantation owner. When the trees become too tall, they are simply cut off about two feet above ground; and new shoots appear from the trunks the following season.'[26] Pruning helped sunlight penetrate the bush, which stimulated the production of fruit and replacement suckers, giving grown coffee trees new vigour. By contrast, stumping was a way to obtain strong young uprights and especially helped to rejuvenate trees that were losing branches and foliage below. It could extend the lifespan of a coffee tree up to eighty years, as Paul Janssens and John Gossweiler witnessed in the 1920s, although yields diminished as trees grew older. Stumping was long preferred over other methods for rejuvenating crops, like replanting or grafting.[27]

AHU, Governo Geral de Angola, Repartição do Gabinete, D2.172.6/06, Chefe de gabinete to US consul, no. 3616, Luanda, 18 Sep. 1952. Richard J. Houk, 'Recent Developments in the Portuguese Congo', *Geographical Review*, 48:2 (1958), 201–21, at p. 209, describes forest clearing, planting, and semi-shading on the 500-hectare Alto Minho estate near Uíge, 1956. Similarly, see Maia Cortezão, 'Breve ensaio sobre o café', *Boletim do Instituto de Angola*, 11 (1958), 135–47, at p. 146; Manoel do Nascimento Lopes da Silva Júnior (ed.), *Testemunos de José Cristovão Henriques (Engenheiro-Silvicultor)* (Lisbon: Junta de Investigações Científicas do Ultramar, 1981), pp. 210–13.

24 Livingstone, *Missionary Travels*, p. 419.

25 Mary Kingsley, *Travels in West Africa: Congo Français, Corisco and Cameroons* (London: Macmillan, 1897), p. 642.

26 William Ukers, *All about Coffee* (New York: Tea and Coffee Trade Journal Company, 1922), p. 230; based on United States, Bureau of Foreign and Domestic Commerce, Department of Commerce, *Daily Consular and Trade Reports*, vol. 3 (Washington: Government Printing Office, 1915), pp. 1697–713, 'Commercial Study of Portuguese West Africa'. In 1908, British consul Mackie argued there was 'no necessity to plant the coffee tree' because growers only needed 'to thin out the superfluous trees'. Great Britain, Foreign Office, *Report for the Year 1908 on the Trade of the Province of Angola* (London: HMSO, 1909), p. 39. It becomes clear that information about the Angolan interior was recycled among European and American residents of Luanda, leading to simplified representations of African agricultural practices.

27 Janssens, *Café*, pp. 59–60; Gossweiler, 'Informação', p. 83; *Nomes indígenas de plantas de Angola*, reprint of *Agronomia Angolana*, 7 (Luanda: Imprensa Nacional, 1953),

Amelioration became the conventional way to grow coffee, although some nineteenth-century immigrants experimented with different methods, with varying degrees of success. One of them, Cândido Augusto Fortunato da Costa, learned to adopt tried and tested cultivation techniques the hard way. In a note written for the colonial government, he explained that after receiving a land grant for a plantation in Cazengo in 1851, he first applied what he called 'Brazilian' planting methods. He cleared forest and planted sixteen thousand seedlings obtained from local stocks three feet apart in straight lines. Within two years, most of these new trees had died from overexposure to sunlight. In addition to insufficient shading, he had also wrongly planted the seedlings in dry gravelly terrain instead of their favourite red loamy soil, ignoring not just local knowledge, but also the advice of eighteenth-century experts who knew that gravelly soils hindered the healthy growth of coffee trees.[28] Costa realized that farmers around him were justified in growing coffee in the shade of the forest canopy. To restart, therefore, he trimmed the remaining indigenous coffee trees in his concession and planted about nine thousand seedlings from a nursery to close the spaces in-between.[29]

Starting around the same time as Fortunato da Costa, the former caravan trader Joaquim Rodrigues Graça used a method known as contour cultivation at his Montalegre estate in Golungo Alto. This involved planting coffee in staggered triangles on hill clearances, following the curves of the hill to avoid soil erosion, and using selected trees for shading.[30] In 1855, Albino José Soares built the fabled Prototypo estate in the same way, but leaving much of the natural forest intact.[31]

p. 296; Hélder Lains e Silva, 'A enxertia do Robusta, com garfos provenientes dos ramos horizontais (plagiotrópicos), na restauração de cafezais decrépitos', *RCP*, 1:4 (1954), 28–36. On pruning, see John Gossweiler, 'Relatório sobre as doenças do cafeeiro da região do Amboim', *BAA*, publicação extraordinária, 1 (1933), 5–31, at pp. 18–19; Haarer, *Modern Coffee Production*, pp. 199–200; Wrigley, *Coffee*, pp. 81, 230.

28 John Ellis, *An Historical Account of Coffee, with an Engraving and Botanical Description of the Tree* (Cambridge: Cambridge University Press, 2013 [1774]), p. 26; Laborie, *Coffee Planter*, pp. 8–9.

29 Cândido Augusto Fortunato da Costa, 'Apontamentos de um agricultor' (Fazenda d'Aguas doces, 16 Nov. 1854), *BOA*, 485 (13 Jan. 1855), 5–7; Souza, 'Brasil para África', pp. 266–7, 278–89, 283. On Angolan coffee soils, see Janssens, *Café*, p. 29. For more on Fortunato da Costa, see José C. Curto, 'A família Fortunato da Costa: de Portugal a Angola, via São Tomé, c.1808 a 1859', *Afro-Ásia*, 67 (2023), 97–141, at pp. 131–8. For a later attempt to introduce Brazilian planting methods in an African coffee landscape, see Diana Garvin, 'The Italian Coffee Triangle: From Brazilian *Colonos* to Ethiopian *Colonialisti*', *Modern Italy*, 26:3 (2021), 291–312.

30 Souza, 'Brasil para África', p. 282; Janssens, *Café*, pp. 44–6; Alec Ernest Haarer, *Coffee Growing* (Oxford: Oxford University Press, 1963), p. 33.

31 Carvalho, *Descripção*, vol. 1, p. 132; Alberto de Souza Maia Leitão, *Relatório da visita sanitária aos concelhos de leste de Loanda mais victimados pela doença de somno* (Porto: Typ. a vapor da Empreza Litteraria e Typographica, 1901), p. 59.

The technique would gain popularity among European planters in the 1920s, although local agronomists warned them about the risks of disforestation.[32]

Rising coffee prices in the 1850s brought more foreign settlers to the coffee forests, specifically in the Cazengo and Golungo Alto districts.[33] In addition to favourable prices, they were supported by a new legal regime for the privatization of land, introduced in 1856 as Portuguese officials, much like the British in Lagos, began to see individual property as a means to encourage territorial expansion and the development of export agriculture in Angola. Unlike in Lagos, however, the right to own property was restricted to Portuguese subjects (including *moradores*) and foreign nationals.[34] Settlers could obtain land by government grant (*sesmaria*), private purchase, or blunt expropriation. Often connecting patches of forest previously cleared by African coffee growers, most colonists created plantations five hundred to one thousand hectares in size, as any concession larger than this required special permission from Lisbon. The coffee plantations that developed in Brazil around this time were of similar size, but there, it was the problem of labour control that hindered further enlargement. In Angola, labour was scarce, which meant that planters normally used only a fraction of their concession for coffee cultivation, a pattern that persisted into the 1950s.[35] The required capital usually came from previous commercial activities, earnings on colonial taxes, or mortgages provided by the Banco Nacional Ultramarino, the only official lender in Angola. The largest nineteenth-century estate was Prototypo, founded in 1855, which covered a thousand hectares and produced 225 tons of dried coffee by the early 1880s.[36]

The arrival of white settlers ushered in a large-scale privatization of land in these colonial districts, as several chiefs and *moradores* felt compelled to formally

32 Laurentino Pereira Coelho, 'Relatório sobre o ataque do Stephanodores Coffea, Hagd. às bagas de café na região do Uige', *BAA*, ser. 6, 1:4 (1929), 3–13; Eurico de Azevedo Noronha, 'Plantação de cafezal em curvas de nivel e linhas cerradas', *RCP*, 2:7 (1955), 18–28.

33 David Birmingham, 'The Coffee Barons of Cazengo', *JAH*, 19:4 (1978), 523–38; Jill R. Dias, 'Changing Patterns of Power in the Luanda Hinterland: The Impact of Trade and Colonisation on the Mbundu ca. 1845–1920', *Paideuma: Mitteilungen zur Kulturkunde*, 32 (1986), 285–318.

34 Candido, *Wealth*, pp. 81–3; Souza, 'Brasil para África', pp. 277, 283; Miguel Rebordão Amaral, 'Angola: Concessões de terra e direitos tradicionais (1856–1973): Análise de legislação' (MA dissertation, Universirsity of Lisbon, 2017), pp. 3–4, 9; A. G. Hopkins, 'Property Rights and Empire Building: Britain's Annexation of Lagos, 1861', *Journal of Economic History*, 40:4 (1980), 777–98.

35 W. Clayton Pickersgill, 'Coffee Cultivation in Angola', *Bulletin of Miscellaneous Information (Royal Botanic Gardens, Kew)*, 89 (1894), 161–3; Tania Andrade Lima, 'Keeping a Tight Lid: The Architecture and Landscape Design of Coffee Plantations in Nineteenth-Century Rio de Janeiro, Brazil', *Review (Fernand Braudel Center)*, 34: 1/2 (2011), 193–215, at p. 198.

36 Freudenthal, *Arimos*, p. 174; Carvalho, *Descripção*, vol. 1, p. 119. According to Janssens, *Café*, p. 82, most Cazengo plantations produced about 200kg per hectare.

register the small farms (*arimos*) they cultivated. By demarcating their land for commercial exploitation, they acquired the official status of farmers (*agricultores*), freeing them from burdensome colonial duties, especially compulsory labour. As a result, the number of registered smallholders in Cazengo increased from merely one in 1850 to more than a thousand six years later, growing a total of around two million coffee stands. Most of them also owned one or two enslaved workers. The main victims of this land rush were African peasants who were by law unable to claim property and often saw their lands appropriated by more powerful neighbours.[37]

Privatization increased competition, theft, and vulnerability. For instance, a prolonged drought from 1873 to 1876 forced many smallholders to sell their farms to better resourced *moradores* or European settlers. In turn, colonial settlers used violence to compel indebted *moradores* to hand over their properties. Extortion often resulted in lawsuits between old landowners and new settlers, with colonial judiciaries normally offering little protection to the less powerful.[38] These conflicts sometimes seeped into the columns of Luanda newspapers, as happened in 1873, when the *Cruzeiro do Sul* gave voice to a dispute over a demarcated property in Cazengo, shedding light on the shady ways of land acquisition in the region.[39] Proto-colonial expansion thus pitted the new settler class against the old *morador* elite. Meanwhile, African rulers saw their authority in matters related to land use eroded by colonial laws that facilitated the transfer of communal land to private tenure and ownership. Many of them were therefore apprehensive about Portuguese policies to promote commercial agriculture. In 1872, several influential chiefs in the Dembos district, north of Golungo Alto, decided to expel all colonial settlers and officials from their lands.[40]

37 Dias, 'Angola', pp. 455–6; Freudenthal, *Arimos*, pp. 153, 177; Secretaria do governo geral da província de Angola, 'Nota demonstrativa do número de escravos registados na província de Angola, e suas dependências, nos termos do Decreto de 14 de Dezembro de 1854' (11 Feb. 1856), *Diário do Governo*, 145 (21 June 1856), 854; Ofício do chefe do distrito do Cazengo, 2 Jan. 1857, transcription from *BOA*, 600 (28 March 1857), 2–4, in Filipe Martins Barbosa de Mascarenhas, *O outro lado da escravatura: Repressão e abolição do serviço de carregadores e do tráfico de escravos* (Luanda: edição do Autor, 2012), doc. 69. Tax breaks and labour exemptions were more widely used to promote coffee cultivation. See Augustine Sedgewick, *Coffeeland: A History* (Dublin: Penguin Books, 2020), p. 41.

38 AHU, SEMU-DGU, Angola, 2ª Repartição, no. 830, GG to MSENMU, no. 218, Luanda, 24 July 1979; Mário António Fernandes de Oliveira and Eduardo Santos (eds), *Angolana (documentação sobre Angola)* (4 vols, Lisbon: Instituto de Investigação Científica Tropical, 1968–95), vol. 1, pp. 188, 337, 357, 403, 453, 684.

39 AHU, SEMU-DGU, Angola, no. 644-2, clippings enclosed in GG interino to MSENMU, confidential, no. 5, 25 Feb. 1874.

40 Dias, 'Angola', pp. 469–70; Freudenthal, *Arimos*, p. 179; Souza, 'Brasil para África', p. 262. For global context, see John F. Richards, 'Toward a Global System of Property Rights in Land', in Edmund Burke III and Kenneth Pomeranz (eds), *The Environ-*

Despite the consolidation of significant estates in settler hands, privatization did not lead to a full-scale monopolization of land by European colonists in Cazengo and Golungo Alto. Rather, it contributed to a culture of property holding in the region, with Europeans generally relying on written documentation to prove ownership, while Africans used both written and verbal contracts to exchange and secure their possessions.[41] Settler estates continued to expand into the 1890s, but most depended on the state for bank loans and land concessions. State support for commercial agriculture thus propped up many large but highly indebted coffee plantations, for whom bankruptcy loomed when prices collapsed towards the end of the century. Meanwhile, mixed cropping and flexible supplies of family and village labour protected African smallholders from market volatility. By 1928, African farmers still accounted for more than a third of all coffee produced in Cazengo, a century of settler expansion in the district notwithstanding.[42]

Outside the settler districts, small-scale farming based on communal land holding prevailed. This system was the bedrock of the growing coffee trade during the nineteenth century. Foreign planters played an important role in Angola's entry into the global coffee market around 1850, but the acceleration that followed was largely due to increasing African participation in export production. Already by the mid-1860s it was clear to most observers that several thousand smallholders were collectively outpacing the settler farmers of Cazengo and Golungo Alto, who only accounted for about a quarter of Angolan coffee exports.[43]

African entrepreneurship

Despite heroic tales of settler 'pioneers' taming the Angolan coffee forest, the expansion of the Angolan coffee frontier during the second half of the nineteenth century owed much to the growing involvement of chiefs, village headmen, and individual households in commercial agriculture.[44] Incentives for African farmers to invest in cash-crop production varied. Generally, growing demand for agricultural and forest products increased opportunities for small producers to

ment and World History (Berkeley: University of California Press, 2009), pp. 54–78, at pp. 60–4.

41 José de Oliveira Ferreira Diniz, *Populações indígenas de Angola* (Coimbra: Imprensa da Universidade, 1918), pp. 26–8.

42 'Mapa da produção de café referente ao ano de 1928', *BAA*, ser. 6, 2:7 (1929), 341.

43 Freudenthal, *Arimos*, pp. 169, 174, 178; AHU, SEMU-DGU, Angola, no. 640 (2), 'Mappa dos géneros mais importantes da agricultura desta província, produzido na última colheita', Luanda, 26 Aug. 1870. For the boom period up to 1895, see Mesquita, *Dados estatísticos para o estudo das pautas de Angola: Exportação pelas alfândegas do Círculo e do Congo nos anos de 1888 a 1913* (Luanda: Imprensa Nacional, 1918), pp. 12, 46; Birmingham, 'Coffee Barons', 529; Dias, 'Changing Patterns', 306.

44 Dias, 'Changing Patterns', 299.

participate in global commerce. Moreover, in the colonial districts of Cazengo and Golungo Alto, smallholders who had the capacity to do so registered their plots with the Portuguese government in return for tax benefits, most notably an exemption from compulsory porterage. The decline of chiefly authority in these regions, orchestrated by the colonial government, removed a potential barrier to the privatization of communal land.[45]

Farmers across the northern coffee belt responded to rising world coffee prices by exchanging knowledge, techniques, and planting material, diffusing coffee cultivation from the proto-colonial enclaves. In 1858, the government of Golungo Alto, which had long struggled to motivate African smallholders to grow cash crops, noted with satisfaction that coffee production was 'increasing by the day'.[46] In the neighbouring district of Ambaca, farmers extended small plantations by planting cuttings from existing stands. Africans preferred this form of vegetative propagation to seeding, because it was an effective way to clone a healthy parent tree and produced fruit-bearing stands relatively fast.[47] In the district of São José de Encoge, the number of coffee growers grew from a few dozen in 1855 to over a hundred a decade later, supporting the coastal trade north of Luanda.[48] By 1875, several farms in Encoge had developed into small estates, whose food requirements fuelled a trade in provisions from neighbouring regions. Commercial exchange also led to plant transfers, as traders collected seedlings and cuttings from growers in Encoge to plant at home.[49] Traces of early cultivation at Bembe, 100km northwest of Encoge, were indicative of the speed at which the coffee frontier spread through northern Angola.[50]

45 João Maria Cerqueira de Azevedo, *Angola, exemplo de trabalho* (Luanda: edição do autor, 1958), pp. 252–3; AHU, SEMU-DGU, Angola, no. 622/2, GG to MSENMU, Luanda, 30 Dec. 1856.

46 José de Almeida Santos, *Apenas um punhado de bravos!* (Luanda: Câmara Municipal, 1971), doc. 93, Extratos dos relatórios mensais, dezembro 1858, Golungo Alto, originally published in *BOA*, 696 (29 Jan. 1859).

47 AHU, SEMU-DGU, Angola, 2ª Repartição, no. 828, GG interino, Relatório, Luanda, 28 Oct. 1873, enclosed in GG interino to MSENMU, no. 282, Luanda, 29 Oct. 1873. On clonal propagation, see Haarer, *Modern Coffee Production*, pp. 32, 98, 112–13, 126–9; Wrigley, *Coffee*, pp. 164–5, 189–91, 416–26.

48 ANA, caixa 4999, 'Mapa do estado e progresso de agricultura, dezembro de 1855', Encoge, 1 Jan. 1856; ANA, caixa 3925, Mapa estatística da população, Encoge, 31 July 1866. For commercial links between Encoge and Ambriz, see Menezes, *Demonstração*, p. 15.

49 AHU, SEMU-DGU, Angola, no. 645-1, Relatório de Encoge, enclosed in GG interino to MSENMU, no. 168, Luanda, 23 June 1875; *ibid.*, Relatório de Encoge, 1 Dec. 1875, enclosed in GG interino to MSENMU, no. 328, Luanda, 24 Dec 1875; *ibid.*, no. 645-2, Relatório de Encoge, 1 Aug. 1875, enclosed in GG interino to MSENMU, no. 225, Luanda 28 Aug. 1875.

50 AHU, SEMU-DGU, Angola, 2ª Repartição, António José de Sousa Barroso to SG, Missão do Congo, no. 27, São Salvador, 8 Nov. 1883.

Soon, most production took place in regions outside formal Portuguese control. 'Almost the only part of Africa that I know of wherein Coffee planting is carried on by the natives of the soil, and not aliens of European or Arabian descent, is Northern Angola', a coastal merchant noted in the 1880s.[51] Smallholder success undermined Portuguese notions of economic development by private ownership, while raising the spectre of a powerful, independent African peasantry from which the colonial government was unable to exact tribute. In 1888, the head of the Encoge station, Inocêncio Matoso da Camara, sourly noted that the contribution of his small jurisdiction to Angola's growing coffee output was 'totally insignificant'.[52] Thirteen years later, da Camara's successor Luís António Nobre Leite reported that the Encoge region 'produces a lot of coffee, but it is important to know that most production happens inland at places far away from here [among] non-allied peoples'.[53] A cash-crop economy flourished from which the colonial state could only benefit by levying export duties, a situation that clearly made some officials uncomfortable.[54]

Moreover, cultivation methods based on communally accepted rights to usufruct confounded officials like da Camara, who responded by denouncing these methods as an inefficient use of land and labour. In what became a typical European dismissal of indigenous coffee production, da Camara claimed that Africans did not cultivate coffee, but only collected berries from the wild. 'There is no expansion of cultivation [so that] whatever existed yesterday exists today, and if there is growth, it is due to some fallen bean or berry that increases the [number of] bushes.' Da Camara ignored the various propagation techniques small farmers used and most settlers subsequently adopted. It also struck him that people appeared to neglect their coffee bushes for most of the year. 'When harvest season comes, however, suddenly the owners arrive ... to collect the fruit'.[55] That peasant producers temporarily abandoned coffee bushes to tend to other crops puzzled European colonists. When colonial laws gave African growers some protection from illegal dispossession during the twentieth century, this practice clashed with the demarcation strategies of white settlers, who discredited indigenous land claims by casting doubt on the age or condition of African farms (see Chapter 4).

By tapping into new reserves and transplanting specimen across the forest belt, enterprising African farmers extended the boundaries of the Angolan coffee

51 Anonymous, quoted in Edwin Lester Arnold, *Coffee: Its Cultivation and Profit* (London: W. B. Whittingham & Co., 1886), pp. 265–6. See also Joachim John Monteiro, *Angola and the River Congo* (2 vols, London: Frank Cass, 1968 [1875]), vol. 1, pp. 133–4.

52 ANA, caixa 4998, Chefe Mattoso da Camara to SG, no. 90, Encoge, 16 April 1888.

53 ANA, caixa 4997, Chefe do concelho to SG, no. 127, Encoge, 22 July 1901.

54 Dias, 'Angola', pp. 409–10.

55 ANA, caixa 5002, Administrador do concelho to SG, no. 87, Encoge 12 April 1888.

frontier. Because São José de Encoge seemed to be the focal point of this expansion, in 1918, the Angolan government instructed its head botanist to explore the region around this old colonial outpost. John Gossweiler's report was the first detailed account of African cultivation techniques in northern Angola.[56] Gossweiler used the new military post of Uíge, 40km east of Encoge, as a base to travel through the hills stretching west, north, and south. The colonial government had only recently occupied Uíge and the place attracted the attention of several coastal traders, who opened stores there to buy coffee from local farmers. Many of these shopkeepers later set up their own plantations in the region, often using techniques that in Gossweiler's view contrasted negatively with the proven methods of African growers.

Gossweiler saw that coffee plantations were usually sheltered by natural forest from exposure to excessive sunlight and dry winds. From the way farmers had stumped the trees about every four years, causing the growth of new stalks at the base, he deducted that many stands were about fifty years old. Cultivation must therefore have started in the 1860s, coinciding with an increase of exports from the coast. Gossweiler also noticed that the size and shape of leaves and berries often differed between coffee trees, even when they grew side by side. As plant scientists later established, this was partly because robusta coffee is self-sterile, outbred, and therefore highly variable by nature, unlike the self-pollinating arabica tree.[57] However, Gossweiler explained this variability through a history of interregional plant transfers. Elders informed him that traders used to take seeds, seedlings, and cuttings from Encoge in the way colonial officers had described in the 1870s. The introduction of planting material from elsewhere was the reason, Gossweiler thought, why some berries in the Uíge area resembled those he had seen in Cazengo, while others looked like the fruit of trees in the Encoge and Dembos regions. By replanting and transplanting trees, he argued, African peasants had transformed the Angolan coffee landscape to such an extent that there were few truly wild stands remaining in the Uíge area. A half-century of domestication and naturalization not only belied the myth that African coffee was typically gathered from virgin forest, but also thwarted botanists' attempts to identify categorically distinct indigenous coffee varieties (see Chapter 3).

The exchange of planting material strengthened the biological ties between Angola's two main coffee zones when, around 1900, foreigner settlers opened the country south of the Cuanza River to cultivation. Although less densely forested than northern Angola, the southern region was home to wild coffee

56 John Gossweiler, 'Um reconhecimento fitogeográfico à região produtora do café Encoje', *Relatórios e Informações*, 1:2 (1918), 19–40. On the centrality of Encoge, see Bernardo de Oliveira Fragateiro, 'O districto do Congo debaixo do ponto de vista agrícola', *Revista Agronomica*, 2 (1904), 240–7, 273–80, 308–14, 339–42, at p. 246.

57 Haarer, *Modern Coffee Production*, pp. 17–18, 21; Wrigley, *Coffee*, p. 71.

Plate 2.2 Robusta coffee of the Amboim variety grown at the Experimental Station of Uíge, 2017. Image by author.

populations.[58] But in contrast to the culture of habitat preservation north of the Cuanza, planters in Seles and Amboim tended to clear the native forest canopy and then used cuttings and seeds from other coffee zones for new plantings. These new trees appeared to produce more fruit than the wild stands nearby.[59] In fact, they produced such good yields that growers elsewhere soon began to import coffee seeds from Amboim, reversing the initial flow of planting material.[60]

Like elsewhere, plant transfers often occurred through informal channels, without the intervention of colonial distribution centres.[61] The establishment

58 John Gossweiler, 'Relatório sobre a viagem à região do Seles', *BAA*, ser. 6, 3:8–12 (1930), 211–21, at p. 213.

59 Fausto Martins Lourenço, 'História do café robusta em Angola', *Revista de Ciências Agrárias*, 15:3 (1992), 57–117, at p. 107; António de Figueiredo Gomes e Sousa, 'Relatório de uma missão de reconhecimento agronómico no Distrito do Cuanza-Sul', *BAA*, ser. 5, 1:4 (1925), 7–32, at p. 19; Raul A. de S. Guardado, 'Breve relatório sobre o Amboim florestal e algumas medidas de fomento florestal a adoptar', *BAA*, ser. 5, 1:5 (1925), 137–41, at p. 139; Gossweiler, 'Viagem à região do Seles', 219.

60 John Gossweiler, 'Reconhecimento agronómico no Distrito de Malanje', *BAA*, ser. 6, 5:16–19 (1932), 19–52, at p. 31; 'Informação', 81; J. Costa Rosa, 'Relatório annual da 6ª Delegação Regional dos Serviços Agrícolas', *BAA*, ser. 6, 6:20–3 (1933), 85–104, at pp. 91–5.

61 William Beinart and Karen Middleton, 'Plant Transfers in Historical Perspective: A Review Article', *Environment and History*, 10:1 (2004), 3–29.

of an experimental station in Cazengo in 1908 contributed significantly to the study and development of indigenous and imported coffees in Angola. Based on trials with different species and varieties, the station offered a range of seeds to interested growers. Yet instead of buying seed from the colonial government, most farmers sourced planting material from commercial plantations where 'the trees are old and healthy', as horticulturalist Alec Haarer explained.[62] Specimens were initially taken from the montane forest north of the Cuanza.[63] Later, however, European settlers in northern Angola started new plantations with robusta variants imported from Amboim, which had a reputation of adapting well to new environments (Plate 2.2).[64] These multi-directional plant transfers disrupted the botanical notion of pure varieties, underlining Gordon Wrigley's argument that it is often 'difficult to know whether a plant is truly indigenous or merely naturalized'.[65]

Farms and estates

African farmers and foreign settlers in Angola long built their coffee plantations in the same way. Both groups ameliorated wild or sub-spontaneous forest coffees and used open woodland areas for additional planting, although by the 1950s some Europeans had begun to clear forest and plant trees in straight lines. Generally, cultivation was extensive, as growth came from greater land use rather than increased productivity.[66] However, settler estates differed from African farms in the scale and organization of production: they were much larger, employed more labour, and were more capital intensive. Since there were few economies of scale in coffee cultivation, these differences handicapped European planters in relation to their African neighbours.[67]

62 Haarer, *Modern Coffee Production*, p. 89; 'Horto experimental de Cazengo, movimento de sementes e plantas, de julho a março de 1912', *BAA*, 1:2 (1912), 138–9. See also Cortezão, 'Breve ensaio', pp. 144–5; Eduardo de Oliveira, *Café (instruções e conselhos práticos): Plantação do café, técnica agrícola, 1961–2011* (Rio Tinto: Mosaico de Palavras, 2012); John William Purseglove, *Tropical Crops: Dicotyledons* (2 vols, London: Longmans, 1968), vol. 2, p. 486.

63 Gossweiler, 'Reconhecimento fitogeográfico', 30.

64 'Cartilha do cafeicultor', *RCP*, 1:4 (1954), 57–65; AHU, Ministério do Ultramar (MU), Inspecção Superior da Adminstração Ultramarina (ISAU), A2.050.05/034.00203, 'Relatório do Governo da Província do Congo no ano de 1953', p. 142.

65 Wrigley, *Coffee*, p. 71.

66 AHU, MU, ISAU, A2.0001.02/012.00062, 'Relatório do Governador do Distrito do Cuanza Norte, António Francisco Neto Parra, respeitante ao período de 25 de outubro 1955 a 31 de dezembro 1956', p. 104; *ibid.*, A2.49.003/44.00300, 'Relatório da Inspecção ao Concelho do Negage, pelo Inspector Joaquim Henriques, 1960', pp. 45–6.

67 Steven Topik and William Gervase Clarence-Smith, 'Conclusion: New Propositions and a Research Agenda', in William Gervase Clarence-Smith and Steven

Small coffee farmers owed their economic advantage mainly to their low capital requirements. First, peasant households had access to communal land and employed tools they already used for food production, specifically baskets, hoes, machetes, and hooked sticks (*monanga*) used for weeding and bush clearing. In addition, there was very little mechanization involved in coffee production. The main technological innovations in this period were a variety of mechanical hullers and sorters, but the short harvest of the coffee crop made such machinery relatively expensive for producers, including several European planters, who therefore hulled manually or relied on larger organizations to process coffee mechanically.[68] Coffee was primarily a labour-intensive crop, as besides the busy harvest season, coffee trees demanded the constant weeding of forest creepers, tropical grasses, and waste shrubs, work that was not easily mechanized. Neither Europeans nor Africans invested in pesticides or fertilizers.

Unlike local farmers, foreign planters usually had to purchase (or lease) land and invest in buildings, equipment, machinery, and means of transport. They were also burdened by higher operating costs, as they required a permanent labour force, including expensive European managers and field supervisors. Indeed, on most plantations, the combined salaries of a few white employees exceeded the cost of African labour. As labour was in short supply, coffee planters in Cazengo and Golungo Alto often kept dozens, sometimes hundreds of workers permanently enslaved on their estates (see Chapter 5). The contract labour system that replaced slavery in the 1910s offered planters greater flexibility in recruitment, as they could release about half the workforce after the harvest, keeping the other half employed year-round for plantation maintenance. Nevertheless, contract workers were expensive to obtain and had to be housed, fed, supervised, and looked after, like the enslaved earlier. Gang labour increased yields – more easily so when rows were aligned, which in Angola they were often not – but was also costly as it required supervision.[69]

Topik (eds), *The Global Coffee Economy in Africa, Asia, and Latin America, 1500–1989* (Cambridge: Cambridge University Press, 2003), pp. 385–410, at p. 389; Paige, *Agrarian Revolution*, pp. 228–30, 252–3.

68 João Carlos Mesquitela, 'Guia do cafeicultor de Angola', *Gazeta Agrícola de Angola*, 10:5 (1965), 212–15, 217; Fausto Martins Lourenço, 'História do café robusta em Angola', *Revista de Ciências Agrárias*, 15:4 (1992), 85–119, at p. 87.

69 Gareth Austin, 'Mode of Production or Mode of Cultivation: Explaining the Failure of European Cocoa Planters in Competition with African Farmers in Colonial Ghana', in William Gervase Clarence-Smith (ed.), *Cocoa Pioneer Fronts since 1800* (London: Palgrave Macmillan, 1996), pp. 154–75; Topik and Clarence-Smith, 'Conclusion', p. 387. On production costs in northern Angola, see João Carlos Mesquitela, 'Determinações do custo da produção do café numa propriedade de tipo médio em Angola', *RCP*, 3:9 (1956), 25–43; António de Sousa Santos, 'Aspectos económicos da cafeicultura angolana: O preço do custo de produção de 1 kg de café comercial', *RCP*, 4:13 (1957), 47–57; Alfredo de Sousa, *Ensaio de análise económica do café* (Lisbon: Junta de Investigação do Ultramar, 1958), pp. 25–31. For an exam-

African producers tended to be more efficient, as their farms were generally self-provisioning, extended family units. When they grew larger, they relied on extra hands from the wider community. A colonial census taken in Encoge in 1910 suggests that families in this coffee-growing region averaged four persons and usually had a husband and wife at their core. Besides having children, the most common way to extend households was to incorporate wards, nephews, and nieces, as well as people labelled as 'servants' by the census but who may have been enslaved.[70] Records of the North Angola Mission, active in the same region from the 1930s, show that young men at the mission school often returned to their villages in the dry season to help with the coffee harvest. These records also demonstrate that, when coffee prices surged after the Second World War, African farms began to receive migrant workers during the harvest season, signalling the emergence of a local wage economy.[71] Most settler estates continued to rely on coerced labour throughout this period, mainly because their owners expected government support and refused to pay above the reservation wage. Many properties remained underutilized as administrators failed to recruit enough workers (see Chapter 6).

Another important difference was the ability of smallholders to adapt to the changing requirements of coffee and food production, based on their habit of multi-cropping to maintain food security. During the first coffee boom, peasant households in the Uíge area grew coffee alongside food crops such as maize, beans, banana, peanuts, and vegetables, as well as other cash crops like tobacco, cannabis (*liamba*), cotton, and castor oil. These crops were typically grown in plots separated from the coffee farms to avoid competition for subsoil moisture. Sheep, pigs, or goats often meandered in the shade of the coffee trees, eliminating grassy weeds and providing natural manure.[72] Settlers rarely mono-cropped coffee. They often invested in one or two other cash cops, like rubber or palm oil. They also let workers cultivate their own food plots – partly to compensate for low cash wages – and they planted palm trees and fruit trees to feed workers. Nevertheless, the main purpose of their estates was to produce coffee. The high fixed costs of these plantations led to inelastic supplies, making them more vulnerable to global price shocks than multi-cropping smallholders.[73]

ple of wage discrepancies, see AHU, MU, ISAU, A2.050.02/016.00106, 'Relatório da Inspecção ao Concelho de Ambaca, pelo Inspector Administrativo, Eduardo B. Lapido Loureiro' (1950).

70 Jelmer Vos, 'Family and Labour in an Angolan Cash-Crop Economy, 1910', *History of the Family*, 29:2 (2024), 280–98.

71 North Angola Mission, Archibald Patterson Papers (privately held), 'News of the Work' (Dec. 1952).

72 Beça, 'Presídio de Encoge', 93; Gossweiler, 'Reconhecimento fitogeográfico'. On mixed cropping, see Haarer, *Modern Coffee Production*, pp. 142, 208.

73 Maria Eugénia Mata *et al.*, 'Success and Failure in Portuguese Colonial Africa: The Case of the Cazengo Agricultural Company (1900–1945)', *Entreprises et histoire*,

Diseconomies of scale became visible in the late nineteenth century as bankruptcies began to plague the Cazengo estate sector. Many plantations were recipients of loans from the Banco Nacional Ultramarino, which had been founded by the Portuguese government in 1864 to subsidize the development of plantation agriculture in Angola and São Tomé and Príncipe. Planters needed these bank loans especially to secure labour.[74] In the wake of a prolonged drought in the early 1870s and declining coffee prices in the early 1880s, several defaulted on their mortgage payments. When harvests proved insufficient to cover the debts, they had no other option than to transfer their property, including the enslaved, to the Banco Nacional.[75] Around 1900, the bank assigned management of some estates – including the aforementioned Colónia São João, Prototypo, and Montalegre – to the newly established Cazengo Agricultural Company, which instantly became the largest coffee company in Angola. However, as prices remained weak, the company struggled to cover its expenses, which included investments in hulling and winnowing machines, irrigation systems, and a permanent labour force of more than a thousand African workers and several dozen European employees. With these came related outlays on housing, healthcare, food, clothing, and furniture. In the early 1900s, the company's plantations looked dilapidated.[76]

All plantations in the Cazengo region felt the strain of low robusta prices, which barely covered the costs of production. High transportation costs, overextension, and overreliance on the coffee crop added to the malaise, and many estates were rented out, sold, or abandoned.[77] The Cazengo Company survived

3 (2017), 53–73, at p. 66; Leitão, *Relatório*, pp. 18–72; Neuparth, *Apontamentos*, p. 23; Houk, 'Recent Developments', p. 210; Sousa, *Ensaio*, pp. 41–3; 'Relatório da Inspecção ao Concelho do Negage' (1960), pp. 45–6. On monocropping, see also Palacios, *Coffee*, p. 93; Verena Stolcke, 'The Labors of Coffee in Latin America: The Hidden Charm of Family Labor and Self-Provisioning', in William Roseberry *et al.* (eds), *Coffee, Society, and Power in Latin America* (Baltimore: Johns Hopkins University Press, 1995), pp. 65–93, at pp. 80–5.

74 Yonah Seleti, 'Finance Capital and the Coffee Industry of Angola, 1865–1895', *Transafrican Journal of History*, 16 (1987), 63–77; United Kingdom, Foreign Office, *Report on the Trade of Loanda, for the Year 1885* (London: Her Majesty's Stationery Office, 1886).

75 AHU, SEMU-DGU, Angola, 2ª Repartição, no. 832, Bispo D. José to MSENMU, confidential, Luanda, 18 June 1882.

76 José Joaquim de Almeida, 'Na Provincia de Angola: Administração colonial debaixo do ponte de vista agrícola', *Revista Agronomica*, 2 (1904), 97–110, 137–48, 161–75, 193–205, at p. 108; Henry W. Nevinson, *A Modern Slavery* (New York: Harper Brothers Publishers, 1906), p. 18; Mata *et al.*, 'Success and Failure', p. 68.

77 Ukers, *All about Coffee*, p. 268; John Gossweiler, 'O horto experimental de Cazengo', *BAA*, 1:1 (1908), 16–21; 'Carpodinus Chylorrhiza: A principal productora da borracha de Angola', *BAA*, 1:4 (1908), 150–61, at p. 158; Amílcar Carreira, 'Estação agronómica de Cazengo: Relatório', *BAA*, ser. 3, 4 (1919), 132–56, at p. 139; Seleti, 'Portuguese Colonialism', pp. 131–4.

mainly by virtue of its valuable properties. In the 1900s, it tried to increase revenue by diversifying production. Rubber, cocoa, and sugar cane were planted, but these measures brought only minimal benefits. After the First World War, the company managed to pay off its debts, but as the value of the Portuguese escudo had sunk during the war, it lacked funds for operational costs. In 1929, the Belgian Hallet group, which already owned half of the capital of the Companhia Agrícola de Angola in the Amboim region, stepped in as majority shareholder. After another decade of fluctuating coffee prices, Hallet sold the company and its four thousand hectares of planted coffee trees to the Chibera consortium of Portuguese entrepreneur António da Costa, who had better luck. The post-war commodity boom and the entrenchment of the contract labour system ensured the company remained one of the largest plantation firms in Angola.[78]

Conflicting views

Smallholder initiative drove the first Angolan coffee boom and kept production afloat after 1895, when growers experienced a long period of depressed and unstable world coffee prices. Despite market volatility, coffee outputs increased on the thinly populated sub-plateau around Amboim and Seles, south of the Cuanza River, where European traders, shopkeepers, and businesses were able to build new plantations around pockets of natural forest and by expropriating indigenous farms.[79] North of the Cuanza, by contrast, planters struggled with labour shortages and competition from African farmers, and for several decades the estate sector barely expanded beyond the old colonial districts of Cazengo and Golungo Alto. In the north, smallholders consistently accounted for nearly 70 per cent of outputs between 1900 and 1930.[80]

While cash-crop agriculture in northern Angola had primarily been a story of successful indigenous entrepreneurship, Portuguese officials struggled to recognize African contributions to economic development. A report on the

78 Gervase Clarence-Smith, 'Business Empires in Angola under Salazar, 1930–1961', *AEH*, 14 (1985), 1–13; *The Third Portuguese Empire, 1825–1975: A Study in Economic Imperialism* (Manchester: Manchester University Press, 1985), pp. 69–70, 97, 171, 176; Banco de Portugal, Arquivo Histórico (Lisbon), BAM/LIS/071/0008, Companhia Agrícola de Cazengo, 1925; Arquivo Nacional da Torre do Tombo (Lisbon), PT/TT/AOS/D-N/6/1/1, Administrador delegado Augusto Lopes Joly to Ministro das Finanças [1927]; AHU, MU, ISAU, A2.050.05/033.00202, José Diogo Ferreira Martins, 'Relatório da Inspecção aos Distritos de Cuanza Norte, Cuanza Sul, 1960–1961', pp. 15, 33.

79 Lourenço, 'História', 15:3, pp. 101–7; Paige, *Agrarian Revolution*, pp. 232–5.

80 Aida Freudenthal, 'Angola', in A. H. de Oliveira Marques (ed.), *O império africano, 1890–1930* (Lisbon: Editorial Estampa, 2001), pp. 259–467, at p. 344 fn. 227; statistics of agricultural production for 1928–31 in *BAA*, ser. 6 (1929–33), and 1932 in *BAA*, ser. 7, 6:24–7 (1934), 180.

state of the Angolan economy by José Firmo de Sousa Monteiro, a Portuguese agronomist who visited the colony in the 1910s, shows that racialized conceptions of African production systems as primitive and inefficient influenced even the views of sympathetic observers. Monteiro admired the flourishing coffee trade near Uíge, but his assessment of the region's 'natural wealth' completely dismissed the agricultural dimension of African export production. He believed the coffee trade was based purely on gathering fruit from sub-spontaneous plants, rather than cultivation.[81]

Quite innocuous on its own, Monteiro's report was symptomatic of broader currents in colonial discourse, which increasingly emphasized the supremacy of Western agronomic knowledge. It came at a time when Portugal's economic policy in Angola was teetering between two models. On one side, there were politicians who sympathized with maintaining the 'peasant economy' that had produced taxable riches like ivory, wax, coffee, and rubber for over half a century. Many of them nonetheless proposed adding a state-funded programme of white settlement to develop intensive agriculture on the Central Plateau. On the other were politicians who strongly supported the creation of a 'plantation colony' based on large-scale private capital investment. Proponents of this model were often apologists of coerced labour, convincing one another that Africans were only productive when forced to work for European colonists, whereas their opponents argued that settler agriculture was compatible with free labour and the promotion of an independent African peasantry. On both sides, however, belief in the economic benefits of white colonization and the superiority of Western 'scientific' approaches to crop production was growing.[82]

Ideas about Africa's economic future circulating in the upper echelons of empire found a local voice in José Cardoso, governor of the rubber-rich Congo district that became the heartland of the Angolan coffee economy. As rubber revenues dwindled in 1912, Cardoso considered ways for local agriculture to sustain the export trade. In his opinion, small-scale peasant production was unhelpful.

81 José Firmo de Sousa Monteiro, *Breve noticia das riquezas naturais de Angola: Possibilidade da sua produção e aspectos regionais agrícolas* (Luanda: Imprensa Nacional, 1921), p. 50.

82 Valentim Alexandre, *Velho Brasil, novas Áfricas: Portugal e o Império (1808–1975)* (Porto: Edições Afrontamento, 2000), pp. 160–1, 174–5; Freudenthal, 'Angola', p. 285; Cláudia Castelo, *Passagens para África: O povoamento de Angola e Moçambique com naturais da metrópole (1920–1974)* (Lisbon: Edições Afrontamento, 2007), pp. 49–54, 65–80; Maria Paula G. Meneses, 'O "indígena" africano e o colono "europeu": A construção da diferença por processos legais', *e-cadernos CES*, 7 (2010) <https://doi.org/10.4000/eces.403>. Eurocentric notions of 'rational' and 'scientific' agriculture became buzzwords in the colonial literature of the early twentieth century. See, for instance, António Lobo de Almada Negreiros, *La main-d'œuvre en Afrique: mémoire presenté au Congrès International de 1900* (Paris: s.l., 1900), pp. 29–31; Vicente Ferreira, *A situação de Angola* (Luanda: Imprensa Nacional, 1927), p. 110.

Cardoso argued that local farmers were culturally inhibited from maximizing production as they attempted to grow just enough to survive, pay colonial taxes, and satisfy a baseless need for imported luxuries. His reasoning expressed the cognitive dissonance of European colonizers who, on the one hand, complained about African producers lacking material incentives (see Chapter 5) but, on the other, conveniently redefined African consumer demand as a 'vice' when they needed to dismiss African economic behaviour as irrational.[83] While proof of well-established coffee and peanut trades was right in front of him, Cardoso believed that local smallholders barely produced for the market, which showed him their inability to respond to the growing demand for cash crops. The solution to the impending collapse of the Angolan export economy was large-scale, intensive agriculture, for which only Europeans had the capital and necessary expertise. According to Cardoso, the future of African labour lay in small-scale food production combined with work for European agricultural companies.[84]

When a new generation of Portuguese settlers in northern Angola began to compete for African land in the 1920s, the most vocal ones used similar racialized ideologies to dismiss African production methods as irrational, inefficient, and unprofitable. 'Vast unexploited resources extend over thousands of hectares of forest, where coffee plants, sown by birds ... live and die smothered by the surrounding vegetation before any human hand takes advantage from nature.' This was how José Roque Martins, one of the first plantation owners in Uíge, described the local coffee landscape in the early 1930s. He continued:

> The African does not farm coffee: he takes care of some bushes that he inherited, [which are] old, ruined by poor harvesting methods, almost fruitless. Most coffee that he sells, he picks from around the bush, pulling the few branches that [managed to] escape the weblike vines smothering the shrubs and still bear fruit. When he has collected enough to satisfy his necessities, he ignores the remainder.[85]

As they appeared to do little more than gather fruit from wild trees to add a little luxury to their subsistence lifestyles, African farmers, according to Martins, were inefficient users of the riches the Angolan coffee forest offered.

83 In 1935 the colonial minister, Armindo Monteiro (1931–35), endorsed promoting African consumer needs because it was good for Portuguese industry. See Cláudia Castelo, 'Developing "Portuguese Africa" in Late Colonialism: Confronting Discourses', in Joseph M. Hodge *et al.* (eds), *Developing Africa: Concepts and Practices in Twentieth-Century Colonialism* (Manchester: Manchester University Press, 2014), pp. 63–83, at p. 65.

84 José Cardoso, *No Congo Português: Viagem ao Bembe e Damba, considerações relacionadas, setembro a outubro de 1912* (Luanda: Imprensa Nacional de Angola, 1914), pp. 151–64.

85 José Roque Martins, João Afonso, and Carlos Alves (eds), *Uige, Songo, Bembe: A circunscrição civil do Bembe, na primeira exposição colonial portuguesa* (Luanda: Imprensa Nacional, 1934), p. 6.

These dismissive views of African production went against historical evidence and the observations of local agronomists, who were generally staunch proponents of indigenous cultivation methods. As this chapter has shown, small farming units in coffee-growing regions were market-oriented, making strategic decisions about investing productive resources in coffee cultivation. In addition to collecting coffee from the wild, farmers integrated coffee in mixed-cropping systems by improving natural stands and taking planting material from healthy trees to extend their farms. Indeed, rather than exploiting a previously idle resource – wild forest coffee – smallholders in Angola were generating new capital in the form of additional trees, as cocoa farmers did in West Africa.[86]

Local botanists and agronomists emphasized the efficiency and sustainability of African ways of coffee growing. These 'field scientists', as Helen Tilley has called them, contrasted African techniques with the wasteful methods of European planters during the interwar period, of which forest clearing was considered the gravest mistake.[87] In this regard, they radically opposed the science that was lectured in metropolitan schools, which defended settler agriculture – and the transformation of the African peasantry into field labourers – in the name of environmental conservation.[88] Some of their accusations were exaggerated, as many settlers continued to follow nineteenth-century patterns of plantation building. Nevertheless, shading and crop diversity, two key themes in modern agroforestry literature, were for John Gossweiler, Angola's first state botanist, defining features of small-scale coffee cultivation that colonial planters ignored at their own peril. Given the economic struggles of the Cazengo estates in the 1910s, it is easy to understand why he suggested Europeans must learn from African growers, not the other way round.[89]

While the political debate about the future of African peasant production continued, on the ground the plantation model prevailed. After the First World

86 Gareth Austin, *Labour, Land and Capital in Ghana: From Slavery to Free Labour in Asante, 1807–1956* (Rochester, NY: University of Rochester Press, 2005), p. 432. Cocoa farming involved the adoption of an exotic crop, which coffee was not.

87 Helen Tilley, *Africa as a Living Laboratory: Empire, Development, and the Problem of Scientific Knowledge, 1870–1950* (Chicago: University of Chicago Press, 2011), pp. 12–13, 115–68; Coelho, 'Relatório'; John Gossweiler, 'Contribuição para o estudo da flora dos Dembos', *BAA*, ser. 6, 3:8–12 (1930), 89–96, at p. 92; Gossweiler, 'Informação', 74.

88 Maria do Mar Gago, 'How Green was Portuguese Colonialism? Agronomists and Coffee in Interwar Angola', in Ana Delicado *et al.* (eds), *Changing Societies: Legacies and Challenges*, vol. 3, *The Diverse Worlds of Sustainability* (Lisbon: Instituto de Ciências Sociais, 2018), pp. 229–46.

89 Gossweiler, 'Reconhecimento fitogeográfico', 32; Shalene Jha *et al.*, 'Shade Coffee: Update on a Disappearing Refuge for Biodiversity', *Bioscience*, 64:5 (2014), 416–28; Louise Meylan *et al.*, 'Evaluating the Effect of Shade Trees on Provision of Ecosystem Services in Intensively Managed Coffee Plantations', *Agriculture, Ecosystems & Environment*, 245 (2017), 32–42.

War, the colonial government introduced new regulations for land concessions and labour recruitment, facilitating the enlargement of the nineteenth-century plantation sector. Significantly, it also recognized the contribution of peasant producers to the Angolan economy and consistently included provisions in land laws to protect African cash-crop agriculture. As later chapters will show, however, settler colonialism as practised was less the result of policies designed in Lisbon than of decisions made by colonists, administrators, and officials in the Angolan departments of agriculture and labour. State support of European coffee plantations led to an uneasy coexistence of settlers and smallholders, turning the metropolitan idea of protecting both in equal measure into a mirage.

3

'Angola Writes New Chapter'

TROPICAL AFRICA was, and still is, home to a wide variety of indigenous coffee species, but before the twentieth century, Africans generally did not cultivate much coffee and the continent exported very little.[1] In fact, while populations in East Africa had long processed small amounts of forest coffees for domestic use, the only region in the continent that produced substantial amounts of wild and naturalized coffees for export before 1900 was Angola.[2] During the colonial period, nonetheless, Africa emerged as a new frontier in the global coffee trade, as the continent's share in world production rose from a little over 1 per cent in 1900 to 15 per cent in 1950 and 23 per cent in 1965.[3] Most growing regions in Africa, Angola included, produced robusta coffee, a species different from the arabica strains that had so far dominated global trade. Although not as desirable in taste, robusta had two advantages over arabica that determined its commercial success in the twentieth century. First, it was resistant to coffee leaf rust, a fungal disease that, since its initial outbreak in Ceylon

1 Aaron P. Davis, Rafael Govaerts, and Diane M. Bridson, 'Annotated Taxonomic Conspectus of the Genus *Coffea* (Rubiaceae)', *Botanical Journal of the Linnean Society*, 152:4 (2006), 465–512.

2 John Hanning Speke, *Journal of the Discovery of the Source of the Nile* (London: William Blackwood, 1863), pp. 357, 377, 636; Cornelis Frederik van Delden Laerne, *Brazil and Java: Report on Coffee Culture in America, Asia and Africa* (The Hague: Martinus Nijhoff, 1885), pp. 458–61.

3 Nationaal Archief (The Hague, henceforth NA), Koninklijke Nederlandse Vereniging voor de Koffiehandel (2.19.012), no. 153, Algemene staat van koffie, thee, rijst en specerijen, opgemaakt door G. Duuring & Zoon, Dalen & Plemp, Kolff & Witkamp en Leonard Jacobson & Zonen, makelaars te Rotterdam (1889–1916); Benoit Daviron and Stefano Ponte, *The Coffee Paradox: Global Markets, Commodity Trade and the Elusive Promise of Development* (London: Zed Books, 2005), p. 58; Jonathan Morris, *Coffee: A Global History* (London: Reaktion Books, 2019), p. 122; Mario Samper and Radin Fernando, 'Appendix: Historical Statistics of Coffee Production and Trade from 1700 to 1960', in William Gervase Clarence-Smith and Steven Topik (eds), *The Global Coffee Economy in Africa, Asia, and Latin America, 1500–1989* (Cambridge: Cambridge University Press, 2003), pp. 411–62, at pp. 450–3.

in 1869, has severely restricted the worldwide expansion of arabica production.[4] Furthermore, because of its poorer taste, robusta was relatively cheap, allowing manufacturers to keep blended and soluble coffee products affordable during the Great Depression (1929–39) and the post-war boom in commodity prices.

Angola was among the early beneficiaries of increased global demand for African coffees after 1900, exploiting its position as leading robusta producer in the continent. As Chapter 1 has shown, the suppression of the transatlantic slave trade, global economic integration, and increasing coffee consumption in the industrializing Global North created the conditions for Angola's entry in the world coffee trade during the nineteenth century, resulting in a record 11,000 metric tons shipped from its shores in 1895. Coffee exports reached new heights of 22,000 tons in 1936 and 90,000 tons in 1956. The current chapter examines the global context of this twentieth-century expansion. It considers ecological conditions favouring robusta cultivation, product innovations and changing consumption patterns in Europe and North America, and subsequent adjustments to coffee processing in Angola. It will show that the Angolan coffee sector developed not through dependency on the Portuguese metropole, but by exploiting demand for robusta in two nations that lacked African colonies: the Netherlands and the United States. Angola was not the only coffee producer on the continent that exported heavily to markets other than the metropolitan, which highlights the need to look for global connections across imperial boundaries for understanding modern African history. At the same time, the relationship between Angolan growers and foreign buyers was critically mediated by the Portuguese Coffee Export Board, a colonial intervention dictated by the requirements of standardization in the coffee commodity chain.

Robusta revolution

An acceleration in the global coffee trade during the 1920s, after decades of stagnation, gave new impetus to coffee cultivation in Africa. Growth was driven primarily by industrial labour specialization and the subsequent growth of urban middle classes in North America and Europe, which created new consumer markets for the caffeinated beverage.[5] Despite dramatic price variations in the interwar period and a dip in global shipments during the Second World War, the new surge continued into the 1950s, as the amount of coffee annually exported and imported around the world grew from roughly 1.3 million metric tons in

4 Stuart McCook, *Coffee Is Not Forever: A Global History of the Coffee Leaf Rust* (Athens: Ohio University Press, 2019).

5 Michael F. Jiménez, '"From Plantation to Cup": Coffee and Capitalism in the United States, 1830–1930', in William Roseberry *et al.* (eds), *Coffee, Society, and Power in Latin America* (Baltimore: Johns Hopkins University Press, 1995), pp. 38–64, at pp. 42–4.

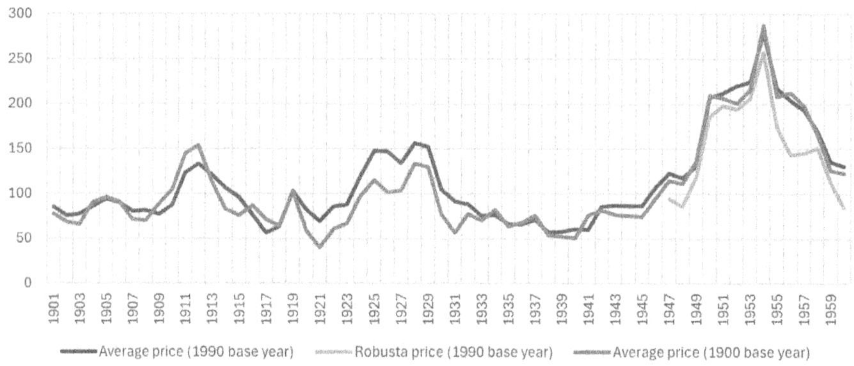

Graph 3.1 Real coffee prices, 1901–60. Source: Samper and Fernando, 'Appendix', pp. 455–8; Jacks, 'From Boom to Bust'.

1920 to more than 2.3 million tons in 1960.[6] Though South America was the main contributor, rising prices after the First World War (Graph 3.1) also pulled the African continent into the world coffee market.

Africa's main impact on the global coffee trade came from its growing robusta coffee output. Scientifically known as *Coffea canephora*, robusta is one of three main commercialized coffee species in the world, the others being *C. arabica* and *C. liberica*. All three species are indigenous to Africa. Before the twentieth century, a small number of arabica cultivars derived from Ethiopian introductions to Yemen dominated global trade. Only Angola produced substantial amounts of a different species, robusta, although botanists had not yet recognized it as such. The outbreak of a leaf blight epidemic in Asia, together with Africa's entry in the world coffee market, broke arabica's global hegemony.

Coffee leaf rust is a fungal disease that reduces the yield of coffee plants by disrupting the production of nutrients that allow the plants and their fruit to develop. It affects mainly arabica, which owing to its low genetic diversity is susceptible to many plant pests and diseases, including coffee leaf rust.[7] The impact is most severe at low elevations, where a combination of heat and humidity allow rust spores to germinate. The fungus (*hemileia vastatrix*) is endemic to many African coffee regions, condemning arabica to highland environments where cooler temperatures keep the fungus in check. During the final decades of the nineteenth century, rust swept across plantations in Asia and the Pacific, causing

6 Samper and Fernando, 'Appendix', pp. 417–19.

7 Jarkko Salojärvi *et al.*, 'The Genome and Population Genomics of Allopolyploid *Coffea arabica* Reveal the Diversification History of Modern Coffee Cultivars', *Nature Genetics*, 56 (2024), 721–31.

the near collapse of arabica production in these regions.[8] In response to the crisis, coffee breeders in the Dutch East Indies, the world's largest exporter after Brazil, began experimenting with alternative, disease-resistant coffees found in Africa. In 1900, they received a robusta sample from a nursery in Brussels, collected several years earlier in the Lower Congo, not far from the border with Angola. Belgian botanists had labelled this new species *C. robusta* because of the plant's hardiness, vigour, fertility, and apparent resistance to known coffee diseases. In Java, it proved tolerant to leaf rust and showed a capacity to grow at low altitudes, where the impact of rust on arabica trees was most severe. Moreover, Dutch coffee breeders found that robusta had a relatively mild taste and was therefore drinkable, a considerable improvement to the West African liberica coffees they had experimented with earlier. As many estate farmers and smallholders in Java and Sumatra replaced their remaining arabica stocks with new robusta stands, by 1935, robusta accounted for more than 90 per cent of Indonesian coffee outputs.[9] In global markets, 'Robusta' came to refer specifically to coffees derived from cultivars developed in Indonesia, whereas African robustas usually received regional designations.

Leaf rust had a major impact on the way coffee growing developed in Africa. Its endemic presence curtailed the expansion of arabica cultivation in the continent at a time when rising global demand for coffee stimulated colonial economies to expand production. As the rust is most devastating at lower elevations, arabica cultivation was largely restricted to a few highland enclaves in East Africa, where white settlers tended to dominate production. Elsewhere, African and European farmers expanded the cultivation of robusta coffee, which was not constrained by rust in the same way. Besides Angola, the main centres of robusta production were Uganda, western Tanzania, and Madagascar in East Africa, the Belgian Congo in Central Africa, and Côte d'Ivoire in West Africa. While growers in Angola and the Lake Victoria region primarily used naturalized indigenous varieties, in other regions cultivation relied on both local and imported cultivars.[10]

8 William Gervase Clarence-Smith, 'The Coffee Crisis in Asia, Africa, and the Pacific, 1870–1914', in Clarence-Smith and Topik, *Global Coffee Economy*, pp. 100–19; McCook, *Coffee Is Not Forever*.

9 P. J. S. Cramer, *A Review of Literature of Coffee Research in Indonesia* (Turrialba: SIC Editorial, Inter-American Institute of Agricultural Sciences, 1957), pp. 12–13, 106–7, 113–18.

10 McCook, *Coffee Is Not Forever*, pp. 108–24; International Institute of Agriculture, *Coffee in 1931 and 1932: Economic and Technical Aspects* (Rome: Printing Office of the Chamber of the Deputies, 1934), pp. 20–1; António Pais dos Santos da Fonseca Ferrão, 'Os principais problemas da cafeicultura na Costa do Marfim', *RCP*, offprint no. 4 (Lisbon: Junta de Exportação do Café, 1955), pp. 10–21; Hélder Lains e Silva,

The increased commercialization of robusta in the early twentieth century caused a major shift in the global coffee trade as well as in consumer palates. Little traded before 1900, except from Angola, by 1956 robusta accounted for over 22 per cent of world coffee exports.[11] Compared to arabica, this was generally a poor-quality coffee, which enjoyed a mixed reception among traders and roasters in Europe and North America. Some critics argued that beverages made from robusta coffee were tasteless and lacked body, while others found them sweet and mild. It was generally considered that robusta had 'no objectionable features', unlike some of the low-grade arabicas from Brazil with which it was competing at the low end of the market.[12] Its neutral taste made robusta ideal for blending with other coffees, especially in times of rising coffee prices. During the global recession of the 1930s, European and North American roasters selling vacuum-packed blends of ground coffee appreciated robusta as a low-cost filler, as did their (unwitting) penny-saving clients. As coffee traders began to pump growing amounts of robusta in the market, consumer tastes changed. One North American coffee expert observed in 1937: 'A few years ago coffee brokers were loath to taste a cup of Robusta. After repeated sippings, however, one finds himself becoming accustomed to them.'[13] With Asian and African robustas now firmly established in the world coffee market, Western consumers had no choice but to adapt.

Angola led the African robusta revolution, building on the coffee economy that myriad peasant households, settler farmers, caravan traders, and coastal merchants had collectively created in the nineteenth century.[14] Exports from the colony rose from about four thousand metric tons at the end of the First World War to more than twelve thousand tons in 1925 and nearly 22,000 tons in 1936 (Graph 3.2). This growth followed the arrival of a new generation of European planters, many of them former shopkeepers, drawn to coffee farming by the high prices of the 1920s and visible improvements in road transportation (see Chapter 4).[15] By this time, white farmers accounted for about two-thirds

'Progressos técnicos da cafeicultura no Congo Belga e na Costa Rica', *RCP*, offprint no. 16 (Lisbon: Junta de Exportação do Café, 1959).

11 Mark Pendergrast, *Uncommon Grounds: The History of Coffee and How It Transformed Our World*, rev. edn (New York: Basic Books, 2010), p. 261.

12 Arno Viehoever and H. A. Lepper, 'Robusta Coffee', *Journal of the Association of Official Agricultural Chemists*, 5:2 (1921), 274–88, at pp. 286–7. See also William H. Ukers, *All about Coffee* (New York: Tea and Coffee Trade Journal Company, 1922), p. 145; Gordon Wrigley, *Coffee* (Harlow: Longman, 1988), 490; McCook, *Coffee Is Not Forever*, p. 103.

13 Cited in Pendergrast, *Uncommon Grounds*, p. 187.

14 *TCTJ*, 57:5 (1929), 763.

15 Angola, Repartição Central de Estatística Geral, *Anuário estatístico de Angola*, 1936 (Luanda: Imprensa Nacional, 1936); José Roque Martins, João Augusto Afonso, and Carlos Alves (eds), *Uige, Songo, Bembe: A circunscrição civil do Bembe, na primeira exposição portuguesa* (Luanda: Imprensa Nacional, 1934), p. 5; David Bir-

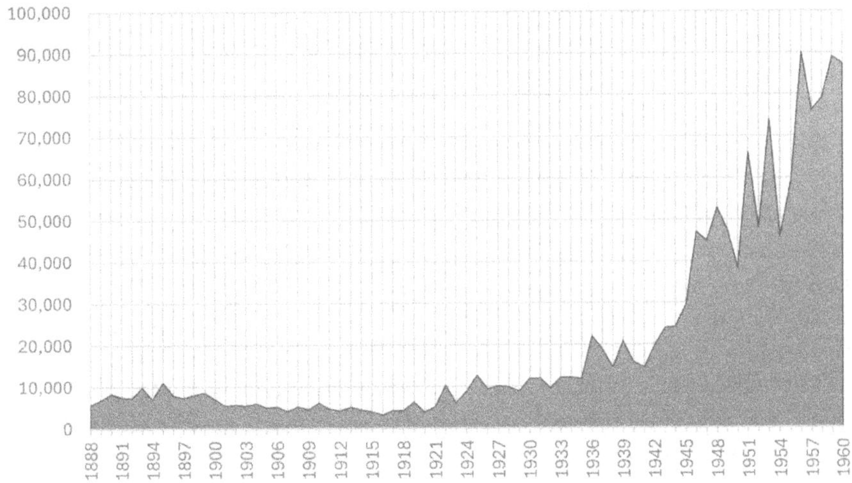

Graph 3.2 Coffee exports from Angola, 1888–1960 (metric tons). Source: Mesquita, *Dados estatísticos*; Ferrão, 'Sobre a lei'; Esteves and Oliveira, *Contribuição*, p. 24.

of Angolan production. Their dominance was most noticeable south of the river Cuanza, in the sparsely populated coffee zones of Amboim and Seles, where, from the 1890s, Portuguese settlers obtained comparatively large concessions from the Portuguese government and few African farmers grew the crop. In northern Angola, by contrast, settlers had to compete with African producers, who remained dominant into the 1930s.[16]

Two companies from the Netherlands and England dominated coffee exporting in Angola, continuing a nineteenth-century pattern of Anglo-Dutch hegemony in the regional commodity trade.[17] A new Amsterdam-based firm, the Zuid-Afrikaansch Handelshuis, locally known as 'Casa Zuid', became the main Dutch player in Angola after the NAHV decided to consolidate their Central African investments in the Belgian Congo. Zuid held stores in Luanda, Ambriz, and Lobito, which they stocked with textiles and other European merchandise. They distributed these wares on credit to smaller traders inland, who exchanged them for coffee and other produce. According to a former company director,

mingham, 'A Question of Coffee: Black Enterprise in Angola', *Canadian Journal of African Studies*, 16:2 (1982), 343–6.

16 Fausto Martins Lourenço, 'História do café robusta em Angola', *Revista de Ciências Agrárias*, 15:3 (1992), 57–117, at pp. 101–7; Jeffery M. Paige, *Agrarian Revolution: Social Movements and Export Agriculture in the Underdeveloped World* (New York: Free Press, 1975), pp. 232–5. For output figures, see *BAA* (1929–32).

17 Delegação do Governo Geral de Angola à Primeira Exposição Colonial Portuguesa, *Angola, café, exportação* (Luanda: Imprensa Nacional, 1934).

Andries Pieter van der Graaf, Zuid were 'the largest coffee exporter [in Angola] before the war'.[18] The Second World War disrupted the company's operations in Southern Africa, and afterwards the company prioritized their imports over their exporting activities.[19]

On the British side, Robert Hudson & Sons filled a vacancy left by old-timers Hatton and Cookson, which, like the NAHV, had downsized their operations in Angola after the trade in wild rubber collapsed in 1913.[20] Hudson & Sons were a Leeds-based subsidiary of Robert Hudson, suppliers of railway technology, focusing specifically on the import and export trade. In the 1930s, they had stores and distributing agents all over the colony and claimed to be 'the largest commercial organisation of Angola'.[21] They also owned plantations, including the thousand-hectare Alto Loge estate near Uíge, an emerging coffee centre in northern Angola, which gave them twenty-six tons of green coffee in 1934.[22] Hudson & Sons exported mainly to markets other than the United Kingdom, where levels of coffee consumption were notoriously low.[23] Like Zuid, they divested from exporting after the Second World War. But their role as agent of international shipping companies, distributor of Unilever products, and dealer of Ford trucks, automobiles, and coffee hulling equipment consolidated their leading position in the import trade.[24]

Angola produced commodities for a diverse international market, but differential tariffs encouraged foreign traders to ship tropical goods via Lisbon. Thus, while statistically Portugal accounted for most coffee imports from Angola in the interwar period, only a small portion remained there. In fact, despite possessing several coffee-growing colonies in Africa and Asia, Portugal was hardly a nation of coffee drinkers. Its population was relatively small and its domestic market

18 Andries Pieter van der Graaf, 'My Years in Angola, 1950–1970' (2012), typescript manuscript published online at <https://www.asclibrary.nl/docs/341217840.pdf> (Africa Studies Centre Library, University of Leiden), p. 12; Martins *et al.*, *Uige*, p. 11.

19 NA, Rotterdamsche Bank (2.18.33), no. 41, Zuid-Afrikaansch Handelshuis, Riemens, 'Reisverslag' (Amsterdam, 26 Oct. 1949).

20 Unilever Archives (Port Sunlight), UAC/2/33/BU/2/1/1, Hatton & Cookson balance sheets, 1915–20. For the NAHV, see NA, Nieuwe Afrikaansche Handels-Vennootschap (2.18.10.09), 57/127, La Vieter to NAHV, privé no. 5, Boma, 12 Feb. 1923; *ibid*, 181–4, balance sheets 1913–16.

21 Robert Hudson & Sons advertisement in Adolfo Pina (ed.), *A Província de Angola: Número extraordinário dedicado à exposição colonial portuguesa e em honra da restauração de Angola* (Luanda: Empresa Gráfica de Angola, 1934).

22 Martins *et al.*, *Uige*, pp. 18–19. In the 1950s, Alto Loge was with 1,500 African employees one of the largest estates in northern Angola. It is unclear if Hudson & Sons still owned it. Richard J. Houk, 'Recent Developments in the Portuguese Congo', *Geographical Review*, 48:2 (1958), 201–21, at p. 210.

23 Ukers, *All about Coffee*, pp. 285–7; 'Survey of Coffee Drinking Habits in U.K.', *TCTJ*, 94:3 (1948), 20.

24 Robert Hudson & Sons advertisement in *Revista do Ultramar*, 1:10 (1948).

easily saturated. Many people could not afford to buy coffee and instead drank substitutes made from roasted cereals, beans, and chicory.[25] A lot of the coffee Portugal imported from Africa moved on to Northwest Europe, especially the Netherlands, as well as the United States.[26]

In 1929, the Netherlands was 'the leading coffee market of Europe', according to the American consul-general in Amsterdam, Charles Hoover.[27] The country was a central point for the receipt and distribution of coffee in the continent, exporting approximately half of all the coffees it imported from around the world to buyers in Germany, France, Sweden, Switzerland, Belgium, and Denmark. Dutch citizens were themselves also keen coffee drinkers, each consuming on average around 4kg per year. Because of the Netherlands' colonial presence in Indonesia, Dutch consumers had developed an early taste for robusta.[28] For instance, a typical Dutch coffee blend in 1929 contained equal measures of Brazilian arabicas and East Indian robustas and a lesser amount (20 per cent) of Central American 'Milds' to enhance the flavour, a composition that would change little over time. Because of the longstanding dominance of Dutch trading firms in Angola, importers and dealers in the Netherlands had also grown familiar with Angolan growths. While these had appeared in Dutch coffee auctions from the late nineteenth century, dealers now advertised them as potential substitutes for Indonesian robustas.[29] Generally, however, the trade in African coffees was still relatively insignificant during the 1930s, amounting to no more than 4 per cent of all Dutch coffee imports.[30]

The Second World War caused a dramatic shift in the Netherlands' relationship with African coffees, especially Angolan robusta. Under Japanese occupation, Indonesian coffee production collapsed as coffee estates were uprooted to make room for food crops.[31] When, after the war, Dutch importers had to look

25 Pedro Cintra Ferreira, *O café no commercio* (Brussels: Generaux, 1908), p. 119; 'Coffee Propaganda Is Begun in Spain and Portugal', *TCTJ*, 57:4 (1929), 489–90; Hélder Lains e Silva, 'Nota sobre o consumo do café na metrópole de 1900 a 1952', *RCP*, 1:1 (1954), 27–31.

26 Ukers, *All about Coffee*, pp. 287–90; Delegação do Governo Geral de Angola, *Angola*; 'Angola Writes New Chapter in the Production of Coffee', *TCTJ*, 73:1 (1937), 11, 36.

27 'Netherlands Is the Leading Coffee Market of Europe', *TCTJ*, 57:4 (1929), 456–60.

28 Pendergrast, *Uncommon Grounds*, p. 153.

29 Stadsarchief Amsterdam, 598, Archief van de Koffiehandel Hofmann, Schöffer & Co., no. 170, brochure no. 26 (30 Sep. 1933).

30 Stadsarchief Amsterdam, 598, Archief van de Koffiehandel Hofmann, Schöffer & Co., no. 170, Annual Review (2 Jan. 1939); NA, Directie Economische Zaken van het Ministerie van Buitenlandse Zaken (2.05.37), no. 4043, Gezantschap der Nederlanden, no. 426/59, Rio de Janeiro, 30 March 1940.

31 'Dutch Tea, Coffee and Cocoa Trades Seek to Regain Pre-War Importance', *TCTJ*, 91:1 (1946), 16; Pierre van der Eng, 'Food Supply in Java during War and Decolonisa-

elsewhere for cheap robustas, they instantly grew their ties with Angola. The Netherlands became so reliant on the Angolan coffee trade that, by the 1950s, the country sourced about 90 per cent of its robusta supplies from the Portuguese colony, which amounted to about a third of total Dutch coffee imports. In some years, Angola was even the Netherlands' main coffee supplier, ahead of Brazil.[32] Dutch dependency manifested in the blends national roasters prepared for their consumers, in which Angolan robusta took the place formerly occupied by Indonesian and even captured a small part of the Brazilian share.[33] While the relative proportions of arabicas and robustas fluctuated slightly every year depending on cost price and quality, the standard 'red' blend of Douwe Egberts, the Netherlands' largest roaster, was sometimes half Angolan.[34] The dependency was mutual. Since Angola produced much more coffee than Portugal could absorb, its export trade relied heavily on importing countries that lacked colonial supply lines of their own, like the Netherlands and the United States.[35]

Angola and the United States

American and Dutch demand for robusta led to a large-scale expansion of the Angolan coffee economy during the 1940s and 1950s. The obstructions to global trade caused by the Second World War barely affected Angolan coffee exports, as the navicert regime allowed Portuguese vessels to continue to ship produce from Angola.[36] Initially, prospects were not good. As world coffee prices dipped in the late 1930s, growers and traders in Angola held back production, causing exports to bottom at 14,000 metric tons in 1941. By the end of the war, however, they were back up to 29,000 tons. From 1945 to 1954, world coffee prices spiralled upward and so did shipments from Angola, which climbed to 47,000 tons in 1946 and 90,000 tons a decade later (Graphs 3.1 and 3.2).[37] Growth was based on an expanding settler economy, which by this time accounted for three-quarters of Angolan outputs, although in absolute terms African production also

tion, 1940–1950' (2008), MPRA Paper No. 8852, <https://mpra.ub.uni-muenchen.de/8852/> [accessed 2 June 2023], p. 20.

32 René Coste, *Les caféiers et les cafés dans le monde* (2 vols, Paris: Éditions Larose, 1955–61), vol. 2, p. 718; Alfredo de Sousa, *Ensaio de análise económica do café* (Lisbon: Junta de Investigação do Ultramar, 1958), p. 105.

33 'Koffieverbruik in Nederland met sprongen omhoog', *Allerhande*, 44 (April 1959), 1.

34 Tresoar (Leeuwarden), 110, Douwe Egberts, no. 254, Jaarrapport 1954; *ibid.*, no. 3471, Pedro Oliveira Leão to Douwe Egberts, Luanda, 22 April 1959. Douwe Egberts dominated the Dutch export market by acquisition of roasters in Germany, Belgium, France, and Scandinavia. See Pendergrast, *Uncommon Grounds*, p. 269.

35 A. G. Mezerik, 'World Coffee Consumption', *TCTJ*, 105:4 (1953), 18–19, 34.

36 'O café de Angola', *BGC*, 18:205 (1942), 96–7.

37 António Teixeira Lopes, *Considerações acerca de alguns aspectos da produção em Angola* (Luanda: Imprensa Nacional, 1951), pp. 6–7.

increased. By 1956, coffee planters had brought more than 250,000 hectares under cultivation, excluding illegal occupations and most African farms. The post-war expansion was most salient in northern Angola, which held about 80 per cent of the colony's cultivated coffee lands. This geographic recalibration of coffee production manifested in the preponderance in Angolan exports of the 'Ambriz' variety, which was the name allocated to coffees grown north of the Cuanza River, outside the old Encoge and Cazengo districts. Ambriz coffee was especially valued by manufacturers for blending well with arabicas.[38]

Like other coffee-growing regions in Africa, Angola benefited from an expanding post-war market for robusta, especially in the United States. American stakes in the Angolan coffee trade had grown during the recession of the 1930s, when coffee manufacturers increasingly turned to robusta to keep their products affordable. This turn brought a lingering unease between robusta and the American coffee industry to an end. In 1912, the New York Coffee Exchange had banned the sale of robusta, officially because the Department of Agriculture's definition of coffee only included arabica and liberica seeds, although there were suspicions that this definition fundamentally served to protect the interests of traders in Brazilian arabicas from the entry of cheaper Asian and African coffees. Despite this prohibition, New York merchants continued to import small batches of coffee from Angola, which went undetected as their botanical status was still unclear and they appeared in the market under other names than robusta.[39] In subsequent years, roasters in the United States complained about illegal sales of Indonesian robusta as 'Java' coffee, a name traditionally associated with arabica. There were even rumours importers tried to sell robusta as 'Santos', the standard Brazilian arabica that was priced slightly higher than robusta but tasted not much better. To clear up the confusion within the industry about the robusta trade, American government officials sought clarifications from their Dutch counterparts about the nature and appearance of the product from Indonesia. These explained that robusta beans looked very different from arabica, that in the Netherlands, 'Java' only applied to arabica imports, and that botanically, robusta was indeed coffee and therefore should be sold as such.[40] In 1929, the Department of Agriculture officially recognized robusta as coffee, allowing the Green Coffee Association of New York to develop new regulations for its trade.

38 Coste, *Les caféiers*, vol. 2, pp. 454, 461; Irene S. Van Dongen, 'Coffee Trade, Coffee Regions, and Coffee Ports in Angola', Economic Geography, 37:4 (1961), 320–46, at p. 330.

39 Viehoever and Lepper, 'Robusta Coffee', 286; Pendergrast, *Uncommon Grounds*, p. 153; João Mesquita, *Dados estatísticos para o estudo das pautas de Angola: Exportação pelas alfândegas do Círculo e do Congo nos anos de 1888 a 1913* (Luanda: Imprensa Nacional, 1918), p. 45.

40 See correspondence in NA, Directie Economische Zaken van het Ministerie van Buitenlandse Zaken, no. 1623. On the use of the 'Java' label by American roasters, see Augustine Sedgewick, *Coffeeland: A History* (Dublin: Penguin Books, 2020), pp. 104, 110–11.

Around the same time, European botanists classified several seemingly different African coffees as pertaining to a single species, *C. canephora,* which became the commonly adopted scientific name for robusta coffee. This provided much-needed clarity about the nature of American imports from the African continent, especially from Angola, which has increased significantly since.[41]

By the mid-1930s, the United States already absorbed up to 40 per cent of Angolan exports.[42] The quota arrangements of the Inter-American Coffee Agreement briefly restricted sales of African coffees to the United States during the Second World War.[43] After the war, however, two developments in the coffee industry, combined with soaring world coffee prices and the collapse of Indonesian production, caused a surge in American imports from Angola. The first was the growing popularity of canned, vacuum-packed coffee. Developed in the 1930s, the vacuum pack lengthened the time between roasting and brewing, which benefited large-scale industrial roasters at the expense of smaller grocers. Industrial roasting reduced the price of ground coffee blends, but also forced roasters to invest in branding and advertising and to keep prices stable to compete in national markets.[44] During the post-war price hike, therefore, large coffee roasters such as Maxwell House (owned by General Foods) and the Great Atlantic & Pacific Tea Company progressively used African robustas as cheap 'fillers' in their popular blends.

The second significant post-war development in the United States was the rise of instant, or soluble, coffee. First developed in the early twentieth century, instant coffee caught on in the 1940s, after companies like Nestlé and Maxwell House had managed to manufacture products with a consistent flavour that satisfied consumers looking for a quick and easy caffeine boost. Because price rather than quality determined demand for instant coffee, manufacturers mostly used coffee extracts from low-cost beans, especially robustas, which offered the additional advantage of high caffeine content. The introduction of vending machines, which mainly dispensed soluble coffee, and the growing popularity of the coffee break at places of work further increased demand for cheap robustas.[45] Nevertheless, while manufacturers transformed ever larger amounts of imported robusta into powder, instant

41 Wrigley, *Coffee*, p. 57; *TCTJ*, 57:3 (1929), 333; Auguste Chevalier, *Les caféiers du globe* (3 vols, Paris: Paul Lechevalier, 1929–47), vol. 1. For statistics, see Delegação do Governo Geral de Angola, *Angola*; José Bento Alves, 'Produção e comércio de café', *Actividade Económica de Angola*, 1 (1936), 59–75, at pp. 67–9.

42 'Angola Writes New Chapter'.

43 Pendergrast, *Uncommon Grounds*, p. 259; Maria do Mar de Mello Gago da Silva, 'Robusta Empire: Coffee, Scientists and the Making of Colonial Angola (1898–1961)' (Unpublished PhD dissertation, University of Lisbon, 2018), p. 157.

44 Elizabeth A. Richards, 'An analysis of the retail coffee market', *TCTJ*, 102:6 (1952), 18, 41–2.

45 Pendergrast, *Uncommon Grounds*, pp. 240–5, 261–2; Jiménez, 'Coffee and Capitalism', p. 49.

coffee remained supplementary to North American diets. Throughout the 1950s, people predominantly drank filtered coffee, usually during meals, and most product sales were still of canned ground coffee. Instant coffee was also very much an American drink that, apart from Switzerland and the United Kingdom, had yet to find a market among European consumers.[46] On a global scale, therefore, robusta largely disappeared into vacuum-packed blends.

With demand for coffee rising after the war, American importers began to source significant amounts of robusta in African colonies other than Angola, notably Côte d'Ivoire, Uganda, Madagascar, and the Belgian Congo, which all produced more than their metropolitan markets needed. Nonetheless, in the 1950s, Angola still supplied about 40 per cent of American robusta imports. Conversely, the United States absorbed about half of all Angolan exports.[47] Such was the level of interdependence between these two markets that American industry representatives repeatedly advised Portugal's Colonial Coffee Export Board (*Junta de Exportação do Café Colonial*) on improvements to its grading system.[48]

Product improvement

With the integration of the global coffee market in the nineteenth century, methods of grading coffee harmonized in ports across the Global South. Grading facilitated trade over long distances as it classified coffees according to specific attributes, using standards that buyers and sellers universally agreed on for determining quality and price. Coffee historians have paid much attention to the opening of coffee exchanges in New York, Le Havre, Hamburg, and Antwerp during the 1880s, the ensuing trade in coffee futures (exchange-traded forward contracts), and the introduction of numerical grades this trade required. It is often forgotten, however, that 'spot' transactions and standard contracts between farmers, traders, exporters, brokers, and roasters remained common in the global coffee trade. In fact, the first futures market for robusta opened in London only in 1958, initially trading only 'Uganda unwashed'. As one of the first countries in Africa, Angola introduced a numerical grading system in 1932, three years after the New York Coffee Exchange allowed trading of robusta. Even so, geographical origin and other descriptive markers, such as 'large' and 'small', or 'fine', 'good', 'fair' and 'poor', were still commonly used in European markets to grade Angolan coffees.[49]

46 Coste, *Les caféiers*, vol. 2, pp. 691–2; J. W. F. Rowe, *The World's Coffee* (London: Her Majesty's Stationery Office, 1963), p. 25; William Kappenberg, 'Solubles Increase Total Coffee Consumption', *TCTJ*, 103:4 (1952), 28; 'Elaboração do café soluvel', *RCP*, 4:13 (1957), 58–66; Jaime de Almeida Loureiro, 'Os cafés soluveis e a sua crescente expansão', *RCP*, 4:14 (1957), 17–23.

47 Coste, *Les caféiers*, vol. 2, p. 690; Sousa, *Ensaio*, pp. 66, 68.

48 Silva, 'Robusta Empire', pp. 166–73.

49 For historical accounts, see Edouard Raoul, *Culture du caféier: Semis, plantations, taille, dépulpation, décorticage, expédition, commerce, espèces et races* (Paris: Augustin

Standardization was in essence a process of homogenization. The coffee plant itself is very heterogeneous: plant scientists have discerned 103 different species, which all behave differently in different environments. To facilitate trade, the global coffee industry first reduced the number of marketable coffee varieties to a manageable scale. In turn, traders limited variability by separating dried beans into bags of uniform quality, usually based on outward appearance.[50] This process was more difficult for robusta coffee than for arabica. Unlike arabica, robusta is self-sterile and outbred. In its natural environment, therefore, the tree appears in many different varieties, their characteristics mainly depending on soil and climatic conditions. Robusta's innate variability, further enhanced by naturalization and introduction, long hampered botanical efforts to identify the species and label its many varieties, confusing traders along the way.[51]

Fortunately, botanical classifications only play a small role in the marketing of coffee. Since the characteristics of different coffees are strongly determined by their habitats, as commodities they 'bear names usually associated with the place grown or port of export', as American food expert Vernon Dale Wickizer explained.[52] The names under which Angolan coffees first appeared in European markets alternated between the vague designation 'African' and the more specific 'Cazengo'.[53] After smallholder production expanded in northern Angola,

---

Challamel, 1897), pp. 194–200; Ukers, *All about Coffee*, pp. 304–6, 327–31; Richards, 'Analysis'; Charles Rufenacht, 'A Review of European Coffee Option Markets', *TCTJ*, 112:3 (1957), 14, 94. On contracts and futures, see Steven Topik, 'The Integration of the World Coffee market', in William Gervase Clarence-Smith and Steven Topik (eds), *The Global Coffee Economy in Africa, Asia, and Latin America, 1500–1989* (Cambridge: Cambridge University Press, 2003), pp. 21–49, at pp. 39–40; Peter H. May *et al.*, 'Sustainable Coffee Trade: The Role of Coffee Contracts' (2004), International Institute for Sustainable Development, <https://www.iisd.org/publications/report/sustainable-coffee-trade-role-coffee-contracts>, accessed 19 Dec. 2023; Alexander Engel, 'Buying Time: Futures Trading and Telegraphy in Nineteenth-Century Global Commodity Markets', *JGH*, 10:2 (2015), 284–306; 'Futures Trading and German Agricultural Markets', in Jonathan Curry-Machado *et al.* (eds), *The Oxford Handbook of Commodity History* (New York: Oxford University Press), pp. 167–85.

50 Davis *et al.*, 'Annotated Taxonomic Conspectus'; Benoit Daviron, 'Small Farm Production and the Standardization of Tropical Products', *Journal of Agrarian Change*, 2:2 (2002), 162–84.

51 Alec Ernest Haarer, *Modern Coffee Production* (London: Leonard Hill, 1958), p. 17; John William Purseglove, *Tropical Crops: Dicotyledons* (2 vols, London: Longmans, 1968), vol. 2, pp. 482–3; Wrigley, *Coffee*, p. 71.

52 Vernon Dale Wickizer, *The World Coffee Economy, with Special Reference to Control Schemes* (Stanford: Food Research Institute, 1943), p. 27.

53 For 'African coffee' see Liverpool Record Office, 380 HOL I 8/8, John Holt, Accounts with Irvine & Woodward, 1871–3; Rhodes House Library (Oxford), Box 12/6,

traders began to distinguish two regional varieties, 'Cazengo' and 'Encoge', which showed minor differences in shape, size, and flavour.[54] As more regions opened to coffee cultivation in the early twentieth century, new Angolan varieties appeared in global markets, most notably 'Amboim' and 'Ambriz'. Colonial agronomists long continued to see these varieties as different subspecies, but they were all the same. Growing conditions were the main determinant of regional variation.[55]

But the variable nature of robusta continued to trouble the Angolan coffee trade, as even within regional denominations homogeneity in appearance was often lacking. A shortage of processing facilities in Angola, where only the better-capitalized plantations were equipped with hulling and winnowing machines, compounded the problem.[56] Shipments of beans of irregular shape and size with high levels of impurities and imperfections were therefore normal. Understanding that international traders attached importance to uniformity, from 1914, the

---

Letters from John Carnegie, Luanda, 1873–4; Francis B. Thurber, *Coffee: From the Plantation to the Cup* (New York: American Grocer Publishing Association, 1881), p. 211. For 'Cazengo' see *The Economist*, 10 Dec. 1864, p. 1522; 11 Nov. 1865, p. 1370.

54 See NA, Koninklijke Nederlandse Vereniging van de Koffiehandel, no. 245, sales advertisements of coffee supplied by the NAHV in 1887 (nos 50, 52, 64); Stadsarchief Amsterdam, 31005, Archief van Geels & Co., no. 9, coffee auction Amsterdam, 5 Aug. 1891. On bean size, see Raoul, *Culture du caféier*, pp. 165–6; John Gossweiler, 'Um reconhecimento fitogeográfico à região produtora do café Encoje', *Relatórios e Informações*, 1:2 (1918), 19–40, at p. 32; José Quintella Pessoa Lopes, *Subsídios para o estudo dos cafés de Angola* (Porto: Tip. Sociedade Papelaria, 1934).

55 Paul Janssens, *Le café robusta dans l'Angola* (Brussels: Imprimerie Industrielle et Financière, 1930), p. 18; Aníbal Coelho de Montalvão, 'Cotações dos principais géneros de exportação de Angola', *BAA*, ser. 6, 1:3 (1928), 241–5. See the differentiation of *C. Canephora* into *Typica* (Encoge), *Welwitschii* (Cazengo) and *Gossweileri* (Amboim, Seles) in Hélder Lains e Silva, 'Programa de selecção de café robusta em Angola', *RCP*, 3:9 (1956), 7–24; Abílio Mendes Gaspar, *Programa de melhoramento do cafeeiro robusta em Angola* (Nova Lisboa: Instituto de Investigação Agronómica de Angola, 1969).

56 Augusto Eduardo Neuparth, *Apontamentos para a história da Companhia Agrícola de Cazengo* (Lisbon: Typographia do Commercio, 1904), pp. 9–10; Ukers, *All about Coffee*, p. 268; Abelardo Pompeu do Amaral, *Cultura prática e racional do cafeeiro* (São Paulo: CMG Editora, 1925), p. 55; Topik, 'Integration', p. 23; Maria Gago, 'Moving Coffee from the Forests of Colonial Angola to the Breakfast Tables of Main Street America, 1940–1961', in John Krige (ed.), *Knowledge Flows in a Global Age: A Transnational Approach* (Chicago: Chicago University Press, 2022), pp. 231–52, at pp. 236–7. For a description of hulling and winnowing machines on plantations in Cazengo and Golungo, see Alberto de Souza Maia Leitão, *Relatório da visita sanitária aos concelhos de leste de Loanda mais victimados pela doença de somno* (Porto: Typ. a vapor da Empreza Litteraria e Typographica, 1901), pp. 18–72.

colonial government introduced laws to stimulate the production of 'clean' coffee and reduce the export of 'dirty' coffee.[57] These measures remained ineffective, however, as European planters often lacked the required capital to invest more in primary processing, and small African farmers the financial incentive. Poor cultivation practices (from a roaster's perspective) like harvesting unripened berries remained common, most farmers still used pestles for hulling dried coffee, and many coastal factories continued to rely on hand-operated devices for cleaning and sorting the product before sale.[58] In 1921, roasters at Van Nelle, a large Dutch coffee manufacturer, compared a sample of Ambriz coffee with clearly visible defects to a sample of clean Bukoba coffee from western Tanzania. This was to show their commercial agent in East Africa what the robusta beans they asked him to procure should not look like.[59] Fortunately, for Angolan exporters, not just their own but most African robustas struggled with consistency.

In an increasingly competitive international market, producing robusta beans of consistent quality became imperative. Uniformity in form and colour was important to traders because it facilitated roasting and blending, which were the coffee manufacturer's main craft.[60] Around 1930, therefore, the Angolan government's Department of Agriculture and Trade began to intervene more directly in product improvement. Under the motto 'produce a lot and better, to sell cheaply', it created Angola's first curing stations as well as technical 'brigades' to offer farmers advice on cultivation methods. However, limited funding reduced the effectiveness of these measures.[61] More important at this stage were new regulations, published in 1932, to standardize exports. These standards enhanced the value of Angolan coffees by limiting variability in appearance and providing international traders advance knowledge of the quality of the product they were to receive.[62] Coffee processed and bagged for export had to bear a certificate

57 'O café de Angola', *O Século*, 10 Oct. 1914; João Maria Cerqueira de Azevedo, *Angola, exemplo de trabalho* (Luanda: edição do autor, 1958), p. 257; Yonah Ngalaba Seleti, 'Portuguese Colonialism, Capitalism and the Angolan Coffee Industry: 1850–1950' (Unpublished PhD dissertation, Dalhousie University, 1987), p. 173; Silva, 'Robusta Empire', p. 164.

58 Gossweiler, 'Reconhecimento fitogeográfico', 34–5; Janssens, *Café*, pp. 90–1.

59 Stadsarchief Rotterdam, 944, Archieven van de Erven de weduwe J. van Nelle, no. 2389, Letter to Van Nelle's Oversea Trading Co. c/o A. L. M. Winkelman (Mombasa), no. 12, 24 June 1921.

60 A. Baião Esteves and F. Santos Oliveira, *Contribuição para o estudo das características dos cafés de Angola* (Lisbon: Junta de Investigações do Ultramar, 1970), p. 44; L. Doyle Peck, 'Product Consistency Key to Roaster's Success', *TCTJ*, 108:3 (1955), 28; Jiménez, 'Coffee and Capitalism', p. 46.

61 Alves, 'Produção', pp. 62, 66; Azevedo, *Angola*, p. 257. For an overview of measures introduced around 1930, see Fausto Martins Lourenço, 'História do café robusta em Angola', *Revista de Ciências Agrárias*, 15:4 (1992), 85–119, at pp. 88–9.

62 Gregory L. Martinez, Jr, 'African Coffees Are Now Firmly Established in the U.S. Market Primarily Due to Solubles', *TCTJ*, 113:4 (1957), 20–1, 59–64, at p. 60.

showing its type and region of origin. Angola contained six different coffee zones, of which Ambriz, Encoge, Cazengo, and Amboim (or Novo Redondo) were the most important. Among types, there was a distinction between peaberry (*moka*), which appeared only seldom, and flat (*chato*) beans. Following the requirements of the New York Coffee Exchange, flat beans were graded on a scale from one to seven based on their shape, size, and number of defects. Because many of the coffees grown by African farmers did not even attain the lowest standard, inspectors dismissed defects in these coffees, provided they were free from impurities or traces of parchment. In fact, most coffees exported through the northern ports of Luanda, Ambriz, and Ambrizete in the early 1930s were graded type 7, as growers continued to invest little in processing. South of the Cuanza, where many of the larger estates possessed their own coffee mills, the quality was generally better.[63]

Following these advancements in grading, Angola began to earn a reputation in global markets for producing coffees that were reliable in appearance and flavour and reasonably priced. In Amsterdam, for instance, the sales brochures of coffee dealers Hofmann, Schöffer & Co. advertised Ambriz and Amboim beans as fine tasting and large, which facilitated even roasting.[64] Importers in southern European countries like Spain favoured Cazengo beans, which were slightly cheaper than the Amboim variety. Local consumers seemed to prefer their taste to that of Indonesian robusta, leading the consul of the Netherlands in Saint-Jean-de-Luz to suggest to the ministry at home in 1939 that coffees from the Dutch East Indies should match the quality of the Angolan product.[65] British consuls in Luanda remained sceptical about the benefits of the new grading system. In their view, Angola still exported little high-grade coffee because producers prioritized quantity over quality.[66] However, according to an American industry publication, Angola was writing a 'new chapter in the production of coffee' in Africa, as the country focused on improving quality, beyond merely increasing volume.[67]

63 Angola, Serviços de Agricultura e Comércio, *Algumas considerações sobre a cultura do café em Angola e regulamento da exportação* (Luanda: Empreza Gráfica de Angola, 1932); Janssens, *Café*, p. 110; International Institute of Agriculture, *Coffee*, p. 99; Alves, 'Produção', 67–74; 'Exportação e melhoria do café de Angola', *BGC*, 24:275 (1948), 212–13. See also Seleti, 'Portuguese Colonialism', pp. 238–9, 284–5, 288.

64 Stadsarchief Amsterdam, 598, Archief van de Koffiehandel Hofmann, Schöffer & Co., no. 170, lijsten.

65 NA, Directie Economische Zaken van het Ministerie van Buitenlandse Zaken, no. 43, Gezantschap der Nederlanden, no. 91/14, St Jean de Luz, 30 Jan. 1939; *ibid.*, Gezantschap der Nederlanden, no. 541/131, St Jean de Luz, 27 Nov 1939.

66 Great Britain, Department of Overseas Trade, *Economic Conditions in Angola (Portuguese West Africa) (March, 1934)* (London: HMSO, 1934), p. 20; *Report on the Economic and Commercial Conditions in Angola (Portuguese West Africa), February, 1937* (London: HMSO, 1937), p. 21.

67 'Angola Writes New Chapter'.

Further improvements came with the establishment in 1940 of the *Junta de Exportação do Café Colonial*, Portugal's imperial Coffee Board. The creation of the Junta followed the establishment of similar boards for cotton and cereals in 1938 and, equally important, the 'Office du Café' in the Belgian Congo in 1939.[68] It reflected a significant shift in the Portuguese state's relation to the Angolan coffee sector. For decades, this sector had grown from the bottom up, with only minimal political intervention apart from the provision of land and labour to European planters. But as exports hit new heights in the 1930s and more white settlers became involved in coffee cultivation, their political influence grew and the state came to see coffee as an important foreign exchange earner, meriting protection. The Junta was partly set up to protect growers from the market volatility they experienced during the 1930s. It regulated exports, shielded farmers from price fluctuations, and promoted their product in international markets. To make Angolan coffee more competitive, however, it also invested in product improvement.[69]

The work of the Junta benefited stakeholders unevenly. By imposing a hefty registration fee, the Junta effectively allowed only a select group of European (mainly Portuguese) plantation companies and specialized trading firms to operate as licensed exporters, consolidating their position as oligopolistic intermediaries in the Angolan coffee market.[70] It purchased coffee at a fixed minimum price, which aided growers during the war, but not so much when world prices rapidly increased thereafter. It helped producers place their coffee in international markets by signing trade agreements with foreign governments, arranging shipping, and developing global marketing campaigns. These included full-page advertisements in the American industry's flagship magazine, the *Tea and Coffee Trade Journal*, starting in 1947 and usually containing a racialized drawing of a black woman accompanied by the slogan 'They are sweet and they will bring down the cost of your blends' (Plate 3.1). Angolan producers also gained a near-monopoly on coffee imports into Portugal. But they were disadvantaged when the Junta decreed that coffee traders had to ship 25 per cent of their exports to Portugal, where prices were kept artificially low during the 1950s.[71]

68 E. Ebale, '"Office du Cafe" a Boon to Congo Coffee', *TCTJ*, 107:6 (1954), 28; Seleti, 'Portuguese Colonialism', p. 319.

69 Arquivo Nacional da Torre do Tombo (Lisbon), SGPCM-GPC/0339/00005, Associação Comercial de Angola, Memorial [1940]; Manuel Ramos de Souza, *A Junta de Exportação do Café Colonial em Angola: 5 anos de actividade* (Luanda: Mondego, 1946); Azevedo, *Angola*, p. 259.

70 A list of exporters was published in *RCP*, 1:3 (1954), pp. 76–8; 2:7 (1955), pp. 75–7.

71 Seleti, 'Portuguese Colonialism', pp. 323–9; Silva, 'Robusta Empire', pp. 116–73. On price fixing, see Armando Castro, *O sistema colonial português em África (meados do século XX)*, 2nd edn (Lisbon: Editorial Caminho, 1980), p. 140; Gervase Clarence-Smith, *The Third Portuguese Empire, 1825–1975: A Study in Economic Imperialism*

Plate 3.1 Advertisement by the Junta de Exportação do Café, 1954. Source: *Tea and Coffee Trade Journal*, 107:6 (Dec. 1954), 25.

An important point of attention was product improvement, which is where the Junta probably did most for small farmers and planters in Angola, especially as it released the burden of coffee processing. The Junta invested in both primary and secondary processing. It established 'technical brigades' in the northern coffee centres of Uíge, Encoge, and Cazengo to distribute hand-operated hullers and grading devices, support small farmers with land registration, and advise them on farm upkeep, coffee picking, and drying. As Chapter 4 will demonstrate, Junta engineers were generally sympathetic to the needs of Afri-

(Manchester: Manchester University Press, 1985), pp. 148–9. On coffee promotion, see Junta de Exportação do Café, *Quatro anos de propaganda do café português* (Lisbon: Junta de Exportação do Café, 1961); Sousa, *Ensaio*, p. 83.

can farmers, reflecting a post-war change in colonial thinking throughout the continent about the economic merits of small-scale agriculture.[72] The brigades, while headed by white technicians, were largely composed of black advisors. One of their main tasks was to help famers combat the spread of the coffee borer, a small beetle that drills into berries to reproduce. However, the brigades were structurally underfunded, leading one colonial inspector, Henrique Galvão, to judge them as mere 'propaganda stunts' in 1945. It was said that in five years they had not delivered a single huller to growers in northern Angola. Junta officials themselves were more optimistic, and believed their work genuinely improved the condition of African farms. However, staff shortages remained a problem until the 1950s.[73]

Much more significant was the establishment of curing works (*fábricas de rebenifício e homogenização*) in six Angolan seaports to reprocess and standardize green coffee. Starting in 1949 with machinery imported from Brazil and Japan, these mills did everything from husking and polishing dried berries to winnowing, sizing, cleaning, and bagging them. They also became large depots, as the creation of Junta brought the practice of re-exporting coffee through Portugal, with its need for warehousing in Lisbon, to an end. The mills especially helped the many small and medium-sized farms that lacked mechanical processing facilities of their own. According to the Junta's president, Camilo Lemos de Mendonça, the mill in Luanda (Plate 3.2), opened in 1953 with a capacity to process twelve tons of coffee per hour, was the second largest in the world at the time. In northern Angola, where growers often sold unhusked sun-dried coffee (*café mabuba*) to local traders, the Junta built several smaller hulling stations.[74]

72 Sara Berry, 'Debating the Land Question in Africa', *Comparative Studies in Society and History*, 44:4 (2002), 638–68, at p. 647.

73 Angola, Concelho de Coordenação Técnica e Económica, *Planos de trabalho para 1943 dos serviços técnicos e organismos de coordenação económica* (Luanda: Imprensa Nacional de Angola, 1943); Junta de Exportação do Café, Delegação de Angola, Serviços Técnicos, *Primeira Conferência Agronómica dos Serviços Técnicos: Programa de trabalhos para o ano de 1955/1956* (Luanda, 1955); Lourenço, 'História', 15:4, p. 89; Galvão cited in Gago, 'Moving Coffee', p. 234. See also Álvaro de Freitas Morna, *Problemas económicos da colónia: Algodão, milho, café, trigo* (Luanda: Imprensa Nacional, 1943), pp. 42–4.

74 'A inauguração da fábrica de Luanda da Junta de Exportação do Café', *RCP*, 1:1 (1954), 33–6; Manuel António Matias, 'Fábricas de rebenefício e homogeneização do Ambrizete e Ambriz', *RCP*, 2:6 (1955), 37–44; 'Africa Coffee Trade Had Good Year in 1953', *TCTJ*, 106:4 (1954), 22–3, 52; Camilo Lemos de Mendonça, 'Review of Angola Coffee Growing, Exports', *TCTJ*, 107:6 (1954), 26; Fernando Pereira Bastos, 'Angola Is Winning "The Battle of Quality"', 113:4 (1957), 28, 68–9; Fernando Pereira Bastos, 'How the Angolan Coffee Board Operates', *TCTJ*, 114:1 (1958), 70, 124; Arquivo Histórico Ultramarino (Lisbon, henceforth AHU), Ministério do Ultramar (MU), Inspecção Superior da Adminsitração Ultramarina,

Plate 3.2 Luanda curing works, c.1950. Source: Agência Geral do Ultramar, Angola, cx. 14, no. 18415, PT/TT/AGU/001/018415. Image provided by Arquivo Nacional da Torre do Tombo.

In many ways the Junta did more for the coffee economy north of the Cuanza than for the big plantation companies near Seles and Amboim, which had their own processing facilities and handled their own shipping and marketing.[75]

The state-owned curing works significantly advanced the standardization of Angolan coffee, as all dried berries passed through the mills before export. Along with the works, the Junta introduced a new grading system in 1945, which maintained the regional designations set in 1932, but changed the number of basic grades to four: first quality, second quality, unselected coffees, and 'waste'.[76] The latter consisted of leftovers from primary processing for which there was an

A2.050.05/034.00207, Governador Hélio Esteves Felgas, 'Relatório do Governo do Distrito do Congo referente a 1957', confidential, pp. 186, 197; Gago, 'Moving Coffee', p. 237.

75 Seleti, 'Portuguese Colonialism', pp. 339, 344, 356, 360–1. On the relation between farm size and processing facilities, see Artur Rocha de Medina, *A tecnologia do café e o tamanho da propriedade* (Lisbon: Junta de Exportação do Café, 1950); Sousa, *Ensaio*, p. 34.

76 Portugal, 'Portaria 10835', *Diário de Governo*, Ser. 1, 9 (12 Jan. 1945), 30–2; also published as *Regulamento para a classificação dos cafés coloniais portugueses* (Porto: Oficinas de O Comércio do Porto, 1945). On the process of grading, see Gago, 'Moving Coffee', p. 238.

industrial use, such as flavouring, caffeine extraction, or the making of fertilizer.[77] With an eye on the expanding North American market, the Junta decreed in 1949 that Angola should export only first-grade coffees to the United States. This ruling upset some Angolan producers because it blocked their lower-grade coffees from entry into the American market. However, with 60 per cent of exports graded first quality in 1954, the new regulations helped build Angola's reputation for producing clean, uniform robustas.[78] The higher prices paid in global markets for the dominant Angolan variety, Ambriz, than for robusta coffees from Indonesia and Côte d'Ivoire reflected the success of post-war Portuguese investments in product improvement.[79]

Food laws in the United States were strict about defects in green coffee beans, but the American coffee industry was less critical and cared more about price. As the market for low-cost blends and instant coffee expanded, large manufacturers like General Foods and Nestlé were mainly interested in obtaining consistent lots of robusta as cheaply as possible. One way to achieve that was to increase imports from other parts of Africa, especially Côte d'Ivoire.[80] Another was to shape the policy of the Portuguese Coffee Export Board in Angola, which was still America's main supplier in the continent. In 1956, the Junta refined its coffee-grading system in collaboration with the American Green Coffee Association to facilitate the trade of lower-grade coffees to North America. The new grading system distinguished between five categories of which only the last, previously known as 'unselected', was barred from direct sale to the United States.[81] Following these new standards, American importers, who controlled half the Angolan export market, bought mainly the least expensive Angolan varieties: Ambriz, Cazengo, and Encoge. By contrast, roasters in the Netherlands developed a liking for the more expensive Amboim and Novo Redondo types, which was partly a response to the American hold over the low end of the market, but

77 AHU, MU, Direção-Geral de Economia (DGECO), Repartição Administrativa (RA), no. 1798, Jorge Velosa, 'O café de Angola e os seus problemas', Luanda, 19 May 1961. On caffeine extraction, see also Bartow J. Elmore, *Citizen Coke: The Making of Coca-Cola Capitalism* (New York: W. W. Norton, 2016), pp. 193–213.

78 Gregory L. Martinez, Jr, 'Growing Importance of African Coffee', *TCTJ*, 101:1 (1951), 72, 74, 76–8; 'Angola e o café', *RCP*, 1:3 (1954), 42–5; Hélder Lains e Silva, 'Exports from Angola in 1954 Show Marked Decline from Previous Year', *TCTJ*, 109:6 (1955), 60; C. Krug and R. A. De Poerck, *World Coffee Survey* (Rome: FAO, 1968), p. 112.

79 Ferrão, 'Principais problemas', 25–7, 34–5; Sousa, *Ensaio*, p. 49.

80 Pierre L. Massin, 'Ivory Coast Tops African Producers in Volume', *TCTJ*, 107:6 (1954), 30, 51.

81 Esteves and Oliveira, *Contribuição*, pp. 29–36; Jaime de Almeida Loureiro, 'A portaria no. 15.913, de 19 de Julho de 1956, e a classificação dos cafés portugueses', *RCP*, 3:11 (1956), 33–44; Paul Falush, 'History of Angola Robustas Enters New Phase in World Coffee Market', *TCTJ*, 107:6 (1954), 43; Martinez, Jr, 'African Coffees', *TCTJ*, 113:4 (1957), 20–1, 59–64.

also satisfied a more discerning consumer market. Portugal absorbed most of the remaining exports, mainly third-grade coffees that neither American nor Dutch traders had an interest in, but which Portuguese manufacturers often blended into classic Portuguese barley and chicory mixtures.[82]

Besides horizontal collaboration on grading, some large roasters, particularly in the Netherlands, became directly involved in local procurement to secure good-quality coffees.[83] No national coffee industry after the Second World War depended as much on Angolan robusta as the Dutch. Roasters in the Netherlands filled their most popular coffee blends for the larger part with varying proportions of cheap Brazilian arabicas and Angolan robustas to keep not only their price constant, but also their flavour.[84] They typically purchased Angolan coffee from different importers headquartered in Amsterdam, including firms like Theobroma and Douqué. Additionally, some developed direct links with Angola through specialized traders, such as Charles Norton & Co., Mário Cunha, and Transagraire. However, after a bad purchase of Novo Redondo beans in the mid-1950s, the Douwe Egberts company went a step further and established a partnership with the Lisbon-based import house of Pedro Oliveira Leão, whose Angolan agents sourced coffee in the different growing regions. Like most coffee merchants, Douwe Egberts recognized that grades alone were not a sufficient guarantee of quality, as they were based on visual criteria and could not account for taste and smell. Uniformity in shape and size facilitated even roasting, but it was not an indication of flavour. Sampling therefore remained important and, according to the purchasing department at Douwe Egberts, it was best done before shipping. The company advanced credit to Leão to procure coffee, but also trained his employees in Luanda in cup tasting, so they knew which beans were best for the range of Douwe Egberts blends. To secure their investments, the company tied Leão to exclusive delivery, controlled his books, and made sure his employees were on long-terms contracts so they would not take their expertise elsewhere. Douwe Egberts continued using other supply networks, but this arrangement gave the organization greater control over the coffee commodity chain.[85] Incidentally, to increase market confidence in the quality

82 Tresoar, 110, Douwe Egberts, no. 254, Jaarrapport 1954; *ibid.*, no. 3471, Pedro Oliveira Leão to Douwe Egberts, Luanda, 16 Feb. 1961; Nina Luttinger and Gregory Dictum, *The Coffee Book: Anatomy of an Industry from Crop to the Last Drop*, rev. edn (New York: New Press, 2006), p. 141; Sousa, *Ensaio*, pp. 48, 55–7.

83 Topik, 'Integration', p. 43; Sedgewick, *Coffeeland*, p. 303.

84 'Vier-smaken-systeem', *Allerhande*, 34 (May 1958), 3.

85 Tresoar, 110, Douwe Egberts, no. 3471; AHU, MU, DGECO-RA, no. 1798, Jorge Velosa, 'O café de Angola e os seus problemas', Luanda, 19 May 1961. On product stability, see Janina Grabs and Stefano Ponte, 'The Evolution of Power in the Global Coffee Value Chain and Production Network', *Journal of Economic Geography*, 19:4 (2019), 803–28, at p. 813; John M. Talbot, *Grounds for Agreement: The*

of Angolan coffee, a 1959 revision of the Portuguese classification system made testing of colour, smell, roast, and flavour part of grading.[86]

Colonial rule

The arrival of African producers was one of the main developments in world coffee trade post-1900. By the late 1950s, African exports accounted for 24 per cent of global trade, and Côte d'Ivoire, Uganda, Angola, and the Belgian Congo – all predominantly robusta producers – were the world's largest suppliers after Brazil, Colombia, and El Salvador.[87] Apart from Angola, none of these African countries had sold much, if any, coffee at the start of the century. The growth of African coffee exports from practically zero to more than half a million metric tons while the continent – Ethiopia excepted – was under European rule raises a thorny question about the role colonization played in 'opening' Africa to the world coffee market.[88]

Colonial states intervened in coffee cultivation in different ways. In some East African regions, during the 1920s and 1930s, European colonizers made coffee a compulsory crop to boost export revenues, demanding African farmers planted a minimum number of trees in exchange for tools, materials, and expertise. In most cases, however, cultivation only increased when farmers took the initiative in response to higher prices.[89] The example of nineteenth-century Angola, where the largest expansion in production happened outside the small pockets of proto-colonial control, shows that African smallholders did not require colonial incentives to start growing coffee.

A more significant contribution of colonial states to economic development was infrastructural. High transportation costs caused by dependence on head

---

Political Economy of the Coffee Commodity Chain (Lanham: Rowman & Littlefield Publishers, 2004), pp. 51–2. On poor Novo Redondo coffee, see 'Classificação e exportação dos cafés angolanos', *RCP*, 2:8 (1955), 51–67. On the continued importance of sampling, see Sousa, *Ensaio*, p. 36.

86 Junta de Exportação do Café, *Regulamento para a classificação dos cafés portugueses: Portaria no. 17330* (Lisbon: Junta de Exportação do Café, 1959).

87 Irene S. van Dongen, 'Coffee Trade, Coffee Regions, and Coffee Ports in Angola', *Economic Geography*, 37:4 (1961), 320–46, at p. 321.

88 Ewout Frankema *et al.*, 'An Economic Rationale for the West African Scramble? The Commercial Transition and the Commodity Price Boom of 1835–1885', *Journal of Economic History*, 78:1 (2018), 231–67, at p. 235.

89 Kenneth Curtis, 'Smaller Is Better: A Consensus of Peasants and Bureaucrats in Colonial Tanganyika', in Clarence-Smith and Topik, *Global Coffee Economy*, pp. 312–34, at p. 318; Sven Van Melkebeke, *Dissimilar Coffee Frontiers: Mobilizing Labor and Land in the Lake Kivu Region, Congo and Rwanda (1918–1960/62)* (Leiden: Brill, 2020), p. 41.

carrying long hampered the development of African coffee economies, notably in regions where export production had started before effective European rule, like Madagascar and Angola. New roads and railways, built by colonial states, opened the African interior to the world coffee trade after 1900. Furthermore, states helped growers compete in global markets by shifting the burden of product improvement, standardization, and marketing to export boards, established in many colonies during the 1930s and 1940s. Interventions like these have led to arguments that European colonization was an important condition for African economic growth, the most convincing being perhaps that only states could raise the capital required for large infrastructural projects. However, there is little evidence that African countries would have missed out on foreign investments if European empires had not colonized them. The case of Ethiopia, which modernized its economy and became a significant coffee exporter during the twentieth century in the absence of colonial domination, indicates that colonization was not a prerequisite for growth. At the same time, Ethiopia's imperial tradition hints at the importance of centralized authority in facilitating external partnerships and securing foreign investment. It could be argued, as European colonizers certainly did, that strong state structures were lacking in many African export regions before the colonial era.[90]

While capital investments under colonial rule may have benefited small-scale farmers in some colonies – notably 'peasant' colonies where Africans owned the land – in settler-elite colonies the state actively restricted opportunities for African producers to participate in global trade. This happened in the coffee economies of Côte d'Ivoire, Madagascar, Kenya, and Angola, where govern-

90 See the discussion in Ralph Austen, *African Economic History: Internal Development and External Dependency* (Oxford: James Currey, 1987), pp. 122–9; Gareth Austin, 'Capitalism and the Colonies', in Larry Neal and Jeffrey G. Williamson (eds), *The Cambridge History of Capitalism*, vol. 2 (Cambridge: Cambridge University Press, 2014), pp. 301–47, at pp. 327–30; 'The Economics of Colonialism in Africa', in Célestin Monga and Justin Yifu Lin (eds), *The Oxford Handbook of Africa and Economics*, vol. 1 (Oxford: Oxford University Press, 2015), pp. 522–35, at pp. 527–9; Johan Fourie, *Our Long Walk to Economic Freedom: Lessons from 100,000 Years of Human History* (Cape Town: Tafelberg, 2021), pp. 129–31. For Ethiopia, see Charles W. McClellan, 'Land, Labor, and Coffee: The South's Role in Ethiopian Self-Reliance, 1889–1935', *AEH*, 9 (1980), 69–83. For more on colonization as a response to political fragmentation, see A. G. Hopkins, 'The "New International Economic Order" in the Nineteenth Century: Britain's First Development Plan for Africa', in Robin Law (ed.), *From Slave Trade to 'Legitimate' Commerce: The Commercial Transition in Nineteenth-Century West Africa* (Cambridge: Cambridge University Press, 1995), pp. 240–64, at p. 248; Stephen Ellis, *Season of Rains: Africa in the World* (Chicago: University of Chicago Press, 2011), pp. 20–1. For an alternative scenario, see A. Adu Boahen, *African Perspectives on Colonialism* (New York: Diasporic African Press, 2011), pp. 1–26.

ment intervention in land and labour markets ensured that resource exploitation advanced white settlers at the expense of African farmers. Most colonial administrations withdrew their support for European growers after the Second World War, leading consistently to increased smallholder outputs.[91] As the next three chapters will demonstrate, the Angolan tragedy was that state aid for white settlers continued throughout the colonial era, stifling the nineteenth-century cash-crop revolution that had raised the material welfare of thousands of coffee-growing peasant households.

91 John Rapley, *Ivoirien Capitalism: African Entrepreneurs in Côte d'Ivoire* (Boulder: Lynne Rienner, 1993), pp. 43–5; Gwyn Campbell, 'The Origins and Development of Coffee production in Réunion and Madagascar, 1711–1972', in William Gervase Clarence-Smith and Steven Topik (eds), *The Global Coffee Economy in Africa, Asia, and Latin America, 1500–1989* (Cambridge: Cambridge University Press, 2003), pp. 67–99; David Hyde, '"Paying for the Emergency by Displacing the Settlers": Global Coffee and Rural Restructuring in Late Colonial Kenya', *JGH*, 4:1 (2009), 81–103.

4

Paths Taken and Not Taken

IN COLONIAL Africa, coffee was generally a smallholder crop, grown by peasant households on communally owned or, sometimes, privatized land. Angola was among the few African countries where coffee became a settler crop grown on medium and large estates.[1] The reasons for smallholder dominance were fundamentally economic. Coffee production on estates involved expensive overheads and salary costs but offered few economies of scale. Meanwhile, smallholders required very little capital, as they had access to land at little or no cost, could rely on unpaid family labour, and used cheap hand tools to grow and process coffee (see Chapter 2). In many African regions, settlers played a role in the early development of coffee cultivation, often experimenting with imported arabica cultivars. But for political, environmental, or economic reasons they often withdrew from coffee growing before African production became globally significant. As William Clarence-Smith has explained, settlers were typically 'opportunistic producers, most likely to turn away from coffee when expenditure was especially high', as happened when coffee prices fell or when colonial governments banned compulsory labour, forcing planters to pay market-rate wages to plantation workers. However, in settler-elite economies like Angola, the Belgian Congo, and Kenya, colonial governments proved willing to intervene in African land and labour markets to ensure the survival of a foreign planter class.[2]

This chapter analyses the twentieth-century transition from smallholding to settler agriculture in northern Angola, where the share of European estates in coffee production jumped from at best one-quarter in 1900 to approximately

1 John M. Talbot, *Grounds for Agreement: The Political Economy of the Coffee Commodity Chain* (Lanham: Rowman & Littlefield Publishers, 2004), pp. 4–7.

2 Paul Mosley, *The Settler Economies: Studies in the Economic History of Kenya and Southern Rhodesia 1900–1963* (Cambridge: Cambridge University Press, 1983); William Gervase Clarence-Smith, 'The Coffee Crisis in Asia, Africa, and the Pacific, 1870–1914', in William Gervase Clarence-Smith and Steven Topik (eds), *The Global Coffee Economy in Africa, Asia, and Latin America, 1500–1989* (Cambridge: Cambridge University Press, 2003), pp. 100–19, at p. 108; Sven Van Melkebeke, *Dissimilar Coffee Frontiers: Mobilizing Labor and Land in the Lake Kivu Region, Congo and Rwanda (1918–1960/62)* (Leiden: Brill, 2020), pp. 52–3.

two-thirds in 1958.[3] It argues that this came about largely through settler initiative, rather than imperial design, although colonists worked within colonial structures developed since the middle of the nineteenth century and the government later coopted their efforts as a demonstration of effective colonization. The chapter first provides a snapshot of the coffee landscape in northern Angola during the 1900s and 1910s, showing the vigour of the smallholder economy before the colonial government let white colonists take over. It subsequently demonstrates how, in typical fashion, bootstrapping immigrants advanced in the absence of central planning and coordination, beginning after the First World War and in larger numbers after 1945.[4] Indeed, from the end of the nineteenth century, politicians and intellectuals in Lisbon devised several grand schemes for the economic development of Angola, usually attributing a pivotal role to white settlers. But these plans often came to nothing and, moreover, coffee barely figured in them. Although the creation of the Junta de Exportação do Café in 1940 (see Chapter 3) was a sign that the Portuguese government recognized the crop's economic importance, the export board never specifically favoured European planters: its mills processed coffee from all producers, while its agronomists often worked to support small African growers.[5] As coffee planters built a settler economy from the bottom up, though, they were buoyed by the favourable conditions of colonial conquest, improved roads and mechanized transport, advances in tropical-disease control, and, most importantly, government laws facilitating labour recruitment and land acquisition. The legal framework for land concessions in Angola protected African smallholders to some extent, but in the absence of proper oversight its main effect was to usher in a process of colonial land grabbing.[6]

Considering the important role of colonists in the development of Angola's colonial economy, it is surprising how little attention historians have so far given them. The literature on settler colonialism in Portuguese Africa has analysed

3 Yonah Ngalaba Seleti, 'Portuguese Colonialism, Capitalism and the Angolan Coffee Industry: 1850–1950' (Unpublished PhD dissertation, Dalhousie University, 1987), p. 136; Angola, Repartição Central de Estatística Geral, *Anuário estatístico de Angola, ano de 1958* (Luanda: Imprensa Nacional, 1959).

4 For a classic study of settler frontier conquest, see James Belich, *Replenishing the Earth: The Settler Revolution and the Rise of the Angloworld* (Oxford: Oxford University Press, 2009). Belich examines societies where settlers became a majority population. In Africa, settler-elite colonies were more common.

5 Richard J. Houk, 'Recent Developments in the Portuguese Congo', *Geographical Review*, 48:2 (1958), 201–21, at p. 207.

6 René Pélissier, *La colonie du minotaure: Nationalismes et révoltes en Angola (1926–1961)* (Orgeval: Pélissier, 1978), pp. 153–6; Jeffery M. Paige, *Agrarian Revolution: Social Movements and Export Agriculture in the Underdeveloped World* (New York: Free Press), pp. 238–42.

imperial plans, political discourse, and migration patterns, but has scarcely studied the lives of white settlers, how they obtained their plantations, and how they managed them.[7] As some Portuguese colonists were keen to document their life story or recount crucial episodes of their time in the Angolan interior, there are nonetheless several first- and second-hand accounts of settler experiences in the northern coffee economy. The third section of this chapter examines some of these accounts, showing that personal initiative, social networks, and colonial privileges shaped their life course in Angola, and thereby imperial space more generally. One thing that settlers rarely discussed, however, was the reality of land capture, which often involved pillaging African farms. The fourth section analyses the methods European planters used to acquire land, their recurring conflicts with local smallholders, and the ambivalent position of the colonial administration regarding settler enterprise. Despite the ad-hoc nature of settler expansion in northern Angola, repertoire – a limited number of known forms of action – played a crucial role in colonial land occupation. The chapter makes clear how little this repertoire changed over time, indicating that land seizure was generally condoned by the colonial state.[8]

Coffee lands

In the early twentieth century, most of what Angola put out for global consumption came from small-scale African producers. This made the country like the

7 Cláudia Castelo, *Passagens para África: O povoamento de Angola e Moçambique com naturais da metrópole (1920–1974)* (Lisbon: Edições Afrontamento, 2007); Bárbara Direito, 'The Land Question in Early Twentieth-Century Portuguese Legal Colonial Thought', *Portuguese Journal of Social Science*, 16:2 (2017), 181–93; Fernando Tavares Pimenta, 'White Settler Politics and Euro-African Nationalism in Angola, 1945–1975', in Edward Cavanagh and Lorenzo Veracini (eds), *The Routledge Handbook of the History of Settler Colonialism* (Abingdon: Routledge, 2017), 277–89; Márcia Gonçalves, 'Of Peasants and Settlers: Ideals of Portugueseness, Imperial Nationalism and European Settlement in Africa, c.1930–c.1945', *European Review of History: Revue Européne d'Histoire*, 25: 1 (2018), 166–86. A settler-focused study is Cláudia Castelo, '"Village Portugal" in Africa: Discourses of Differentiation and Hierarchisation of Settlers, 1950s–1974', in Duncan Money and Danelle van Zyl-Hermann (eds), *Rethinking White Societies in Southern Africa* (London: Routledge, 2020), pp. 115–33.

8 On repertoires, see Charles Tilly, *Roads from Past to Future* (Lanham: Rowman & Littlefield, 1997), p. 11; Manali Desai, 'Colonial Legacies and Repertoires of "Ethnic" Violence: The Case of Western India, 1941–2002', *Journal of Historical Sociology*, 22:2 (2009), 147–79; Miguel Bandeira Jerónimo, 'Repressive Developmentalism: Idioms, Repertoires, and Trajectories in Late Colonialism', in Martin Thomas and Andrew S. Thompson (eds), *The Oxford Handbook of the Ends of Empire* (Oxford: Oxford University Press, 2018), pp. 537–54.

'peasant' colonies of British and French West Africa, where Africans retained control of most of the land despite the influx of a small number of foreign entrepreneurs.[9] The farmers who accounted for the bulk of Angola's coffee production lived in the hill country stretching north of the proto-colonial settler districts of Cazengo and Golungo Alto through the lands of the independent Dembo (*Ndembu*) chiefs into southern Kongo. Although Portugal maintained political alliances with some Dembo rulers and built fortifications in São José de Encoge, near the home of Dembo Mbwila, and in São Salvador, the capital of the Kongo kingdom, the northern region remained largely free of colonial rule until the 1910s. Some coastal traders established temporary factories in the coffee areas, which they supplied with trade goods during harvest time, but most produce came to the coast through African traders.

Accounts of early twentieth-century colonial campaigns to occupy the Dembos and southern Kongo regions provide a snapshot of the Angolan coffee landscape spreading out around Encoge, Portugal's fortified settlement on the border between both regions. First, in 1907, military officer João de Almeida led a force from the safe colonial haven of Golungo Alto through rugged, forested mountains to Encoge to gather intelligence on agriculture and transport routes in the Dembos region. Like Ensign David Magno after him, Almeida noticed the absence of Europeans in the region. Some Portuguese colonists had built plantations or opened stores in the district during the mid-nineteenth century but had to flee when tax revolts broke out in 1872, which closed the region to white settlement for decades.[10] Although the region enjoyed a reputation as an impenetrable refuge for runaway slaves, criminals, and convicts, local leaders maintained close commercial, political, and cultural ties with their neighbours. A flourishing trade in forest coffee, rubber, and agricultural produce gave visible material and cultural benefits to the people who controlled this commerce. In several villages, Almeida found European-style homes with thatched gable roofs, doors and windows made of wood, and pottery and wooden furniture inside. Women wore bracelets of imported copper and iron. Merchant families taught their children the Portuguese language so they could communicate with traders on the coast. In the region, coffee was not only important as a commodity, but also played a role in social relationships, especially in the exchange of gifts.[11]

9 Gareth Austin, 'Capitalism and the Colonies', in Larry Neal and Jeffrey G. Williamson (eds), *The Cambridge History of Capitalism*, vol. 2 (Cambridge: Cambridge University Press, 2014), pp. 301–47, at p. 315.

10 Jill R. Dias, 'Angola', in Valentim Alexandre and Jill Dias (eds), *O império africano, 1825–1890* (Lisbon: Editorial Estampa, 1998), pp. 319–556, at p. 470.

11 João de Almeida, *Operações militares nos Dembos em 1907* (Lisbon: Typographia Universal, 1909), pp. 3–9; Henrique Galvão, *Dembos* (3 vols, Lisbon: Agência Geral das Colónias, 1935), vol. 1, pp. 24–35; David Magno, *Relatório dos serviços militares do Lombige* (Luanda: Governo Geral de Angola, 1910), pp. 109–32.

From São José de Encoge, coffee forests stretched in all directions. In September of 1916, the colonial government ordered two military units to cross this part of northern Angola and meet one another in Encoge. One started in the north from Tando, a recently occupied post near Bembe, the other from the Lucala railway station, about 300km south of Encoge. The government hoped pacification, as colonials called these military exercises, would open the region to lorry transport and attract European trade. Significantly, the campaign led to the occupation of Uíge, a group of villages east of Encoge that became a thriving hub in the Angolan coffee trade.[12] Meanwhile, the reports from both missions provided colonial officials with rich descriptions of local coffee production, motivating the Angolan government to send their head botanist, John Gossweiler, to revisit Uíge in 1918.[13]

The commander of the northern squadron, Amaro Gomes Duarte, spent most of his campaign navigating the mountain ranges around Uíge. He came across several indigenous coffee plantations, often located in lush woodlands between hills. He spoke with chiefs who had travelled for coffee business to Ambriz or Caxito, a commercial settlement on the road to Luanda, or had worked as trade brokers at one of the coastal factories. Throughout the region, men wore European clothes or garments made of imported white cloth, reflecting their involvement in the export trade. For them, coffee was also a means to pay the colonial hut tax, which some chiefs led by Dembo Mbwila had grudgingly accepted.[14] But there was still little sign of European commercial penetration. A few years earlier, the factory of Santos, an immigrant trader in Massarele, east of Bembe, had been plundered. In a fragile economic climate, incidents like this discouraged coastal merchants from setting up shop in this vast and fertile coffee region.[15] Before colonial occupation, therefore, coffee was sold mainly outside the growing areas.

South of Encoge, there was a similar geographical separation of coffee cultivation from coffee trading. The commander of the southern regiment, João Fran-

12 Arquivo Histórico Miltar (Lisbon, henceforth AHM), caixa 44, doc. 12, Relatório de ocupação [M'Pozo, 1916].

13 John Gossweiler, 'Um reconhecimento fitogeográfico à região produtora do café Encoje', *Relatórios e Informações*, 1:2 (1918), 19–40. Gossweiler had joined a colonial economic mission to the region in 1915. See A. Galvão, 'Relatório duma viagem ao Congo em agosto e setembro de 1915', *Boletim da Sociedade de Geografia de Lisboa*, 36:4–6 (1918), 81–155.

14 AHM, caixa 44, doc. 8, Relatório da coluna de polícia à regiao do Ambuila, Bembe, 10 Nov. 1916. In 1855, Encoge chiefs paid the colonial *dízimo* tax to Portugal in slaves. Portugal later accepted rubber as tax payment. See Arquivo Nacional de Angola (Luanda, henceforth ANA), caixa 4999, Mapa dos Dembos e sobas do presidio, 2° semestre de 1855, Encoge, 1 Jan. 1856; ANA, caixa 5000, Imposto de cubata, 1909–11; ANA, caixa 5002, Ofício do chefe Alves Fernandes, Encoge, 19 June 1913.

15 AHM, caixa 21, doc. 8, Relatório, Bembe, 23 Nov. 1914; Seleti, 'Portuguese Colonialism', pp. 137–8.

cisco, described a busy commercial landscape along the road up from Lucala to Quisseque, a village located about 50km southeast of Encoge on the fringe of the Angolan coffee forest. Small traders, often agents of larger houses on the coast, had opened shops in several places to exchange imported merchandise for produce, including coffee. Most shopkeepers were European, but some were Cape Verdean, while others were Africans from the region, including an Ambaquista woman who cultivated and traded food crops and lived 'European style' in a stone house with a zinc roof in Samba Cajú. Francisco witnessed significant land clearing – removing thicket rather than forest – for agriculture and livestock farming along the road up to Quisseque. By contrast, forested mountain ranges characterized the landscape further north, with coffee bushes growing from low down to higher up the hills. Commercial establishments were noticeably absent here. In the wake of Portugal's aggressive military campaigns in northern Angola in recent years, producers were wary of foreign invaders and preferred to sell their produce to European traders at a safe distance rather than inviting them to settle in their communities.[16]

By separating cultivation from trade, the Dembos and Kongo regions differed substantially from the old colonial enclaves of Cazengo and Golungo Alto, where hundreds of Portuguese colonists kept shops to sell textiles, rum, and other wares to African coffee growers and plantation workers.[17] Further north, by contrast, there were 'neither taverns nor shops', according to the administrator of Encoge. But a handful of itinerant retailers peddled imported hoes, salted fish, gunpowder and fuses, Dutch gin, denims, African cloth (*panos da costa*), leaf plates, and a range of other goods.[18] In 1918, to expedite coffee, producers in the northern and eastern districts still organized their own transport

16 ANA, caixa 1841, Coluna movel de reconhecimento dos caminhos entre Camabatela e Encoge, Relatório do comandante, João Francisco, Dalatando, 30 Nov. 1916. For the military campaigns, see René Pélissier, *História das campanhas de Angola: Resistência e revoltas 1845–1941* (Lisbon: Editorial Estampa, 1997). On the Ambaquistas, see also José Joaquim de Almeida, 'Na Provincia de Angola: Administração colonial debaixo do ponte de vista agrícola', *Revista Agronomica*, 2 (1904), 97–110, 137–48, 161–75, 193–205, at p. 108; Mădălina Florescu, 'Post-Abolition Angola in a Post-Colonial Mission Archive: A Preliminary Contextualisation of a Photograph from the Spiritans' Mission in Malange, Northern Angola, 1904', *Social Dynamics*, 40:1 (2014), 66–84.

17 ANA, caixa 2168, Secretaria-geral do Governo, Mapas de comerciantes, 1904; Alberto de Souza Maia Leitão, *Relatório da visita sanitária aos concelhos de leste de Loanda mais victimados pela doença de somno* (Porto: Typ. a vapor da Empreza Litteraria e Typographica, 1901), p. 17.

18 ANA, caixa 3387, Mapa dos comerciantes e industriais deste concelho, Encoge, 31 Dec. 1898; *ibid.*, Nota dos artigos de importação que tem mais consumo neste concelho e no sertão limítrofe, enclosed in Administração do concelho de Encoge to SG, no. 46, Encoge, 31 March 1900.

or sold their produce, packed in palm-fibre bags, to ambulant traders operating on behalf of European buyers.[19] But these ways of organizing production and trade ended abruptly during the 1920s. The merchant community of Ambriz took advantage of the colonial occupation of northern Angola to open the first European stores in Uíge, eliminating the African middleman traders if not yet the need for head carriers. Soon thereafter, shopkeepers throughout the region used the profits from rising coffee prices to request land from the colonial government and build their own plantations, starting a new wave of settler expansion in northern Angola.[20]

Settler advancement

During the interwar period, coffee in Angola changed from a crop of smallholders to one mainly grown by foreign settlers. In the nineteenth century, the share of colonial estates in the country's overall coffee output was small compared to African contributions (see Chapter 2). After world coffee prices plummeted in 1896, European companies in Angola generally steered clear of coffee farming, while many estates in the Cazengo and Golungo districts were sold, abandoned, or merged into the Cazengo Agricultural Company. Against a backdrop of smallholder dominance, the influx of white settlers to northern Angola after the First World War was nothing short of dramatic.

Rising coffee prices after 1918 and the effective suppression of anti-colonial tax revolts attracted many new traders and planters to the region, ending decades of European withdrawal from the local coffee economy. Colonial land registry data show that from 1920 to 1943, the central government in Luanda received 1,162 requests for land concessions from settlers in Cazengo, Ambaca, Dembos, and Bembe, the main coffee districts north of the Cuanza River. Most requests were for demarcations of several hundred to five thousand hectares, which applicants promised to develop into cash-crop plantations. Other colonists requested small plots to build a shop to trade with local producers. The government eventually suspended most of these applications, as the volatility of world coffee prices disrupted the business plans of many colonial settlers.[21]

19 ANA, caixa 3400, Capitania-mor dos Dembos, Relatório annual relativo ao ano económico de 1915–16, Cacula Caenda, 28 Aug. 1916; ANA, caixa 4952, Processo no. 1031, Comissão municipal do Bembe, acta no. 8, 15 June 1918; Fausto Martins Lourenço, 'História do café robusta em Angola', *Revista de Ciências Agrárias*, 15:3 (1992), 57–117, at p. 112.

20 David Birmingham, 'A Question of Coffee: Black Enterprise in Angola', *Canadian Journal of African Studies*, 16:2 (1982), 343–6.

21 Angola, Repartição Central dos Serviços de Cadastro, *Relação geral dos processos organizados para a concessão de terrenos do estado, desde 1912 até 31 de dezembro de 1943* (Luanda: Imprensa Nacional, 1944).

The frenzy of European settlement after 1920 paled in comparison with the land rush that unfolded after the Second World War. Spurred on by the post-war commodity boom, which tripled world coffee prices, the number of registered European coffee plantations on the northern sub-plateau increased from 215 in 1948 to 1,268 in 1959 – not counting hundreds of illegal demarcations. These estates belonged to 1,180 different owners, some of whom did not live on the farm themselves and had delegated day-to-day management to a caretaker. By this time, the coffee estates in Angola together covered an estimated 266,000 hectares, which was about a quarter of Angolan land in use for cash-crop cultivation and generated half of the country's export earnings.[22] Four-fifths of these coffee lands were north of the Cuanza. Sociologist Jeffery Paige has calculated that in some northern sub-districts (*concelhos*), European concessions occupied 10 to 16 per cent of the total land area. Northern Angola was especially attractive to new settlers as they still found plenty of non-demarcated land there, thinking they could occupy this land although Africans often used it for farming. South of the Cuanza, in contrast, the area suitable for coffee cultivation was smaller and already heavily colonized by European plantation firms. As mentioned in Chapter 2, nineteenth-century planters often entered coffee farming through other colonial careers, seeing coffee as an opportunity to invest fortunes amassed in trade, warfare, or governance. Likewise, most twentieth-century plantation owners had initially come to Angola for reasons unrelated to agriculture. Many were shopkeepers who used their know-how of the coffee trade and their connections with importers, exporters, and creditors to establish their own estates. Typically, they offered their commercial establishments as collateral for the loans they needed to pay for plantation labour, buildings, and machinery.[23]

Given the enormous growth of settler agriculture in northern Angola, it is remarkable what little role centralized planning played in this expansion. At the turn of the twentieth century, few in the upper reaches of the Portuguese empire suspected that within decades Angola would encompass Africa's largest settler-based coffee economy. Because world coffee prices were low and many plantations struggled to survive, coffee rarely featured in official discourse on Angola's economic development. It was long seen as an African forest crop of

22 Angola, Repartição Central de Estatística Geral, *Anuário estatístico de Angola, ano de 1948* (Luanda: Imprensa Nacional, 1950); *Anuário estatístico de Angola, ano de 1959* (Luanda: Imprensa Nacional, 1960); Alfredo de Sousa, *Ensaio de análise económica do café* (Lisbon: Junta de Investigação do Ultramar, 1958), pp. 11–12, 37–8. Figures of land occupation and coffee production are estimates, as the government failed to keep up with new concession requests and to register most African farms. On the commodity boom, see Marian Radetzki, 'The Anatomy of Three Commodity Booms', *Resources Policy*, 31:1 (2006), 56–64.

23 Paige, *Agrarian Revolution*, pp. 235, 241–2.

marginal importance.[24] Policymakers focused on other products and other regions. While officials a century earlier had favoured cotton, sugar, and tobacco as cash crops that could offset the loss of the slave trade (see Chapter 1), many of them now pinned their hopes on cotton cultivation and ranching.[25] Moreover, plans for white settlement in Angola, considered crucial to the colony's economic progress by politicians and opinion makers from the First Republic (1910–26) through the Estado Novo (1933–68), focused rather narrowly on the central and southern highlands, and even there were only sparingly implemented. Settler colonialism in Angola was, therefore, more ideology than policy.[26]

Settler expansion in northern Angola occurred not by design, but by improvisation, as shopkeepers took advantage of rising coffee prices and the opportunities Portuguese colonialism provided in the form of land concessions, labour supplies, and bank loans. These colonial provisions, which were theoretically available to most white settlers and Western businesses in Angola, built on nineteenth-century precedents, which colonial rulers reshaped to meet twentieth-century requirements. Colonial land policy, first codified in 1856, followed the old *sesmaria* model, in which the state claimed ownership of all African land and leased plots to private developers.[27] Similarly, Portugal's infamous contract labour system evolved from older forms of coerced labour, notably slavery and forced porterage, which were abolished during the nineteenth century (see Chapter 5). Colonists themselves followed in the footsteps of previous generations, who provided examples, inspiration, and a way of thinking about exploiting African resources.[28]

24 Portugal, *A agricultura em Angola: Breve resumo sobre os recursos agrícolas da província de Angola* (Lisbon: Agência Geral de Angola, 1922), pp. 53–5.

25 Maria Cândida Proença, 'A questão colonial', in Fernando Rosas e Maria Fernanda Rollo (eds), *História da Primeira República Portuguesa* (Lisbon: Tinta-da-china, 2009), pp. 205–28, at pp. 209–10.

26 Castelo, *Passagens*, pp. 49–143; Gonçalves, 'Of Peasants and Settlers'; United Nations General Assembly, 'Document A/6000/REV.1: Report of the Special Committee on the Situation with Regard to the Implementation of the Declaration on the Granting of Independence to Colonial Countries and Peoples' (New York, 1965), <https://digitallibrary.un.org/record/732453?ln=en>, accessed 21 Dec. 2023, pp. 272–3. Emblematic of the continued fixation on the Central Plateau is the work of the former colonial minister and High Commissioner to Angola, Vicente Ferreira, *Estudos Ultramarinos* (3 vols, Lisbon: Agência do Ultramar, 1953–5). Ferreira favoured migration of rural working-class families, but until the 1940s most advocates of white settlement had large-scale, capital-intensive enterprise in mind. See Castelo, 'Village Portugal'.

27 Aida Freudenthal, *Arimos e fazendas: A transição agrária em Angola* (Luanda: Chá de Caxinde, 2005), pp. 138–44.

28 Ewout Frankema *et al.*, 'Endogenous Processes of Colonial Settlement: The Success and Failure of European Settler Farming in Sub-Saharan Africa', *Journal of Iberian and Latin American History*, 34:2 (2016), 237–65, at p. 239.

Although there was no imperial master plan for white settlement in northern Angola, the Portuguese state had, from the mid-nineteenth century, developed colonial laws to facilitate land acquisition. As pressure on African agricultural land increased during the transition to 'legitimate' trade, Portugal began to design a legal structure to regulate land ownership in the African colonies. This structure was built on the premise that all land previously unclaimed by private individuals, companies, or organizations was 'empty' and therefore state property, which the state could relinquish through sale, lease, or rent. Leasing (*aforamento*) became the most common form of land concession, with tenants being given the option of permanent ownership after a few years. Legislation from 1919 stipulated that the Angolan government could independently grant concessions of up to five thousand hectares, with the condition that the holder had to prove effective occupation within ten years.[29] Although the idea of *terra nullius* effectively refuted indigenous land ownership, it did not directly legitimize private European ownership. As Mariana Candido has argued, the push for privatization in Angola occurred in the context of dramatic economic changes in the wake of the abolition of the slave trade and paralleled the legalization of individual property in Portugal.[30]

Africans featured minimally in colonial land policy, which Portugal designed mainly to regulate European ownership. Portuguese nationality, or equivalent legal status, was a requirement to apply for a concession. In general, the view was that indigenous land use deserved protection, but that Africans were not sufficiently civilized to enjoy the right to individual property, apart from *moradores* (in the nineteenth century) and *civilisados* (in the twentieth century). Land policy thus provided a legal platform to articulate racist ideologies of difference.[31]

29 For an overview of the most relevant laws, see Miguel Rebordão Amaral, 'Angola: Concessões de terra e direitos tradicionais (1856–1973): Análise de legislação' (MA dissertation, University of Lisbon, 2017), <http://hdl.handle.net/10400.5/13879>, accessed 21 Dec. 2023; United Nations General Assembly, 'Report', pp. 263–7.

30 Mariana Pinho Candido, *Wealth, Land, and Property in Angola: A History of Dispossession, Slavery, and Inequality* (Cambridge: Cambridge University Press, 2022). The concept of *terra nullius*, ingrained in Portuguese imperial history, was inherent in settler colonialism and state centralization generally. See John F. Richards, 'Toward a Global System of Property Rights in Land', in Edmund Burke III and Kenneth Pomeranz (eds), *The Environment and World History* (Berkeley: University of California Press, 2009), pp. 54–78, at pp. 56–8; Lorenzo Veracini, *Settler Colonialism: A Theoretical Overview* (Basingstoke: Palgrave Macmillan, 2010), pp. 87–8.

31 Bárbara Direito, 'African Access to Land in Early 20th Century Portuguese Colonial Thought', in João Vicente Serrão *et al.* (eds), *Property Rights, Lands and Territory in the European Overseas Empires* (Lisbon: Imprensa de Ciências Sociais, 2014), pp. 255–63; Maria Paula G. Meneses, 'O "indígena" africano e o colono "europeu": A construção da diferença por processos legais', *e-cadernos CES*, 7 (2010), <http://journals.openedition.org/eces/403>, accessed 22 Dec. 2023.

Legal scholars based the denial of private property to Africans on the idea that land in Angola belonged to clans and not to individuals. Thus, individual clan members could claim ownership of trees on common land through usufruct, but not the land itself. By denying Africans the opportunity to own private land, the argument went, the colonial state was merely continuing an indigenous legal tradition.[32] The First Republic briefly allowed private ownership of small plots of land by Africans. However, difficult prerequisites for ownership meant that in Angola less than three hundred smallholders had received fully legalized concessions from the Portuguese government in 1916.[33] From 1919, when Portugal issued its first comprehensive land concessions law, Africans could apply for title to a few hectares of land if they could prove effective and continuous occupation. Such titles provided legal protection against European encroachment but did not give Africans the right to sell or transfer land to others. In other words, Africans had the right to use their land but could never take full ownership of it. In this respect, Portuguese policy differed little from that of other colonial powers in Africa.[34]

However, unlike Britain's strategy in Kenya, Portugal did not ban Angolans from producing valuable export crops, and instead protected African usufruct by law.[35] From 1911, European applicants had to report evidence of African occupation, especially homes and farms, in areas provisionally demarcated for a concession. Removal of occupants was legally impossible without consent and compensation, and so it was common for Africans to continue to live on land enclosed by a settler estate. Moreover, from 1944 onwards the government would no longer grant a concession if the applicant demarcated land that was more than 40 per cent in African use.

Portugal's ambivalent policy towards African land use, denying full ownership but securing usufruct, reflected its dual approach to Angolan economic development, which on the one hand supported white settlement, but on the

32 Oliveira Santos, 'O problema das terras em Angola', *Estudos ultramarinos*, 7 (1957–8), 61–81, at pp. 62–3. For context, see Candido, *Wealth*, pp. 91–5; Joana Dias Pereira, 'Colonialism and Customary Land Tenure in Africa: Portuguese Representations and Policies during the 19th and 20th Centuries', *African Studies*, 82:3–4 (2023), 332–47.

33 Aida Freudenthal, 'Angola', in A. H. de Oliveira Marques (ed.), *O império africano, 1890–1930* (Lisbon: Editorial Estampa, 2001), pp. 259–467, at p. 285; Angola, *Negócios Indígenas: Relatório do ano de 1913* (Luanda: Imprensa Nacional de Angola, 1914), pp. 38–41; *Relatório do ano de 1914* (Luanda: Imprensa Nacional, 1915), pp. 10, 18–19, 93; *Relatório do ano de 1915* (Lisbon: Tipografia Universal, 1918), pp. 4–5; *Relatório do ano de 1916* (Lisbon: Typ. do Annuario Commercial, 1917), p. 6.

34 Sara S. Berry, 'Debating the Land Question in Africa', *Comparative Studies in Society and History*, 44:4 (2002), 638–68, at p. 642.

35 Mosley, *Settler Economies*.

other recognized the value of African agricultural production (see Chapter 2). As Sara Berry has noted, colonial regimes generally recognized that retaining Africans on their land, instead of forcing them to migrate, provided the benefit of a stable labour supply.[36] For example, the British government dispossessed Africans in Kenya to reserve land for white settlement, but then allowed them to squat on this land as labour tenants.[37] In northern Angola, the government chose to partially protect African agricultural lands. In theory, this benefited colonists in two ways: peasant households sold their coffee harvests to settlers for onward sale to export houses, while the same households also provided labour, which the government extracted by force if necessary. However, because the colonial administration lacked personnel to implement official land policies, small farmers were typically on the losing end of disputes arising from Portugal's concession regime, surrendering both land and labour to white settlers.

Shopkeepers

In 1959 there were more than a thousand European coffee farmers in northern Angola. Few had started out as agriculturalists. What initially attracted most of them to Africa was trade, as this 'promised quick success', one official explained.[38] The life stories of four male Portuguese colonists shed light on the transition from shopkeeping to coffee cultivation. These stories, written down in biographies, personal documents, and fictional accounts, contain some common threads. They illustrate that coffee traders and planters often came to Angola at a young age, either as wards of relatives who had migrated earlier or as apprentices of traders who hailed from the same home region. Official settlement schemes barely played a role in Portuguese migration before the 1950s.[39] Furthermore, the colonial system provided opportunities for upward mobility that these immigrants rarely enjoyed in Portugal, as many came from poor backgrounds and had few qualifications. By restricting issuance of trade licences, land concessions, bank loans, and labour supplies to white settlers and a handful of 'civilized' Africans, colonial rule ensured that Europeans became dominant producers and intermediaries in the Angolan coffee economy. Portuguese nationals even occu-

36 Berry, 'Debating', p. 642.

37 Christopher Youé, 'Black Squatters on White Farms: Segregation and Agrarian Change in Kenya, South Africa, and Rhodesia, 1902–1963', *International History Review*, 24:3 (2002), 558–602.

38 Angola, Repartição Central de Estatística Geral, *Anuário estatístico de Angola, ano de 1959* (Luanda: Imprensa Nacional, 1960). Arquivo Histórico Ultramarino (Lisbon, henceforth AHU), Ministéro do Ultramar (MU), Inspecção Superior da Administração Ultramarina (ISAU), A2.050.05/033.00202, José Diogo Ferreira Martins, 'Relatório da Inspecção aos Distritos de Cuanza Norte, Cuanza Sul, 1960–1961', pp. 36–7.

39 Castelo, 'Village Portugal', p. 116.

pied the position of petty traders that indigenous merchants were able to keep in other African colonies.[40] Settlers thus managed to capture most of the profits generated in times of high prices, although not all of them were continuously successful.

The first case is António Cordeiro de Oliveira, who left his home in Cagido, a small village in the Viseu district of northern Portugal, for Angola in 1915 at the age of thirteen.[41] His life course shows how the coffee trade allowed Portuguese immigrants to overcome disadvantaged socioeconomic backgrounds and become people of considerable wealth and standing. At home, Oliveira faced a life of rural poverty, having completed just three years of primary education. In Angola he started as an apprentice to Joaquim da Cunha, a Portuguese trader in Ambriz who, like him, came from the municipality of Santa Comba Dão. On a salary of twenty escudos a month, Oliveira occasionally worked for other Portuguese merchants in Ambriz. Through his interactions with African traders, he learned rudimentary Kikongo and gained critical experience in the organization of Afro-European trade. In 1919, Cunha entrusted him with the task of turning a seasonal factory in Tando, a small garrison town northwest of Uíge, into a permanent trading point for the local coffee-growing communities. The Tando factory was an extension of Cunha's main store in Uíge, which was quickly becoming northern Angola's main commercial hub because of its close ties with the Portuguese merchant community in Ambriz and Ambrizete.[42] In 1921, Oliveira, now a business associate of Cunha, moved the Tando factory to Songo, another emerging coffee centre 40km by road from Uíge. Four years later, in his early twenties, Oliveira had earned enough income from the coffee trade to separate his factory from the parent company and establish himself as an independent merchant.[43]

Oliveira's rise in the coffee trade coincided with the construction of new colonial roads and the arrival of the first trucks in Uíge around 1924. Their introduction significantly reduced transportation costs, attracting more traders to the region. That year, about twenty factories were operating in Uíge and surrounding towns, most of them owned by young Portuguese companies founded after the collapse of the wild rubber boom in 1913. Together they bought about six hun-

40 Anthony I. Nwabughuogu, 'From Wealthy Entrepreneurs to Petty Traders: The Decline of African Middlemen in Eastern Nigeria, 1900–1950', *JAH*, 23:3 (1982), 365–79.

41 Fernando Paula Vicente, *Angola, Colonização, Descolonização: António Cordeiro de Oliveira, pioneiro do Norte, fundador do Songo* (Lisbon: edição do autor, 2014).

42 Armando Carneiro, *Honra e glória ao fundador do Uige: Júlio Thomaz Berberan* (Rio Maior: Armando Carneiro, 1962), pp. 22–5, 43.

43 A population count in 1922 lists Antonio Cordeiro de Oliveira as an unmarried trader in Songo. ANA, caixa 3640, Recenseamento nominal, Bembe, Songo, 1922.

dred tons of coffee from local African producers.[44] As coffee prices rose, some of these firms decided to expand into agriculture, using their connections with local rulers to make labour previously used in head carrying available to the new plantations.[45] In 1929, there were fifteen coffee plantations in the Uíge region owned by individual businesses or corporations.[46] Oliveira only began growing coffee after 1930, avoiding that year's price slump that brought many European planters to the brink of bankruptcy. In 1933, he registered a demarcation next to his residence in Songo for a 127-hectare plantation called Lengue, which included approximately 75,000 coffee stands.[47] The proceeds from his commercial activities and this relatively small plantation provided the means to expand his landholdings in the following decades. From several people struggling with debt or legal problems in the Songo area he acquired three medium-sized plantations, giving him access to more than a million coffee stands that produced about 450 tons of dried berries annually. The post-war coffee boom also allowed him to extend his activities to Luanda, where he invested in real estate and founded the Sociedade Angolana de Comércio in 1951, whose portfolio, not coincidentally, included Volvo Trucks' Angola agency.

Oliveira's case makes clear that the success of some settlers was predicated on the failure of others. The story of Portuguese immigrant Francisco Teixeira da Fonseca is an example of commercial triumph followed by frustration.[48] In 1911, Fonseca founded a trading house in Zavula, in the Cazengo district, to exchange goods for coffee with local African growers. A flourishing coffee trade gave Fonseca access to bank loans to acquire several medium-sized plantations near his factory and begin a programme of extensive coffee planting.[49] In 1924, his firm produced 145 metric tons of coffee, a record it would not achieve again. At the

44 José de Almeida Mattos, *O Congo Português e as suas riquezas* (Lisbon: Simões, Marques, Santos & Cia, 1924), pp. 164, 203–20; Augusto Casimiro, 'O nosso Congo: Esboço dum relatório', *BGC*, 2:17 (1926), 23–56, at pp. 23–33.

45 José Roque Martins, João Augusto Afonso, and Carlos Alves (eds), *Uige, Songo, Bembe: A circunscrição civil do Bembe, na primeira exposição portuguesa* (Luanda: Imprensa Nacional, 1934), p. 5.

46 ANA, caixa 4995, Mapa nominal das firmas comerciais, industrais e agrícolas existentes no distrito [do Congo], Maquela do Zombo, 25 Oct. 1929; Sociedade de Geografia de Lisboa, Reservados 2-B-36, Jaime R. Sepúlveda Rodrigues, Relatório annual, 1929–30, Maquela do Zombo, 16 Nov. 1929.

47 Angola, Repartição Central dos Serviços de Cadastro, *Relação geral*, p. 28, lists only a demarcation of 0.2 hectares, which must have been for the residence rather than the farm.

48 Francisco Teixeira da Fonseca, *Á volta da falência da minha firma Teixeira da Fonseca & Cia, Lda (Angola)* (Luanda: Lusitana, [1933]).

49 Angola, Repartição Central dos Serviços de Cadastro, *Relação geral*, lists four demarcations registered by Fonseca: one of 279 hectares in Caculo in 1916 (granted), two of 300 hectares in 1918 (archived), and one of 400 hectares in 1929.

same time, the firm purchased almost double that volume from independent African farmers. However, years of financial mismanagement exacerbated by falling coffee prices forced Fonseca to apply for bankruptcy in 1931.

Although the biographies of Oliveira and Fonseca demonstrate the fragility of colonists' careers in the interwar period, they provide little insight into plantation management. For this we turn to *Tonga: Epopeia do café*, a fictional account of the travails of António da Mata, an immigrant from Gouveia, northern Portugal, who became a coffee farmer in the Dembos region in the late 1930s, written by the Portuguese journalist and politician António Pires.[50] Born in Portugal in 1916, but living in Angola from early adulthood, Pires wrote *Tonga* (a Kimbundu term for 'plantation', or a gang of plantation workers) in 1959, drawing on information from coffee planters whom he knew and his own observations on the ground. The promotion of Pires' fictional hero from plantation manager to plantation owner mirrored the real-life case of Manuel Cadete, who first administered and then acquired the Flor de Cazengo estate from Teixeira da Fonseca when the latter went bankrupt in 1931.[51] Although the work's literary qualities are debatable, *Tonga* is unique for its informed and detailed account of plantation life in the montane forest of northern Angola, as seen through settler eyes.

One notable quality of *Tonga* is the attention paid to the physical environment of the coffee plantation. The story focuses on Esperança, a semi-abandoned estate near Pango Aluquém, in the heart of the Angolan coffee forest, which its owner struggled to maintain during the economic depression of the 1930s, but which Mata returned to life when world coffee prices picked up during the Second World War. Contrary to the image of colonial plantations as neatly demarcated and choreographed spaces, the plantation in *Tonga* spread across several hills, with populations of sub-spontaneous coffee trees growing in forest patches scattered throughout the estate, only some of them turned into cultivated farms (*lavras*).[52] The main house, built of brick with a zinc roof, stood on a hill in the middle of the plantation, from where the plantation manager had a wide, but still incomplete, view of the grounds. From the main house, several paths and small trails led through tall grass and shrubs to the various coffee farms. When Mata arrived at the plantation as its newly appointed manager around 1939, he found thousands of long neglected and uncultivated coffee trees in the shade of the forest canopy, overgrown with creepers, Roselle, and other unwanted scrub. The survival of the plantation hinged on turning these semi-wild stands into productive trees. The central message is that planting coffee was hard work: it

50 António Pires, *Tonga: Epopeia do café* (Luanda: Edições Lello, 1959).

51 Aniceto Gourgel, *A povoação de Zavula na época colonial: Província do Kwanza-Norte (principio do sec. XX até 1974)* (Luanda: edição do autor, 2012), p. 27.

52 On 'legible' colonial landscapes, see James C. Scott, *Seeing Like a State: How Certain Schemes to Improve the Human Condition Have Failed* (London: Yale University Press, 2020).

required the clearing of undergrowth, followed by constant weeding and pruning. In his appreciation of coffee's natural habitat, Mata – whose character Pires perhaps created to fit the *Estado Novo*'s idealized image of an industrious but humble peasantry – was the opposite of the real-life colonial planters scorned by local botanists for disrespecting this environment (see Chapter 2).[53]

Second, *Tonga* highlights different categories of plantation labour. Mata found about thirty disgruntled labourers living on the estate, including temporary wage workers (*voluntários*) and government-contracted workers (*contratados*). The former were day labourers from the Dembos region who had come for the duration of the harvest, many bringing with them wives and children to help with picking. But they had overstayed their term of service as wages were three months in arears. The other workers were Ganguelas from the east of the Bié Plateau, about 800km south of Dembos. They were on the plantation because 'the government called' and had a contractual obligation to stay for twelve months.[54] Their duties during the year consisted mainly of farm upkeep, including weeding. The *contratados* also wanted to go home, but their wages were overdue, and the plantation owner had not yet arranged their transport. The workers grew their own food, although this was generally insufficient.[55] Their contracts entitled them to rations of cassava flour (*fuba*), salted fish, beans, and rice. The planter's own meals were mainly chicken and rice, or pasta with chorizo.

Finally, *Tonga* captures the various social, political, and economic hierarchies that planters had to navigate. First, they depended on the goodwill of local administrators, who oversaw all formalities related to labour recruitment. Mata eventually became the owner of the estate, obtaining the title deed and a recruitment licence from the previous owner. This licence was compulsory for all farmers needing more than thirty contract workers.[56] Since Mata could ill afford a private recruitment agent, influence and good standing with local authorities were required to gain access to labour. Next, *Tonga* vividly describes an economic pyramid in which major import and export houses in Luanda were nestled at the top, settlers formed the middle tier, and African growers and plantation workers sat at the bottom.[57] Small European planters like Mata were financially dependent on the Luanda merchants, who sold provisions and merchandise on credit, which was normally repaid with the next coffee harvest. Credit obligations thus tied up a significant portion of the coffee produced on the Esperança estate. Meanwhile, the plantation shop sold wine and fabrics (Dutch printed textiles, denim, and checked cotton from Vizela, a manufactur-

53 Gonçalves, 'Of Peasants and Settlers', 176.

54 Pires, *Tonga*, p. 113.

55 Seleti, 'Portuguese Colonialism', p. 149.

56 AHU, MU, 2243/1, Angola, 'Relatório do ano de 1936 do Curador Geral dos Indígenas' (Luanda, 30 June 1937), p. 12.

57 Seleti, 'Portuguese Colonialism', pp. 231, 234.

ing town in northern Portugal) to workers and African farmers in exchange for, respectively, wages and unhusked coffee (*café mabuba*).[58] European commercial penetration and the gradual replacement of head carriers by trucks in the 1920s had reconfigured the coffee supply chain by eliminating African middlemen and forcing small farmers to sell to local planters or retailers. Many planters thus combined agricultural activities with commercial ones, buying coffee and selling merchandise, and therefore did not necessarily view African growers as competitors.[59]

Because African producers often purchased goods on credit, planter-traders could exploit defaulters by absorbing their farms.[60] On this mechanism of estate building *Tonga* remains silent, as it aims to show the planter as an honest, hard-working farmer. In fact, none of the accounts discussed so far problematize the acquisition of African land by white settlers. *Um colono e coisas do Golungo* differs in this respect. This messily constructed memoir by colonist Francisco Gonçalves Afonso illustrates that many shopkeepers developed plantations by buying out indebted African smallholders.[61] Born in Alijó, in the northern Portuguese district of Vila Real, Afonso came to Angola in 1912, when he was fifteen years old. In 1917, he was working as plantation manager near Malange for the firm of Afonso & Sobrinho (Afonso and nephew), which suggests family ties had brought him to Central Africa. In 1920, he moved to the Golungo region, where he built a successful business in timber, coffee, and palm oil production, centred on three medium-sized plantations. His arrest for attempted homicide in 1947 prompted the writing of this account, a lengthy chronicle of his relationships with fellow colonists, interspersed with transcripts of correspondence, government investigations, and witness statements. It is fundamentally a reckoning with adversaries in the Golungo community who were, Afonso believed, trying to discredit him after he accused them of crimes against African farmers, including land theft, extortion, and kidnapping. The subjective narrative makes it difficult to assess the validity of Afonso's claims. Nevertheless, the book's many pieces of anecdotal evidence and official documents, when put together, highlight the casual violence underlying everyday interactions between white Europeans – traders, planters, administrators, and truck drivers – and black Africans in Angola. They also convey some of the permanent anxieties and tensions within the settler community, who always feared that internal rivalry and

58 For salary payment in textiles, see 'Relatório do ano de 1936 do Curador Geral dos Indígenas', p. 16. For Vizela, see Fernando Pimentel, *Investigação commercial na província de Angola* (Porto: Typographia a Vapor da Empreza Guedes, 1903), p. 115.

59 Martins *et al.*, *Uíge*, p. 6; Gourgel, *A povoação de Zavula*, p. 32.

60 'Relatório da Inspecção aos Distritos de Cuanza Norte, Cuanza Sul, 1960–1961', p. 56.

61 Francisco Gonçalves Afonso, *Um colono e coisas do Golungo* (2 vols, Porto: Tipografia Modesta, 1958), vol. 1, pp. 25–30.

conflict would break the façade of unity and racial superiority they maintained to oppress colonized populations.[62]

Repertoires of dispossession

Land theft and land disputes were common in Angola under colonial rule. These conflicts, sometimes voiced before district administrators, in courtrooms, or in newspapers, but often going unrecorded, became increasingly widespread in the Luanda hinterland during the coffee boom of the 1870s and 1880s.[63] Despite legal provisions introduced by the Portuguese government to protect indigenous land use during the first half of the twentieth century, settlers continued to encroach on African coffee farms, including officially registered properties.

The work of António de Assis Júnior, a black Angolan lawyer in N'dalatando, the administrative centre of Cazengo, demonstrates how sinister strategies of colonial land occupation often were. In the 1910s, Assis Júnior took on the defence of several smallholders who were threatened with expropriation by more powerful landowners. This made him unpopular with local authorities, who in 1917 plotted to have him arrested on charges of leading a 'nativist' uprising against the colonial regime. While in prison, he wrote an account of his persecution, describing various ways in which large planters drove people from their land or confiscated their coffee crops. These included land invasions, bodily assault, and various devious methods, such as furtively including other people's farms in formal demarcations or in legal transfers of ownership. Taken together with earlier and later evidence, Assis Júnior's account shows how little the colonial repertoire of dispossession changed over time.[64]

The most striking case related by Assis Júnior concerned Francisco Cristóvão Rodrigues Pimenta and Pascoal de Lima Canguezeze, two residents of Cazengo who owned a plantation called Catome. The men had inherited this property from their parents, registered it with the colonial government, and had lived on it for thirty years when a new neighbour laid claim to it in 1916. Mário José Gonçalves, also known as Kipexi (Kimbundu for 'smoking pipe'), had just taken possession of an adjacent property, Cango, neatly separated from Catome by a small stream. Twice that year, Gonçalves sent between thirty and forty of his contract workers, armed with machetes and bludgeons, across the river to invade Catome, steal the coffee harvest, and intimidate the owners. Many of the

62 Nancy Rose Hunt, *A Nervous State: Violence, Remedies, and Reverie in Colonial Congo* (Durham: Duke University Press, 2016).

63 Jill R. Dias, 'Changing Patterns of Power in the Luanda Hinterland: The Impact of Trade and Colonisation on the Mbundu ca. 1845–1920', *Paideuma: Mitteilungen zur Kulturkunde*, 32 (1986), pp. 285–318.

64 António de Assis Júnior, *Relato dos acontecimentos de Dala Tando e Lucala* (Lisbon: Mercado de Letras Editores, 2014), pp. 81–5.

invaders hailed from central and southern Angola and had recently completed an extended period of indentured servitude in São Tomé and Príncipe. Rather than ensuring their return home, as labour recruitment laws required, colonial administrators often sent repatriated *santomistas* to coffee plantations in northern Angola to alleviate local labour shortages, a practice that continued into the 1950s. Uprooted, undernourished, and demoralized, these workers became willing pawns in the corrupt schemes of land-hungry planters.[65]

Conflicts over plantation boundaries spread across northern Angola from the moment white settlers began to build estates in regions outside the old Cazengo district. A clause in the 1919 regulations, allowing the removal of African occupants from European concessions, contributed to a brief land rush and a worrying number of forced expropriations. This alarmed the Portuguese High Commissioner for Angola, José Norton de Matos (1921–3), who immediately removed this provision from the legislation. Laws enacted in 1923 and 1927 prohibited the inclusion of land cultivated by Africans in concessions and required that an area at least five times the size of a cultivated plot be left free for African use, although neither settlers nor administrators observed these rules consistently. Rising commodity prices after the Second World War ushered in a new land rush. Because the government's Land Registry could not keep up with the increasing number of applications for concessions, applicants often occupied land by force, causing frequent litigations. Indeed, limited bureaucratic capacity, resulting in a lack of administrative oversight and intervention, was a fundamental problem for a government that aimed in principle to protect African agricultural interests from illegal European encroachment.[66]

For the first three decades after the introduction of the 1919 legislation, the procedures for verifying the presence of African farms on land demarcated for a concession were relatively simple and favoured white settlers. The only authority involved in this process was the local administrator (*chefe de posto*), who, with the interests of the settlers at heart, usually vowed that any evidence of prior coffee cultivation in new demarcations were vestiges of abandoned farms rather than signs of continued land use. However, to accommodate potential African land claims, from 1950 onward the Angolan government ruled that three different authorities, one after the other, had to inspect a demarcation before the central government issued a provisional concession (which became definitive after five years of effective occupation). This now became a lengthy process. The first step for a starting planter was to obtain permission from the district government to demarcate a piece of land, which the government normally granted if the applicant could demonstrate they had sufficient credit to develop their business, and the size of the planned demarcation remained within legal limits. The Land Registry then issued a provisional licence, which the applicant took to the local

65 Júnior, *Relato*, pp. 27–9, 78–81, 86, 127.

66 United Nations General Assembly, 'Report', pp. 270–1.

administration. This allowed the applicant to stake out their demarcation with markers showing their initials and authorization number and, crucially, begin farming. Within a year, the planter had to produce a map and description of the land, showing the location of African farms in the area. After receiving these materials, the local administrator arranged to survey the demarcation to give his approval. Then a technician of the *Junta de Exportação do Café* came to examine the land, after which it was the turn of an official of the Department of Agriculture. Since these two government departments were chronically understaffed, inspections proceeded at a slow pace, causing application files to pile up at the Land Registry. From start to finish, the process of legalizing a demarcation could take up to six years, and even longer if litigations intervened.[67]

The Congo district, especially the coffee-rich township (*concelho*) of Uíge, became a hotbed of settler activity in the 1950s. The contemporary pun 'wild Uíge' conveyed the explosive, unregulated nature of economic development in the region. After a spike in world coffee prices, demand for land completely overwhelmed the colonial administration. For example, between 1954 and 1957, the Congo government received 989 concession requests, two-thirds of which came from Uíge. Together, these requests covered an area of 111,000 hectares, which came in addition to the 288,000 hectares already under concession in the Congo (representing 3 per cent of the total size of the district). But during the same period, only fifty-three applicants received a provisional concession. Highlighting the administrative backlog, in 1957, Land Registry officials faced a stack of nearly two thousand unfinished concession processes in Congo alone.[68] Unwilling to wait for years for the outcome of their application, most planters began harvesting coffee as soon as they received their first permit, often confiscating coffee from African farms based on the claim that the land was theirs.

According to a police report from Uíge in 1955, settlers used several methods to dispossess African farmers. For example, in the outline and description of their demarcation they deliberately undercounted the number of farms. Or they claimed they found farms abandoned, while the owners were temporarily away on labour duty. Or they moved the signposts of their demarcation to land used by Africans, after the authorities verified there was no conflicting overlap

67 Arquivo Histórico Diplomático (Lisbon, henceforth AHD), ser. 135, no. 35 (MU/GM/GNP/135/Pt.35), Governador do Congo to Chefe da repartição do Gabinete do Governo geral de Angola, no. 790/1ª/41, Carmona, 4 June 1956. For a description from a former Junta land inspector, see Fausto Martins Lourenço, 'História do café robusta em Angola', *Revista de Ciências Agrárias*, 15:4 (1992), 85–119, at p. 94.

68 A. E., 'A demarcação de terrenos de estado no distrito do Congo', *BGU*, 35:405 (1959), 63–70; AHU, MU, ISAU, A2.050.05/034.00207, Governador Hélio Esteves Felgas, 'Relatório do Governo do Distrito do Congo referente a 1957 (Confidencial)', p. 8; AHU, Governo geral de Angola (GANG), Repartição do Gabinete, D2.172.6/06, Felgas to GG, no. 61, Carmona, 1 March 1958.

between the two. Alternatively, they removed farmers by force.[69] According to the governor of the Congo district, Hélio Esteves Felgas, many planters purposely demarcated land where Africans were cultivating coffee, especially in the months preceding the annual harvest. Since the first official inspection of the demarcation would only take place a year or two later, this ploy allowed them to steal at least one or two crops from African farmers whose protests were habitually silenced by administrative drudgery and corruption.[70]

Legal disputes often took years to resolve. In 1951, a plantation company called Alto Minho received a permit to demarcate a thousand hectares of forest near Songo. The demarcation included sixty-nine farms pertaining to growers from nearby towns. To minimize compensation claims, the plantation manager, Álvaro Capaz da Silva, alleged that most of these farms had long since been abandoned, a view the local *chefe de posto* was willing to support. However, when a technician of the Junta do Café visited the plantation in 1953, he found the forest 'full of farms [*cheio de lavras*]', some of which looked abandoned, but others were clearly under cultivation. District administrators subsequently argued that, since these farms were located at different places in the forest and each farmer had the right to use an area five times as large, technically little of the planned demarcation could remain. In 1954, the Congo District Land Registry therefore withdrew the licence issued three years earlier and ordered the removal of all signposts. But Capaz da Silva challenged this outcome, delaying the litigation process. By 1955, he was still harvesting the crop, about eighty tons a year, from farms that were not his.[71]

Around the same time, the *chefe de posto* of Bembe was helping the owner of a coffee mill in Uíge, Eduardo Rolando da Fonseca, to demarcate a large coffee estate in the Massarele mountains, northwest of Uíge. Portuguese military officers had already recognized Massarele as an extensively cultivated coffee region in 1914.[72] Colonists who later settled nearby also knew this. In fact, most felt that concessions in this area were impossible to obtain owing to the large number of African coffee farms. But Fonseca thought differently and moved in with the help of the local administrator. After he marked out his intended property, several Massarele elders travelled to Uíge to file a complaint with the gov-

69 AHD, ser. 135, no. 35, Comando da Polícia de Segurança Pública de Angola, Informação, Luanda, 7 March 1955.

70 AHD, ser. 135, no. 35, Governador do Congo to Chefe da repartição do Gabinete do Governo geral de Angola, no. 790/1ª/41, Carmona, 4 June 1956.

71 AHD, ser. 135, no. 35, Nota no. 149, Songo, 23 June 1953, followed by documentation of demarcation process, 1951–55; quote from Capataz da Junta do Café, João Batista Alves de Oliveira, Informação, Songo, 22 June 1953; *ibid.*, Administrador do concelho do Bembe, José Paulo Paixão Barradas, to Governador do Distrito do Congo, no. 38, confidential, Carmona, 6 Aug. 1955.

72 AHM, caixa 21, no. 8, Relatório, Bembe, 23 Nov. 1914.

ernment, stating that Fonseca had taken possession of 110 coffee farms by moving the signboards of his original demarcation. The *chefe de posto* defended Fonseca by maintaining that these farms had been abandoned, causing the owners to lose their usufruct rights to the land. When a lawyer examined the demarcation on behalf of the farmers and confirmed they had a legitimate claim, a lengthy dispute loomed. Subsequent investigations by the Bembe district administrator revealed that the *chefe de posto* used various methods to silence plaintiffs and witnesses, including physical abuse, incarceration, and public shaming, demonstrating the depth of his complicity in Fonseca's illegal endeavours.[73]

Seizures of land and coffee continued also on a smaller scale, following the repertoire described by Assis Júnior earlier in the century. For instance, in 1951, several smallholders in Cazengo complained to the government that a European individual they knew as Carlos had occupied their coffee farms. In 1953, Domingas Borges, from the Mussengue chiefdom near Golungo Alto, protested that a Portuguese colonist named Figueiredo had stolen a farm from her, which had yielded twenty-four bags of dried coffee the year before. In 1958, the government of the Congo district learned that another Portuguese settler, named Ferreira, had seized approximately fourteen bags of coffee from an African grower, Dombache Nulungo, when the harvested berries were drying in his village.[74]

Settlers typically defended their actions on the grounds that African claims to land were illegitimate. Their most effective argument was that farmers often began cultivating wild coffee stands within demarcations only after the first signboards were erected, so that they could claim ownership and compensation when government officials came to conduct their surveys.[75] In the eyes of colonists, Africans took advantage of the difficulty of distinguishing between new, old, and abandoned farms, which lay observers had struggled with since smallholders began transforming the coffee forest in the nineteenth century.[76]

73 AHD, ser. 135, no. 35, Comando da Polícia de Segurança Pública de Angola, Informação, Luanda, 7 March 1955; *ibid.*, Administrador Barradas to Governador do Distrito do Congo, no. 38, confidential, Carmona, 6 Aug. 1955, including letter from planter José d'Almeida Vaz Geada, Songo, 3 Aug. 1955; *ibid.*, Auto de notícia, Carmona, 9 Aug. 1955; *ibid.*, Barradas to Director Distrital de Administração Civil do Congo, no. 65, confidential, Carmona, 1 Sep. 1955.

74 AHU, GANG, D2.172.6/06, Telegrama de António Manuel to GG, Lucala, 4 July 1951; *ibid.*, Chefe de gabinete to governador do Uíge, no. 770, 13 March 1953; *ibid.*, Distrito do Congo, ofício no. 1493/1ª/18, Carmona, 19 April 1958.

75 AHD, ser. 135, no. 35, Governador do Congo to Chefe da repartição do Gabinete do Governo geral de Angola, no. 790/1ª/41, Carmona, 4 June 1956; AHU, MU, ISAU, A2.050.05/034.00203, 'Relatório do Governo da Província do Congo no ano de 1953', p. 175; ANA, caixa 2170, Chefe de posto Lopes Martins to Administrador, no. 163, Caculo Cabaça, 22 July 1956.

76 ANA, caixa 5002, Administrador do concelho, Inocêncio Matoso da Camara, to SG, no. 87, Encoge, 12 April 1888.

But according to a surveyor in the Congo district, it was easy to determine the age of an African plantation in relation to a European demarcation and thus to verify claims about African land use. Additionally, some conflicts involved accusations that farmers had occupied abandoned estates, which the old owners, or new ones, pretended to revive.[77] However, most officials agreed that white settlers were mostly to blame and that small farmers were frequently cheated. District governor Felgas underlined that demarcation requests typically peaked in April and May, as settlers sought to access African coffee farms before the annual harvest. In 1956, he therefore decided to stop issuing licences between April and August, except for demarcations in open, non-forested land where no coffee could be stolen.[78]

Compensation was a non-violent way to prevent or resolve land disputes, especially when government officials supported the claims of African land users. This could take the form of financial compensation, new coffee trees, or making land available at another location. For example, in 1949 Manoel Dias Teixeira obtained a licence to demarcate a plantation near Caculo Cabaça. Upon inspection, the Junta do Café concluded that in the demarcated area there were four occupied farms and nineteen abandoned ones, the owners of which Teixeira had previously bought out. By 1955, Teixeira had compensated all the remaining farmers except one, who refused to sell or trade his farm.[79] To obtain a concession near Quiculungo, Paiva, Marcelo & Companhia compensated thirty-two farmers by planting a total of 110,600 new coffee stands outside the proposed demarcation, but then immediately seized the existing farms within it.[80] In 1957, Armindo Cunha, a settler in the Dembos town of Bula Atumba, agreed to add between fifteen hundred and two thousand new coffee stands to African farms within his demarcation. This allowed the African owners to stay on their land and increase their capital, while Cunha could reap the benefits of buying and selling their coffee.[81] It is difficult to determine the incidence of compensation. Anecdotal evidence suggests that land conflicts, exacerbated by administrative incapacity, were much more common.[82]

77 AHU, MU, ISAU, A2.050.04/027.00167, 'Relatório do Governador do Distrito do Quanza Norte, António Francisco Neto Parra, 1957', pp. 17–18.

78 AHD, ser. 135, no. 35, Hélio A. Esteves Felgas, 'Relatório annual do distrito do Congo referente a 1956, 1° volume', pp. 91–101.

79 ANA, caixa 2170, Chefe de posto Lopes Martins to Administrador, no. 77, Banga, 20 Feb. 1956.

80 AHU, MU, ISAU, A2.050.02/016.00106, 'Relatório da Inspecção ao Concelho de Ambaca, pelo Inspector Administrativo, Eduardo B. Lapido Loureiro' (1950), p. 125.

81 AHU, GANG, D2.172.6/06, Chefe de Gabinete, no. 4900, Luanda, 26 June 1957.

82 AHU, MU, ISAU, A2.0001.02/012.00062, 'Relatório do Governador do Distrito do Cuanza Norte, Antonio Francisco Neto Parra, respeitante ao período de 25 de outubro 1955 a 31 de dezembro 1956', p. 7.

From an economic perspective, it was immaterial whether colonists acquired their land legally or illegally, for settler agriculture remained an inefficient way to produce coffee. In addition to the diseconomies of scale associated with coffee plantations, there was the enduring problem of underdeveloped estates. To obtain a permanent concession, settlers had to demonstrate effective use of the lease, but the criterion for this was notoriously weak. According to legislation from 1923, concessionaires had to cultivate at least 10 per cent of the land they had demarcated. This rule allowed settlers to occupy large tracts of fertile coffee land but leave most of it undeveloped as they struggled to find the requisite labour.[83] The average concession size applied for by settlers in the Congo district in the mid-1950s was approximately one thousand hectares. Such large plantations were not, the Angolan governor-general Horácio Rebelo admitted, an efficient way of using land.[84] Junta engineers knew this, too, but despite their general sympathy for African smallholders and apathy towards large planters, they never dared to question the principle of settler colonialism. Their solution for land underuse due to overextension and labour shortages was to facilitate the permanent settlement on European coffee plantations of free African wage workers from economically disadvantaged regions, or to allow the cultivation of coffee lands by small European family units. The first proposal was an improvement of the current system; the second a variation on the Brazilian *colono* model. Returning the land to African smallholders was unthinkable.[85]

In the end, to minimize land waste and allow a greater number of white immigrants to settle in the region, the Congo government imposed a fifty-hectare limit on demarcations in the Uíge subdistrict, a hundred hectares in the emerging coffee zones of Damba and Negage, and 250 hectares elsewhere.[86] However, such properties were still significantly larger than most African holdings. These often covered only a few hectares, which farmers managed to exploit effectively by using mostly family and village labour.

Settler habits and political choices

The transition to settler agriculture in the Angolan coffee economy after 1920 was anarchic and marred by conflict, violence, and bureaucratic ineptitude. Although white settlement was a tenet of the Portuguese colonial project in Africa, official discourse regarding the European colonization of Angola concen-

83 United Nations General Assembly, 'Report', p. 271.

84 Horácio de Sá Viana Rebelo, *Angola na África deste tempo* (Lisbon: edição do autor, 1961), p. 76.

85 Lourenço, 'História', 15:4, pp. 93, 98–9; Jorge Trancoso Vaz, 'Problemas da cafeicultua no Congo e a mão de obra', *RCP*, 3:11 (1956), 26–32.

86 AHD, Ser. 135, no. 35, Felgas, 'Relatório annual do distrito do Congo referente a 1956, 1° volume', pp. 91–101; Houk, 'Recent Developments', p. 207.

trated mainly on the central highlands. During the first half of twentieth century, colonial thinkers and planners largely ignored an agrarian sector that, dominated by white planters, accounted for 47 per cent of Angolan exports in 1956, while coffee occupied roughly 26 per cent of all Angolan land under cash-crop cultivation.[87] Settler expansion in northern Angola was a grassroots phenomenon led by individual entrepreneurs who were usually drawn to plantation ownership after stints in the coffee trade. To build their estates, these colonists often used unlawful means, including theft, intimidation, extortion, and legal manipulation, to expropriate African smallholders who were on average more efficient coffee growers. Planters had developed and refined this repertoire of dispossession in Angola since the mid-nineteenth century.

The colonial state played an ambivalent but decisive role in this transition. Most importantly, it chose to support settlers by facilitating access to land and labour. At the same time, land concession laws had from the early twentieth century included provisions protecting African land use, which officials at higher district level and within the Junta do Café proved willing to enforce. However, two structural problems disadvantaged African smallholders. First, administrative incapacity allowed illegal demarcations to proliferate. More fundamentally, despite earlier evidence of settler failure and smallholder success, the triumphs of the Angolan coffee economy after the Second World War reinforced belief among government officials in the superiority of large-scale, plantation-based agriculture, creating a false sense of economic dependence on white settlers. While the colonial government was keen to supress excessive exploitation of African land and labour by colonists and low-level administrators and was often concerned about African food and cash-crop production, the system of settler agriculture itself was never questioned. On the contrary, as the next chapters will show, after helping planters obtain land, officials of all ranks felt compelled to support them with labour supplies, extracted from African communities by force if necessary.

87 Sousa, *Ensaio*, pp. 11, 37–8.

5

Out of Slavery

ACROSS AFRICA, Asia, and the Americas, commercial coffee growing has involved a range of farm sizes, land ownership and tenure arrangements, and labour relations. Variations in land and labour regimes existed between coffee economies but, crucially, also within them. From a global perspective, therefore, the coexistence in Angola during the nineteenth and twentieth centuries of African smallholders using family and village labour and European settler estates supported by coerced labour was hardly exceptional.[1] Nevertheless, in the African context, Portugal's persistent support of the estate sector with land concessions and labour supplies distinguished Angola from other coffee economies under colonial rule. Smallholding was the norm in coffee farming throughout the continent, to which even notable settler-elite colonies such as Côte d'Ivoire, Madagascar, and Kenya eventually yielded.

In Angola, Africans were recruited for unpaid or low-paid plantation labour through extra-economic means since the first coffee estates were established during the 1830s. This initially took the form of slavery, replaced in 1869 by the *liberto* apprenticeship regime, which from 1875 onward gave way to a system of contract labour. Coercion was both cause and corollary of the planters' refusal to attract workers through wage incentives. In this regard, the plantation sector differed from the diamond-mining company Diamang, which compensated coercion with material and health gains in line with developments on the African Copperbelt.[2] Although politically contentious, coercion was considered necessary as it

1 William Gervase Clarence-Smith and Steven Topik (eds), *The Global Coffee Economy in Africa, Asia, and Latin America, 1500–1989* (Cambridge: Cambridge University Press, 2003); William Roseberry *et al.* (eds), *Coffee, Society, and Power in Latin America* (Baltimore: Johns Hopkins University Press, 1995).

2 This explains the different approaches to forced labour taken by Jeremy Ball, *Angola's Colossal Lie: Forced Labour on a Sugar Plantation, 1913–1977* (Leiden: Brill, 2015) and Todd Cleveland, *Diamonds in the Rough: Corporate Paternalism and African Professionalism on the Mines of Colonial Angola, 1917–1975* (Athens: Ohio University Press, 2015). See also Dácil Juif and Ewout Frankema, 'From Coercion to Compensation: Institutional Responses to Labour Scarcity in the Central African Copperbelt', *Journal of Institutional Economics*, 14:2 (2018), 313–43.

allowed coffee planters to survive in the face of strong smallholder competition. Unlike the British in Kenya, the Portuguese government never banned African farmers from coffee growing. While the state supported settlers with land concessions and steady supplies of relatively inexpensive workers, by law it also protected African land rights, though not to the extent that it allowed non-assimilated Africans to own land privately (see Chapter 4). As a result, there were tens of thousands of small coffee farmers in Angola, especially in the north, who accounted for about a quarter of the country's coffee production in the 1950s. There were few economies of scale in coffee cultivation, which placed large capital- and labour-intensive plantations at a disadvantage compared to smallholders.[3] Settlers in Côte d'Ivoire and Madagascar found this out when France abolished its forced labour regime in Africa in 1944, suddenly making estate production economically unviable.[4] Around the same time, the British government in Kenya recognized the higher efficiency of small-scale coffee farming. After initially excluding African farmers from growing coffee to protect settler interests, in the 1950s it lifted the ban to boost the production of higher-quality coffees and thereby generate more revenue to help cover the costs of the counterinsurgency during the Mau Mau war.[5] In Angola, however, state subsidies in land and labour to white settlers continued until decolonization in 1975.

While the previous chapter analysed the development of settler colonialism during the twentieth century, this chapter and the next examine the evolution of the plantation labour regime in the wake of slavery and its abolition. Together, these three chapters demonstrate how Portuguese land and labour policies in Angola in the modern colonial era were deeply influenced by nineteenth-century legacies. As Chapter 4 showed, new land concession laws developed in the early twentieth century formalized an archaic leasing model that had initiated a process of land privatization in several proto-colonial enclaves from the 1850s onward.

3 Steven Topik and William Gervase Clarence-Smith, 'Conclusion: New Propositions and a Research Agenda', in Clarence-Smith and Topik, *Global Coffee Economy*, pp. 385–410, at pp. 389–91.

4 Hubert Fréchou, 'Les plantations européennes en Côte d'Ivoire', *Cahiers d'outre-mer*, 8:29 (1955), 56–83; A. G. Hopkins, *An Economic History of West Africa* (New York: Columbia University Press, 1973), p. 219; Fredrick Cooper, *Decolonization and African Society: The Labor Question in French and British Africa* (Cambridge: Cambridge University Press, 1996), pp. 185–202; Gwyn Campbell, 'The Origins and Development of Coffee production in Réunion and Madagascar, 1711–1972', in Clarence-Smith and Topik, *Global Coffee Economy*, pp. 67–99.

5 David W. Throup, 'The Origins of Mau Mau', *African Affairs*, 84:336 (1985), 399–433; David Hyde, '"Paying for the Emergency by Displacing the Settlers": Global Coffee and Rural Restructuring in Late Colonial Kenya', *JGH*, 4:1 (2009), 81–103.

These new laws mainly ensured that white settlers retained access to African land, which Portuguese rulers considered state property. In a similar vein, colonial labour laws introduced after Portugal abolished slavery in the empire in 1869 were originally intended to guarantee colonists control over the labour of the formerly enslaved. The question historians have subsequently asked is to what extent the contract labour system erected on these laws resembled the system of slavery it replaced. This chapter critically intervenes in this debate by examining the transition from slavery to contract labour on the northern coffee estates between approximately 1875 and 1920. During this period, contracts long provided a legal façade for thinly veiled plantation slavery, until colonial governments had the capacity to implement the contract system as originally designed. The chapter concludes that the origins of contract labour lay not so much in slavery, but in a combination of globally evolving labour regimes and Angola's proto-colonial regime of forced porterage. The next chapter studies labour relations on the coffee plantations from 1920 onward, interrogating the commonly used concept of 'forced labour'.

Legacies of slavery

The spectre of bondage haunted the Portuguese labour system in Angola throughout the colonial era. Foreign journalists like Henry Nevinson and Basil Davidson used the term 'modern slavery' to bring the horrors of forced labour to the attention of an international audience.[6] Other observers pointed to a fundamental difference between contract labour and historical slavery. In their eyes, contract workers were treated like 'disposable people', to use the term by which activist and scholar Kevin Bales defines modern-day slavery.[7] For instance, American sociologist Edward Ross, when visiting Angola in 1924, heard workers from Ambaca say they 'would rather be slaves than what they are now. As slaves they have value and are not underfed, but now nobody cares whether they live or die.'[8] These contemporary critiques set the tone for later academic discussions of Angolan labour history. In this context, scholars like Michel Cahen and Maria da Conceição Neto have suggested caution when comparing forced labour to slavery, noting that they substantially differed from one another in legal terms, scope, and method.[9]

6 Henry W. Nevinson, *A Modern Slavery* (New York: Harper Brothers Publishers, 1906); Basil Davidson, 'Africa's Modern Slavery', *Harper's Magazine,* 209:1250 (1954), 56–63.

7 Kevin Bales, *Disposable People: New Slavery in the Global Economy,* rev. edn (Berkeley: University of California Press, 2012).

8 Edward Alsworth Ross, *Report on Employment of Native Labour in Portuguese Africa* (New York: Abbott Press, 1925), p. 12. See also Henrique Galvão, *Santa Maria: My Crusade for Portugal* (Cleveland: World Publishing Company, 1961), p. 64.

9 Michel Cahen, 'Seis teses sobre o trabalho forçado no império português continental em África', *África* (São Paulo), 35 (2015), 129–55; Maria da Conceição Neto,

In a fresh departure from these established debates, recent research in Portugal has focused attention on long-term continuities in the racialist ideologies underpinning the country's forced labour policies in Africa. These studies have shown how a new colonial dogma of civilizational guardianship grew out of the abolition of slavery in Portuguese Africa, echoing experiences in the Colony of Sierra Leone earlier in the century.[10] The question at the heart of this new scholarship is to what extent the Portuguese government adjusted its approach to solving labour shortages in the colonies to placate international criticism. Analysing political debates in Lisbon, João Pedro Marques has argued that radical Smithian ideas of free labour barely played a role in nineteenth-century Portuguese discourse about abolition. The measures Portugal introduced in Africa in response to British pressures to emancipate the enslaved were primarily designed to appease slaveowners. The Marquis of Sá da Bandeira, Portugal's main architect of abolition, was convinced that Africans would supply their labour freely if employers offered attractive wages, as the 'desire to own goods would create the necessity to work'. But the view that coercion was necessary to make Africans productive prevailed.[11] As legal enslavement became increasingly indefensible after mid-century, slavery in Portuguese Africa gradually made way for colonial guardianship, a system that made sure freed persons remained tied to their former masters as *libertos* (freed Africans) for a period of at least seven years. To underline the continuity with slavery, in 1864, the Minister of the Colonies, José da Silva Mendes Leal, explained that 'labour can be compulsory without being slavery'. In 1875, compulsory contracts for freed Africans replaced the *liberto* apprenticeship arrangements, until legislation in 1878 abolished all forms of servitude. Although the new labour regulations banned the notion of bonded labour, they introduced five-year contracts and the legal tool of vagrancy to keep Africans from abandoning their former enslavers.[12]

'De Escravos a "Serviçais", de "Serviçais" a "Contratados": Omissões, perceções e equívocos na história do trabalho africano na Angola colonial', *Cadernos de Estudos Africanos*, 33 (2017), 107–29.

10 Padraic X. Scanlan, 'The Colonial Rebirth of British Anti-Slavery: The Liberated African Villages of Sierra Leone, 1815–1824', *American Historical Review*, 121:4 (2016), 1085–113.

11 Bernardo de Sá Nogueira de Figueiredo Sá da Bandeira, *O trabalho rural africano e a administração colonial* (Lisbon: Imprensa Nacional, 1873), p. 73. For the opposite view, see Antonio Leite Mendes, *Abolição da escravatura em Angola e organisação do trabalho* (Lisbon: Typographia Jornal de Lisboa, 1867).

12 João Pedro Marques, *Sá da Bandeira e o fim da escravidão: Vitoria da moral, desforra do interesse* (Lisbon: Imprensa de Ciencias Sociais, 2008), quote at p. 106. For an overview of labour laws, see Margarida Seixas, 'O trabalho escravo e o trabalho forçado na colonização portuguesa oitocentista: Uma análise histórico-jurídica', *Revista Portuguesa de História*, 46 (2015), 217–36.

In Angola these colonial policies mainly concerned an enslaved population of approximately 66,000 men and women in 1856, reduced to 42,000 by 1866.[13] This was just a fragment of the Angolan population. Nevertheless, the ideology of guardianship underpinning the transition out of slavery influenced the legal framework of contract labour, which would affect a much larger populace during the twentieth century. As Miguel Bandeira Jerónimo has argued, Portugal kept referring to its civilizational duty in Africa when the ways colonial governments facilitated recruitment for private enterprise came under increasing international scrutiny in the early twentieth century. The standard Portuguese reply to outside criticism was that neither the foundational labour code of 1899, nor its revision in 1914, allowed the use of coercion in labour contracting, but colonial administrators could legitimately enforce the 'obligation to work' that these laws had imposed on African subjects. Indeed, to the damning report on the labour situation in Portuguese Africa that Edward Ross submitted to the League of Nations in 1925, Portuguese officials responded that 'if labour must be free, then idleness must not have the same privilege', wilfully ignoring that low remuneration was the main cause of African resistance to waged employment.[14]

The labour code of 1928, which provided the legal basis for the mass conscription of contract labour, addressed international concerns about forced labour in the Portuguese colonies by banning government recruitment for private enterprise, articulating the freedom of workers to choose their employer, and establishing a minimum wage. However, the 'moral duty to work' remained a central tenet of the law. Meanwhile, by setting the minimum wage as a percentage of annual taxation, the government ensured that a significant number of Africans had no choice but to accept waged employment in the colonial economy for at least part of the year. Significantly, Portugal refused to sign the International Labour Organization's (ILO) Forced Labour Convention of 1930 until 1956. As José Pedro Monteiro has demonstrated, after the Second World War, discussions with the ILO had a profound impact on internal Portuguese debates about forced labour in the colonies. But despite growing concerns within imperial ranks about the systemic abuse of African workers and the continued involvement of colonial administrators in private-sector recruitment, official policies changed little before 1962, when Portugal abolished the *Indigenato*, or 'native' code, which provided a legal basis for forced labour. Until then, Portuguese officials continued to defend their increasingly archaic labour regime by referring

13 Arquivo Histórico Ultramarino (Lisbon, henceforth AHU), Secretaria de Estado da Marinha e Ultramar (SEMU), Direcção Geral do Ultramar (DGU), Angola, no. 638/2, 'Nota demonstrativa do número de escravos'; *BOA*, 7 (16 Feb. 1867), 76–7.

14 Miguel Bandeira Jerónimo, *The 'Civilising' Mission of Portuguese Colonialism, 1870–1930* (Basingstoke: Palgrave Macmillan, 2015), quote at p. 183. For this period, see also Valdemir Zamparoni, 'Da escravatura ao trabalho forçado: Teorias e práticas', *Africana Studia*, 7 (2004), 299–325.

to an imaginary psychological disposition that gave black Africans an aversion to work. This, in their view, warranted the treatment of Africans as a separate legal category – 'indigenous subjects' instead of 'civilized citizens' – to whom post-war doctrines of universality and equality did not apply.[15]

These studies show that racist notions of civilizational guardianship and developmental correction informed Portuguese colonial attitudes toward African labour throughout the nineteenth and twentieth centuries. Portugal toed the international line by legally abolishing slavery in its empire in 1869 and all forms of servitude in 1878. However, longer than most colonial powers in Africa, Portugal kept exploiting the muddled boundaries between free and coerced labour, always referring to African 'idleness' when pressed to defend its policies, even after theories of racial differentiation had lost international currency during the Second World War.[16] Moreover, systemic inability to enforce laws that prohibited coercion in labour contracting and government intervention in private-sector recruitment meant that abusive practices went by and large unchecked. Labour regimes in Angola changed as colonial rule progressed, but the adjustment of workers' legal status from enslaved, to freed, to servant initially appeared to have little impact on local labour relations. A study of the coffee estates, the largest plantation sector in the country, will demonstrate that slavery continued with minor adjustments until the 1910s, when the new Republican administration implemented the contract system designed in previous decades.

Legal and illegal slavery

For much of the nineteenth century, commercial agriculture in Angola's nascent settler economy fundamentally depended on slave labour.[17] Until the abolition of slavery in 1869, few people in Portuguese imperial ranks found this problematic and most thought it was inevitable if plantation agriculture had to be the new foundation of Angola's export economy in lieu of the slave trade. For example, in 1839, the colonial traveller and later governor of Angola Pedro Alexandrino da Cunha told the emancipationist former Prime Minister Sá da Bandeira that, although the export slave trade was rightfully banned, 'slavery within [Angola] will have to continue' because, he argued, 'from free blacks you will never draw much labour'. Recasting economic development as a racial problem, da Cunha

15 José Pedro Monteiro, *Portugal e a questão do trabalho forçado: Um império sob escrutínio (1944–1962)* (Lisbon: Edições 70, 2018).

16 Daniel Roger Maul, 'The International Labour Organization and the Struggle against Forced Labour from 1919 to the Present', *Labour History*, 48:4 (2007), 477–500.

17 Roquinaldo Ferreira, 'Agricultural Enterprise and Unfree Labour in Nineteenth-Century Angola', in Robin Law *et al.* (eds), *Commercial Agriculture, the Slave Trade and Slavery in Atlantic Africa* (Woodbridge: James Currey, 2013), pp. 225–42.

placed the blame for the slow pace of legitimate commerce in Angola specifically on African producers. In his opinion, they were non-responsive to economic incentives, particularly because they lacked material needs, an argument apologists of forced labour would often regurgitate.[18] Around the same time, the military officer and colonial statistician José Joaquim Lopes de Lima expected slave labour to be more cheaply available in Angola when captives were no longer traded to the Americas, and that was a good thing. In a well-known treatise first published in 1844, Lopes de Lima predicted that, if the illegal slave trade to Brazil were successfully suppressed, slave owners in Angola would use their captives for domestic production instead. 'The number of slaves [in Angola] should increase as soon as the inhabitants of our cities and inland districts decide to build plantations rivalling those of Brazil.'[19]

The view that Angolan economic development should follow the Brazilian model of slavery-based plantation agriculture was widely accepted.[20] However, the predicted retention of captives for domestic agriculture and industry did not immediately materialize after the closing of the export slave trade. Commodity production remained sluggish throughout the 1850s, leading some slaveowners to ship their human property illegally to São Tomé, where demand and prices for enslaved people were higher than in Angola.[21] The forecast of settler dependence on slavery was nevertheless correct. This scenario played out most notoriously in the coffee districts of Cazengo and Golungo Alto, the main centres of European agricultural enterprise in Angola until the early twentieth century. Responding to a rally in world coffee prices in the late 1850s, planters in both regions expanded production by adding privately purchased enslaved people and publicly provisioned *libertos* to their workforce, with the larger estates employing somewhere between two and four hundred enslaved workers in 1867.[22] For seasonal tasks, especially harvesting and replanting, settlers received support from local government officials who requisitioned temporary labour from local

18 AHU, SEMU-DGU, Angola, no. 825, P. A. da Cunha to Sá da Bandeira, Luanda, 4 June 1839.

19 José Joaquim Lopes de Lima, *Ensaios sobre a statística das possessões portuguezas na África occidental e oriental, na Ásia occidental, na China e na Oceania* (3 vols, Lisbon: Imprensa Nacional, 1844–46), vol 3, p. 7. See also Mariana Pinho Candido, *Wealth, Land, and Property in Angola: A History of Dispossession, Slavery, and Inequality* (Cambridge: Cambridge University Press, 2022), pp. 74–5.

20 Clarence-Smith, *The Third Portuguese Empire, 1825–1975: A Study in Economic Imperialism* (Manchester: Manchester University Press, 1985), p. 2.

21 James Duffy, *A Question of Slavery* (Oxford: Clarendon Press, 1967), p. 34; Jelmer Vos and Paulo Teodoro de Matos, 'The Demography of Slavery in the Coffee Districts of Angola, c. 1800–70', *JAH*, 62:2 (2021), 213–34.

22 Aida Freudenthal, *Arimos e fazendas: A transição agrária em Angola* (Luanda: Chá de Caxinde, 2005), p. 234; AHU, SEMU-DGU, Angola, no. 825, Arsénio P. P. de Carpo to Luís [Travassos] Valdez, Lisbon, 20 May 1863.

village chiefs, ostensibly in exchange for wages.[23] Reliance on bondage was so prevalent that Britain's main diplomat in Angola, Edmund Gabriel, doubted in 1858 'whether any large plantations would be made ... without having recourse to slave labour'.[24] In 1869, enslaved people were given the official status of *libertos*, but that did little to change their captivity.

The labour laws of 1875 and 1878 announced a legal end to servitude in Portuguese Africa and replaced the *liberto* regime with a system of contract labour. This apparently had little effect in Luanda, where an illicit trade in *liberto* services continued openly, including sales to coffee planters in the interior.[25] But from Cazengo came rumours that plantation owners had secured continuing rights over the labour of their former slaves, now called *serviçais*, by offering them small grants of land and token wages.[26] For the settlers, this was an affordable solution to the threat of workers leaving the plantations, while for many *serviçais* these small improvements in their lives on the plantation looked better than the alternative of a precarious existence on the outside. But to the extent that these arrangements existed, they had little to do with free labour. Everyone knew that few Africans signed labour contracts of their own volition and understood their contracts were time-bound. Slaveowners were too stuck in 'the sad tradition of yesteryear', as one Angolan official put it, to see any value in provisions that would not guarantee them long-term rights over African labour.[27]

The coffee estates continued to replenish their workforce by purchasing people in the market of Dondo, on the Cuanza River, where a government agency registered trafficked young men and women as purportedly 'free' contract workers. The causes that used to push vulnerable people into slavery were now driving them into the hands of labour recruiters: debt, famine, misdemeanours, witchcraft accusations, and the greed of village chiefs.[28] Portuguese officials were fully aware of these similarities and in the early years referred to recruitment as ransoming (*resgate*). As the head of the labour office (*Curado-*

23 AHU, SEMU-DGU, Angola, no. 622/2, Petition, Cazengo, 29 Sep. 1856, enclosed in GG to MSENMU, Luanda, 30 Dec. 1856; *Jornal da Sociedade Agrícola do Porto*, ser. 4, 10 (1861), 291–2.

24 The National Archives (Kew, henceforth TNA), FO84/1043, Gabriel to Clarendon, no. 25, Luanda, 3 April 1858.

25 Duffy, *Question*, p. 63; Mário António de Oliveira, 'Para a história de trabalho em Angola', *Trabalho*, 2 (Luanda, 1963), offprint.

26 TNA, FO84/1448, Carnegie to FO, no. 1, Luanda, 9 March 1876; AHU, SEMU, Angola, no. 829, Curador geral to MSENMU, no. 82, Luanda, 29 Aug. 1876.

27 AHU, SEMU-DGU, Angola, no. 646-2, Curador geral to MSENMU, no. 31, Luanda, 29 July 1876. Planter obduracy was transatlantic. See Richard Follett, 'Legacies of Enslavement: Plantation Identities and the Problem of Freedom', in Richard Follett, Eric Foner, and Walter Jonson, *Slavery's Ghost: The Problem of Freedom in the Age of Emancipation* (Baltimore: Johns Hopkins University Press, 2011), pp. 50–84.

28 Duffy, *Question*, pp. 81–2, 100, 180.

ria) in Angola, Francisco António Pinto, explained to the Minister of Colonies in Lisbon in 1878, in the eyes of the African trader 'who gives us the *serviçal* in ransom, this act is pure slavery ... for his part, there is no difference between ransoming with us and trafficking with others'.[29] Pinto's predecessor in the labour office feared that Portuguese recruitment encouraged African authorities to enslave by orchestrating witchcraft trials and other judicial proceedings.[30]

According to the British consul in Luanda, Cohen, who visited Dondo and Cazengo in 1880, many of the plantation workers hailed from the Libolo region immediately south of the Cuanza River and had been sold by their chiefs to labour hustlers with ties to local Portuguese authorities. Upon arrival at the estates, overseers housed the *serviçais* in barracks, separating men from women, and seasoned them to fieldwork. When sufficiently accustomed to the plantation labour regime, workers received their own homes as well as weekly wages – supposedly half in cash and half in rations, although cash tended to be currency for exclusive use in the plantation store, where workers could buy rum, cottons, and special foods like tinned meat.[31] The new head of the labour office, Sebastião Rodrigues Barbosa Centeno, claimed that in general salaries were paid regularly, with some planters paying more than the legally required minimum, although others paid less.[32] In theory, Cohen continued, the workweek consisted of five days, giving *serviçais* two days to tend to their own crops. 'In general, they appeared happy and contented', he reflected in a cautiously optimistic tone. But, he added, 'knowing they were bought, they do not look forward to any other position or future than being bondspeople of their employers'. In fact, Cohen was more concerned about recruitment practices than about conditions on the plantations. He was convinced that 'children and adults are obtained by barter, and this practice ... if not an actual traffic in [enslaved people], is tantamount to slavery'.[33]

Rising coffee prices in the late 1880s initiated a fresh wave of settler competition for land and labour in the Luanda hinterland. Every year, hundreds of *serviçais*, recruited in Libolo, Bailundo, and further afield, were added to the Cazengo

29 AHU, SEMU-DGU, Angola, 2ª Repartição, no. 830, Curador geral to MSENMU, Luanda, 30 Dec. 1878.

30 AHU, SEMU-DGU, Angola, 2ª Repartição, no. 828, Curador geral to SG, no. 182, Luanda, 25/4/77. For political discourse on slavery and witchcraft, see João de Castro Maia Veiga de Figueiredo, 'Política, escravatura e feitiçaria em Angola (séculos XVIII e XIX)' (Unpublished PhD dissertation, University of Coimbra, 2016), <http://hdl.handle.net/10316/29906>.

31 Manuel José Martins Contreiras, *A província de Angola* (Lisbon: La Bécarre, 1894), pp. 58–9; Nevinson, *Modern Slavery*, p. 20.

32 AHU, SEMU-DGU, Angola, 2ª Repartição, no. 832, Curador geral to MSENMU, no. 3, Cazengo, 13 July 1881; no. 4, Cazengo, 22 July 1881.

33 TNA, FO541/48, p. 190, no. 167, Cohen to Earl Granville, no. 3, Luanda, 20 July 1880.

estates and ostensibly placed on salaried contracts.[34] To mitigate seasonal labour shortages, the district government furthermore assigned African military recruits and pressed free villagers into temporary wage labour on nearby plantations. At the height of the first coffee boom, in 1895, twenty-eight plantations together employed 3,798 *serviçais* on five-year contracts as well as 850 workers drafted locally.[35] Labour registers in Angolan archives give the appearance of a methodically enforced recruitment system, detailing workers by number, name, employer, term of service, and monthly wages. These ledgers demonstrate that the movement of *serviçais* to the coffee estates was a relatively minor branch of a much larger migration flow from the Angolan central highlands to São Tomé.[36] However, a crucial identifier of workers, the names of their parents, an essential link for their eventual return home, was generally missing. This indicated that most *serviçais* were recruited under conditions analogous to slavery and were expected to remain on the plantations indefinitely. To cut recruitment costs, estate managers used to recontract workers without their consent, a method also used by cocoa planters in São Tomé.[37] In addition to automatic rehiring, other similarities between contract labour and slavery included the use of gang labour for field clearing and pressing children born on the plantations into servitude.[38]

The coffee estates and their enslaved populations were described in detail by medical officer Alberto de Souza Maia Leitão, who visited the Golungo Alto and Cazengo districts around the turn of 1901 to examine the demographic impact of an ongoing sleeping sickness epidemic. Most of the estates seen by Leitão had populations of twenty to a hundred *serviçais,* while only a handful, like Colónia São João, Prototypo, Monte Alegre, and Monte Bello, had more than a hundred in their employ. *Serviçal* was still a euphemism for 'slave', as a couple of planters revealed by saying they did not employ *serviçais* but only free people (*forros*) and day labourers (*gente de ganho*). The enslaved lived permanently on the plantations, either in designated quarters or in their own villages, and many were born and raised there. Generally, women outnumbered men, mirroring the feminization of agricultural work witnessed on Caribbean coffee plantations in the early nineteenth century. As in the Caribbean, children over five were expected to work. Sleeping sickness, smallpox, jigger, dysentery, anaemia, pneumonia, and diarrhoea

34 Arquivo Nacional de Angola (Luanda, henceforth ANA), códice no. 3388, Delegação da Curadoria Geral, registos de contratos effectuados, Cazengo, pp. 1887–904.

35 David Birmingham, 'The Coffee Barons of Cazengo', *JAH*, 19:4 (1978), 523–38, at p. 529; Great Britain, Foreign Office, *Report for the Year 1908 on the Trade of the Province of Angola* (London: HMSO, 1909), p. 40.

36 ANA, caixa 130, Registo de contratados, 1886–8. Contreiras, *Província*, p. 90, argues that Angolan planters often had to settle for second choice in terms of selection.

37 William Gervase Clarence-Smith, 'Labour Conditions in the Plantations of São Tomé and Príncipe, 1875–1914', *Slavery & Abolition*, 14:1 (1993), 149–67.

38 Duffy, *Question*, pp. 100, 188–9; Nevinson, *Modern Slavery*, pp. 33–8.

were common diseases that either killed or incapacitated workers, with plantations experiencing annual death rates as high as 10 per cent. Because of the slump in world coffee prices, the plantations were no longer expanding. However, several tried to maintain production levels by replacing deceased workers and runaways with new recruits from Libolo, Quiçama, and Bailundo.[39]

The labour regulations of the 1870s had ushered in a system of legalized human trafficking, which alarmed British humanitarians when it became clear this system enabled the large-scale shipment of *serviçais* from Angola to the cocoa plantations of São Tomé and Príncipe.[40] Portuguese officials knew straight away that the new regulations would raise suspicions internationally. In defence, some pointed out that contract labour liberated Africans from slavery by 'putting them under the protection of laws that guarantee their freedom', echoing the arguments of French officials around 1860 who tried to shield the recruitment of so-called labour migrants (*émigrés*) in the Congo River against accusations that it perpetuated the local slave trade.[41] But others harboured concerns about the political fallout of the new labour laws. In 1877, the recently appointed governor of Angola Caetano Alexandre de Almeida e Albuquerque observed that 'the recruitment of [Africans] is nothing more than the buying and selling of them', warning his superiors in Lisbon that, when brought to light, this practice would harm Portugal's international reputation.[42] Little would change until the early twentieth century, when a labour scandal in the 'chocolate islands' of São Tomé and Príncipe forced Portugal to suppress slavery in its colonies.[43]

39 Alberto de Souza Maia Leitão, *Relatório da visita sanitária aos concelhos de leste de Loanda mais victimados pela doença de somno* (Porto: Typ. a vapor da Empreza Litteraria e Typographica, 1901), pp. 18–72. On mortality, see also Maria Eugénia Mata *et al.*, 'Success and Failure in Portuguese Colonial Africa: The Case of the Cazengo Agricultural Company (1900–1945)', *Entreprises et histoire*, 3:88 (2017), 53–73, at p. 58. For Caribbean comparisons, see James A. Delle, 'Women's Lives and Labour on Radnor, a Jamaican Coffee Plantation, 1822–1826', *Caribbean Quarterly*, 48:4 (2002), 27–40, at pp. 28–9; William C. Van Norman, Jr, *Shade-Grown Slavery: The Lives of Slaves on Coffee Plantations in Cuba* (Nashville: Vanderbilt University Press, 2013), pp. 44–62.

40 Kevin Grant, *A Civilised Savagery: Britain and the New Slaveries in Africa, 1884–1926* (New York: Routledge, 2005).

41 AHU, SEMU-DGU, Angola, no. 645-1, GG interino, José Baptista de Andrade to MSENMU, no. 36, Luanda, 20 Feb. 1875; Jelmer Vos, '"Without the Slave Trade, No Recruitment": From Slave Trading to "Migrant Recruitment" in the Lower Congo, 1830–1890', in Benjamin N. Lawrance and Richard L. Roberts (eds), *Trafficking in Slavery's Wake: Law and the Experiences of Women and Children in Africa* (Athens: Ohio University Press, 2012), pp. 45–64.

42 AHU, SEMU, Angola, no. 829, GG to MSENMU, confidential, Luanda, 26 April 1877; confidential, Luanda, 26 Oct. 1877.

43 Catherine Higgs, *Chocolate Islands: Cocoa, Slavery, and Colonial Africa* (Athens: Ohio University Press, 2013).

The end of slavery

The establishment of the First Republic in Portugal in 1910 ushered in the end of human trafficking in the colonies. Republican administrators oversaw the effective occupation of Angola, pushed through an array of administrative and legal changes, and were fervent opponents of slavery. Indeed, historians have often credited the Republican government for introducing new legislation to curtail the illegal enslavement of Africans and trying to enforce the freedom of contract enshrined in the labour code of 1899.[44] However, there were several contemporaneous developments motivating the Portuguese government to act. First, growing anxiety in Europe about labour abuses in the African colonies forced imperial governments to stamp out coercive practices that had the whiff of slavery. In this context, Portugal was compelled to interrupt the recruitment of indentured labourers for the cocoa plantations in São Tomé and Príncipe in 1909 because of clear signs it involved slave ransoming in Angola and the enslavement of workers in the archipelago. Especially after Protestant missionaries and the British Anti-Slavery Society began to scrutinize labour conditions in Angola, the recruitment system on which the coffee plantations in Cazengo and Golungo Alto depended became increasingly difficult to sustain.[45] At the same time, through a series of military campaigns, the colonial state extended its control of African populations far beyond the old proto-colonial enclaves. As a result, the state's capacity to press Africans into low-paid contracts increased just as the lull in the flow of indentured servants to São Tomé freed up workers in Angola. Government support reduced European settlers' dependence on Angola's once extensive trafficking networks.[46]

The growing power of the colonial state ensured labour supplies were relatively cheap and forthcoming, which allowed the contract system to work. Nev-

44 William Gervase Clarence, 'Capital Accumulation and Class Formation in Angola', in David Birmingham and Phyllis M. Martin (eds), *History of Central Africa, Volume Two* (London: Longman, 1983), pp. 163–99, at pp. 168, 179; Douglas L. Wheeler, 'The Forced Labour "System" in Angola, 1903–1947: Reassessing Origins and Persistence in the Context of Colonial Consolidation, Economic Growth and Reform Failures', in Centro de Estudos Africanos da Universidade do Porto (ed.), *Trabalho forçado africano: Experiências coloniais comparadas* (Porto: Campo das Letras, 2006), pp. 367–93, at p. 372; Maria Cândida Proença, 'A questão colonial', in Fernando Rosas e Maria Fernanda Rollo (eds), *História da Primeira República Portuguesa* (Lisbon: Tinta-da-China, 2009), pp. 205–28, at p. 223.

45 Duffy, *Question*, p. 225; Clarence-Smith, 'Labour Conditions'; Suzanne Miers, *Slavery in the Twentieth Century: The Evolution of a Global Problem* (Walnut Creek: AltaMira Press, 2003), pp. 47–53.

46 René Pélissier, *História das campanhas de Angola: Resistência e revoltas 1845–1941* (Lisbon: Editorial Estampa, 1997); Jelmer Vos, *Kongo in the Age of Empire, 1860–1913: The Breakdown of a Moral Order* (Madison: University of Wisconsin Press, 2015), pp. 109–27.

ertheless, government intervention was necessary to break old recruitment habits, as a conflict between the newly created Department of Native Affairs (*Negócios Indígenas*) and the Cazengo Agricultural Company demonstrated. Incorporating the older office of the *Curadoria Geral*, Native Affairs became, from 1913, the agency overseeing the mobilization of labour in the colonial economy. It issued licences to recruitment agents and, based on population censuses and employer needs, indicated where and how many workers these agents were allowed to recruit. The department's first director, José de Oliveira Ferreira Diniz, intended to make a clean break with the past, when colonial laws and policies helped businesses keep hold of their former slaves and *libertos*.[47] A main beneficiary of the old regime was the Cazengo Company, one of the largest employers of African labour in Angola, whose practice of involuntary rehiring continued unchecked into the 1910s. Company records from the early twentieth century demonstrate that the firm kept a relatively stable workforce of fifteen hundred *serviçais* on its coffee plantations, as many were permanently settled on company grounds and contracts were automatically renewed. Meanwhile, workers dying from disease, hard labour, or poor diet were replaced by new recruits at a cost of a hundred *milreis* (about twenty pounds sterling) each. The company needed a stable workforce to maintain production, especially in times of slump when minimizing losses caused by the high fixed costs of the plantations was imperative.[48]

Diniz first became aware of possible labour abuses in 1913, when his office received complaints from a group of Libolo workers that the company was holding them on the plantations against their will. When questioned about this, the local manager, Alberto de Pastro Ferreira, claimed that the Libolos had entered their contracts voluntarily, that some returned home when their terms of employment expired, and that those who re-contracted were informed about their legal rights. They were protesting, Ferreira argued, mainly because they saw that fellow countrymen recruited by the government for work on the Golungo branch of the Ambaca railway, running through company lands, were paid higher salaries. Ferreira insisted the company could not afford to pay more. He added that plantation wages of sixteen cents per day, with incremental bonuses during the coffee harvest, were fair and comparable to what landlords in the Alentejo region of Portugal paid to migrant labourers from the northern Beira district.[49] Ferreira was stretching the truth on all accounts, most importantly regarding recruitment and rehiring. Contracting in the Libolo region took place at the

47 Angola, *Negócios Indígenas: Relatório do ano de 1913* (Luanda: Imprensa Nacional, 1914), pp. 54–6, 68–9.

48 Companhia Agrícola de Cazengo, *Relatório da Companhia Agricola de Cazengo do anno de 1908* (Lisbon: Typ. A. M. Antunes, 1909); *Relatório da Companhia Agricola de Cazengo do anno de 1909* (Lisbon: Typ. Sport, 1910).

49 ANA, caixa 2924, Secretaria dos Negócios Indígenas, processo no. 209, Inquérito sobre as condições de trabalho indígena, Cazengo (1913).

behest of the government, which passed on labour demands from Cazengo planters to local administrators, who in turn engaged village chiefs. Escapes during transit and after showed that many workers resented their recruitment. Indeed, Libolos and other migrants frequently voted with their feet to resist work on the Cazengo plantations.[50]

Colonial labour regulations issued in 1914 required the Cazengo Company to renegotiate the contracts of all *serviçais* whose employment terms expired the following year. The company planned to do this informally, that is, by verbal agreement and without seeking the authorization of the local *curador*, the government agent charged with ratifying labour contracts. At this point, Diniz intervened, arguing that the company's conduct amounted to re-contracting, which was illegal. Diniz wanted the practice of verbal contracts to end and have all workers placed on written ones. He therefore instructed the company to formally rehire all workers who wished to remain on the plantations, and to do this in accordance with the new law, which stipulated shorter contracts, a nine-hour workday, and a 5 per cent wage increase. Moreover, he told the company to either repatriate or resettle those who wished to leave. He also insisted that salaries be calculated monthly, including rest days, against the company's current cost-cutting practice of paying workers for 'effective working days', as if they were all day labourers.[51]

The new company manager, José Caetano de Almeida Costa Real, decided to appeal against Diniz's order to reform expiring contracts and repatriate some of the workers. In his statement to the Angolan government, Real explained that verbal agreements were the most convenient way of re-contracting, for workers and management. Many workers had settled on company lands and, indeed, some were even born there. They considered these lands their home and, according to Real, could not imagine working anywhere else. There was therefore no need to formalize the existing informal arrangements. Furthermore, offering formal contracts to workers in accordance with the new regulations would increase wages to unsustainable levels, especially as coffee prices were falling. Finally, Real argued that repatriation and resettlement were unrealistic scenarios.

50 ANA, caixa 2925, Secretário geral do governo to Circunscrição administrativa do Libolo, no. 2072, 11 Oct. 1910; ANA, códice no. 8383, Administração do concelho de Cazengo, Registo de telegramas expedidos, 1917–18; ANA, códice no. 8376, Administração do concelho de Cazengo, Registo de telegramas recebidos, 1918–19; Angola, *Negócios Indígenas: Relatório do ano de 1916* (Lisbon: Typ. do Annuario Commercial, 1917), p. 11. On Beira migrants in Alentejo, see José da Silva Picão, *Através dos campos: Usos e costumes agrícolo-alentejanos* (Lisbon: Etnográfica Press, 1983), pp. 225–45. See also Conceição Andrade Martins, 'Trabalho e condições de vida em Porugal (1850–1913)', *Análise Social*, 32:142 (1997), 483–535.

51 ANA, caixa 385, Diniz to Agente do curador em Dondo, no. 18/797, circular, Luanda, 10 Aug. 1916.

Even if workers wanted to leave their jobs, most would not have a home to return to and would also find it difficult to settle elsewhere in the country.

The government's advisory council partially sided with the Cazengo Company, but ultimately rejected the appeal. Contrary to Diniz's views, they agreed that verbal agreements were a legitimate form of contracting, although they added that the authorities should intervene if the execution of such contracts was found to be illegal or unethical. On the question of wages, most council members argued that *serviçais* already working for the company should not receive higher wages unless they claimed them. They thus valued the economic health of the company over the wellbeing of its workers but recognized that denying *serviçais* the wages they were legally entitled to was impossible. In the end, the company was forced to release part of its workforce.[52]

As the government clamped down on automatic rehiring, the end of slavery in Cazengo and Golungo Alto was in sight. A new system of recruitment emerged, which was nonetheless rooted in earlier ways of labour procurement. Migrants from the central highlands, hired on fixed-term contracts, filled a large part of the labour needs of European coffee plantations, while colonial administrators conscripted local villagers to meet seasonal demand.[53] While long-term captivity on the plantations became uncommon, coercion still played a role in recruitment despite legislation to reduce it. The debate between apologists and critics of forced recruitment echoed nineteenth-century discussions about African attitudes to work. Employers who wanted the state to mobilize labour on their behalf argued that Africans were averse to physical exertion and that coercion was therefore inevitable. But according to Diniz, much-maligned labour shortages in Angola were mainly caused by wages that were unattractive to workers who could 'obtain better profits by their own means [*motu proprio*]'.[54] Intentionally or not, Diniz highlighted the challenge that independent African farmers posed to the viability of large-scale European agriculture in Angola. Settler estates could only survive if the colonial state was willing to support them with affordable supplies of labour forcibly extracted from African economies.

Old and new forms of coercion

As plantation agriculture expanded in Angola during the twentieth century, contract labour replaced slavery as the dominant mode of labour mobilization. This change followed a global trend in labour regimes emerging in the wake of abolition,

52 ANA, caixa 206, Secretaria geral do governo, processo no. 825, Recurso da Companhia Agrícola de Cazengo sobre recontrato de serviçais, 1915; Angola, *Negócios Indígenas: Relatório do ano de 1915* (Lisbon: Tipografia Universal, 1918), pp. 20–5.

53 Angola, *Negócios Indígenas: Relatório do ano de 1913*, pp. 55, 60–1, 84; *Relatório do ano de* 1914 (Luanda: Imprensa Nacional, 1915), p. 115; *Relatório do ano de 1915*, pp. 18–19; *Relatório do ano de 1916*, p. 11.

54 Angola, *Negócios Indígenas: Relatório do ano de 1916*, pp. 8–10, quote at p. 10.

as the contract became a common mechanism to extract labour from workers who were defined as 'free' on the one hand but as 'servants' on the other.[55] Michel Cahen has argued that in the Portuguese empire compulsory contracts were a radically new form of organizing labour, dictated by the needs of large export-oriented agrarian companies. In his view, plantation-based labour coercion barely existed in Portuguese Africa before the rise of the modern colonial state and the development of capitalist enterprise.[56] However, commercial farms worked by enslaved Africans were widespread in nineteenth-century Angola. The later expansion of coerced labour was, therefore, not a 'rupture' with the past. In fact, the notion of guardianship that underpinned the transition to contract labour was primarily an ideological response to the supply problems the plantocracy experienced after the abolition of slavery.[57] But, in addition to the growing racialization of European discourse on labour productivity in the colonies, there was another, more fundamental, continuity between the two eras. Contract labour had a concrete historical precedent in the age-old system of labour requisitioning for porterage, roadwork, and military service, which was integral to Portuguese proto-colonial rule in Angola. Like contract labour, this system was based on the notion that all Africans, not just the enslaved, were eligible for compulsory labour.

Labour shortages were a vexing issue for settlers and politicians in Angola long before African labour became a 'problem' for twentieth-century imperial rulers. From the beginning of Portuguese settlement in Africa, colonial governments and businesses experienced difficulties in attracting workers for transport jobs, infrastructural projects, and military service. The wealthy Luso-African residents (*moradores*) of Portugal's proto-colonial enclaves in the Angolan interior owned enslaved people, but they typically employed them in permanent occupations, for instance as field workers or skilled craftsmen. For fear of capital losses, they avoided using the enslaved to man their trade caravans, relying instead on the capacity of the local Portuguese authorities, the *capitaes-mores*, to requisition labour from chiefs. The government also conscripted villagers for roadwork, building projects, and military service. These different kinds of forced labour went under the collective name of 'porter service' (*serviço de carreto*).[58]

55 Amy Dru Stanley, *From Bondage to Contract: Wage Labor, Marriage, and the Market in the Age of Slave Emancipation* (Cambridge: Cambridge University Press, 1998), pp. 1–26; Alessandro Stanziani, 'Introduction: Labour Institutions in a Global Perspective, from the Seventeenth to the Twentieth Century', *International Review of Social History*, 54 (2009), 351–8.

56 Cahen, 'Seis teses', 138.

57 Freudenthal, *Arimos*; Marques, *Sá da Bandeira*.

58 Joseph C. Miller, *Way of Death: Merchant Capitalism and the Angolan Slave Trade, 1730–1830* (Madison: University of Wisconsin Press, 1988), pp. 265, 268–73; Esteban Salas, 'Making Portuguese Colonial Governance: Slavery, Forced Labor, and Racial Ideology in the Interior from Benguela, 1760–1860' (Unpublished PhD dissertation, University of Notre Dame, 2021).

It was widely recognized that Africans abhorred forced porterage. In the early 1850s, for example, the inhabitants of Encoge resisted an order by the colonial administration to transport coffee loads of 45kg to Luanda and take the same weight in merchandise on the two-week return journey.[59] In fact, one Portuguese official who made this journey in 1854 wondered 'how you can force an [African] to carry 100 pounds of coffee on the terrible path I had to walk by'. His proposed solution was to exempt chiefs with proven loyalty to Portugal from this service.[60] Colonial rule in Angola became an exercise in balancing labour obligations for all with legal exemptions for the few.

The problem of compulsory labour in Angola became entrenched in Portuguese politics during the middle decades of nineteenth century. While generally accepting that coercion – rather than pay – was the most effective method to resolve labour shortages, politicians in Lisbon debated how the state could legitimately force nominally free Africans to work and whether private enterprise should have access to the coercive powers of the state. In 1839, the colonial ministry banned government recruitment of carriers for colonial traders, hoping this would force the latter to negotiate wages, although the ban had little effect on the behaviour of colonial officers on the ground.[61] At the same time, vagrancy became a key term in colonial discourse on African economic development. This was an elusive concept, but well into the twentieth century it helped Portuguese officials in their mental acrobatics to legitimize coercion.[62] In abstract terms, vagrancy was considered the anti-thesis of productivity. In practice, it was often measured by the capacity of Africans to pay colonial taxes. In 1840, the Portuguese Prime Minister, José Lúcio Travassos Valdez, decreed that vagrancy was a legitimate cause for compulsory wage labour in agriculture or porterage.[63]

When the institution of slavery came under attack during the 1850s, justifications for coerced labour in general were questioned. In 1856, Sá da Bandeira, in his position as Minister of the Colonies, took the drastic measure of abolishing

59 AHU, SEMU, Conselho Ultramarino, Processos de consultas, caixa 29, doc. 982, Francisco de Salles Ferreira to Sá da Bandeira, Lisbon, 8 Jan. 1856.

60 AHU, SEMU-DGU, Angola, no. 827, Carregadores, Extracto do diário da viagem feita pelo Mayor Salles Ferreira em dezembro de 1854 de Loanda a Encoge.

61 António Carreira, *Angola – da escravatura ao trabalho livre: Subsidios para a história demográfica do século XVI até à independência* (Lisbon: Arcadia 1977), pp. 97, 101.

62 Alexander Keese, 'The Constraints of Late Colonial Reform Policy: Forced Labour Scandals in the Portuguese Congo (Angola) and the Limits of Reform under Authoritarian Colonial Rule, 1955–61', *Portuguese Studies*, 28:2 (2012), 186–200, at p. 194; 'Searching for the Reluctant Hands: Obsession, Ambivalence and the Practice of Organising Involuntary Labour in Colonial Cuanza-Sul and Malange Districts, Angola, 1926–1945', *Journal of Imperial and Commonwealth History*, 41:2 (2013), 238–58.

63 AHU, SEMU-DGU, Angola, no. 592, Conde de Bonfim, no. 143, 13 July 1840; no. 443, Paço das Necessidades, 10 Oct. 1840.

compulsory porterage and all other forms of corvée labour, except for military service and road works. This legislation was ostensibly intended to encourage African cash-crop production by freeing up labour, but there was a caveat. Officials argued that labour withdrawn from forced porterage could become productive in local agriculture, but only if farmers and chiefs were given the right kind of fiscal encouragement. In districts like Cazengo and Golungo, the colonial authorities therefore increased taxes, which they expected chiefs to pay in crops like coffee and cotton, while non-payment was punishable with forced labour.[64] It was a public secret that administrators in these regions continued to supply colonial settlers with farmhands conscripted by force.[65]

The 1856 decree found support among smallholders and even among some larger planters. Cândido Fortunato da Costa, owner of the Aguas-doces plantation and chief administrator of the Cazengo district, argued that planters should not have to rely on the forced-porterage system, as they could easily 'ransom' enslaved people from the unoccupied interior of Angola. He compared the price of a captive with the cost of feeding a forced labourer and concluded the latter was higher, ignoring that captives also had to be fed unless they were given the opportunity to grow their own food. More convincing was his argument that relieving farmers from compulsory labour duties would free up energies for cash-crop production, benefiting the Angolan economy.[66] In most colonial circles, however, the abolition of forced porterage caused dismay. There were complaints from Dembos and Golungo Alto that carriers left their work and that products did not reach Luanda. Colonists unwilling to negotiate wages with village heads peddled old arguments against free labour, saying that Africans lacked material needs and had no interest in seeking paid work to raise their incomes above subsistence level.[67] In 1858, Sá da Bandeira responded to these pressures by refining his policy, on the one hand emphasizing that wages had to be freely negotiated, but on the other allowing that forced-labour penalties for substandard harvests could be used for the benefit of private enterprise.[68] As

64 Duffy, *Question*, pp. 16–18. Decree published in *BOA*, 603 (18 April 1857), 3, transcription in José de Almeida Santos, *Vinte anos decisivos da vida de uma cidade (1845/1864)* (Luanda: Câmara Municipal, 1970), doc. 293.

65 AHU, SEMU-DGU, no. 825; Sebastião Lopes de Calheiros e Menezes, *Relatório do Governador Geral da Provincia de Angola, referido ao anno de 1861* (Lisbon: Imprensa Nacional, 1867), p. 43.

66 Cândido Augusto Fortunato da Costa to GG, Cazengo, 2 Jan. 1857, transcription from *BOA*, 600 (28 March 1857), 2–4, in Filipe Martins Barbosa de Mascarenhas, *O outro lado da escravatura: Repressão e abolição do serviço de carregadores e do tráfico de escravos* (Luanda: edição do Autor, 2012), doc. 69.

67 AHU, SEMU-DGU, Angola, no. 825, Secretário de Estado dos Negócios da Marinha e Ultramar, synopse da portaria no. 198, 24 July 1857.

68 AHU, SEMU-DGU, Angola, no. 825, Sá da Bandeira, portaria 22 Sep. 1858. Transcription from *BOA*, 686 (20 Nov. 1858), 4–8, in Mascarenhas, *Outro lado*, doc. 66.

a result, coercion was still tolerated to extract labour from legally free African workers.

Although there were signs of an emerging wage economy in some colonial centres during the 1850s and 1860s, forced labour never went away.[69] Since the state retained the right to requisition workers for public purposes or punish tax defaulters, and local administrators were easily corruptible, labour coercion persisted in various manifestations into the twentieth century. A fundamental problem for free labour advocates was the belief permeating all colonial ranks that settler enterprise merited political intervention in African labour markets. In the nineteenth century, this view legitimized compulsory porterage; in the twentieth, it transformed parts of the contract labour system into forced recruitment. The results were at odds with Liberal visions of a colonial economy based on wage labour and a free African peasantry. As the Angolan writer José de Fontes Pereira told Sá da Bandeira in 1874, abolishing slavery was relatively straightforward; a far greater challenge was to protect the productive lives of free people from the demands of unscrupulous government agents.[70]

69 AHU, SEMU-DGU, Angola, no. 825, Diversos, Carregadores de Caboco, April 1868; *ibid.*, Arsénio P. P. de Carpo to Luís [Travassos] Valdez, Lisbon, 20 May 1863.

70 AHU, SEMU-DGU, Angola, no. 824, José de Fontes Pereira to Sá da Bandeira, Luanda, 23 March 1874.

6

'Slaves on Their Own Land'

THE COLONIAL conquest of Angola, largely complete by 1920, allowed the Portuguese government in Luanda to install a countrywide system to distribute low-wage contract labour, helping coffee estates expand in the face of smallholder competition.[1] The Department of Native Affairs (*Negócios Indígenas*) used tax rolls, census data, and labour requests supplied by district administrators to organize the movement of African wageworkers within and between colonial districts. The resulting labour flows often followed established geographical patterns, with the Angolan Central Plateau remaining an important source of migrant workers. Nevertheless, the scale and scope of recruitment expanded as a growing settler economy needed more labour and governments applied pecuniary and non-pecuniary measures to push an ever larger number of Angolans into wage contracts. While there were about ten thousand *serviçais* in the coffee sector around the turn of the century, the number of contract workers annually hired by European coffee planters had officially grown to ninety thousand in 1959.[2]

Since the introduction of contract labour in the Portuguese empire during the late nineteenth century, scholars and journalists have compared it to the

1 Arquivo Nacional de Angola (ANA), caixa 796, Repartição superior dos Negócios Indígenas, 3ª Secção, 'Registo dos trabalhadores indígenas fornecidos de uns para outros distritos, 1925'; Douglas L. Wheeler, 'The Forced Labour "System" in Angola, 1903–1947: Reassessing Origins and Persistence in the Context of Colonial Consolidation, Economic Growth and Reform Failures', in Centro de Estudos Africanos da Universidade do Porto (ed.), *Trabalho forçado africano: Experiências coloniais comparadas* (Porto: Campo das Letras, 2006), pp. 367–93, at p. 376.

2 For early figures, compare *BOA*, 42 (15 Oct. 1870), 596–7; Guilherme Augusto de Brito Capelo, *Relatório do Governador Geral da Província de Angola em 1887* (Lisbon: Imprensa Nacional, 1889), p. 40; Angola, *Negócios Indígenas: Relatório do ano de 1914* (Luanda: Imprensa Nacional, 1915), p. 115; David Birmingham, 'The Coffee Barons of Cazengo', *JAH*, 19:4 (1978), 523–38, at p. 529; Jill R. Dias, 'Changing Patterns of Power in the Luanda Hinterland: The Impact of Trade and Colonisation on the Mbundu ca. 1845–1920', *Paideuma: Mitteilungen zur Kulturkunde*, 32 (1986), 285–318, at p. 306. For 1959, see Angola, Repartição Central de Estatística Geral, *Anuário estatístico de Angola, ano de 1959* (Luanda: Imprensa Nacional, 1960).

system of bondage it replaced, variously describing it as 'modern slavery', 'slavery by another name', or 'forced labour'.[3] Historians of labour in colonial Africa generally prefer using the latter term. They emphasize that the direct involvement of colonial states in recruitment led to a variety of coercive practices that had little in common with enslavement defined narrowly in terms of ownership. Under colonial rule, as Suzanne Miers and Julia Seibert have shown, slavery gradually disappeared while new forms of coercion emerged, which could be crueller than slavery because employers no longer had to treat workers as capital assets.[4] This chapter proposes that neither slavery nor forced labour fully captures the complexity of the contract labour system. Contract labour involved different kinds of coercion, of which forced labour was one.[5]

In the Forced Labour Convention of 1930, the ILO defined forced labour as 'all work or service which is exacted from any person under the menace of any penalty and for which the said person has not offered himself voluntarily'.[6] The notion of work under threat of 'penalty' alluded to the growing role of states in labour coercion, whereas the reference to unfreedom signalled that, at least in the colonial context, forced labour had replaced slavery as the anti-thesis of 'free' labour.[7] In the Angolan coffee sector, forced labour as the ILO defined it existed in a mixture of requisitioning, prestation, and outright conscription.[8]

3 Henry W. Nevinson, *A Modern Slavery* (New York: Harper Brothers Publishers, 1906); Basil Davidson, 'Africa's Modern Slavery', *Harper's Magazine*, 209:1250 (1954), 56–63; James Duffy, *A Question of Slavery* (Oxford: Clarendon Press, 1967); Eric Allina, *Slavery by Any Other Name: African Life under Company Rule in Colonial Mozambique* (Charlottesville: University of Virginia Press, 2012); Jeremy Ball, *Angola's Colossal Lie: Forced Labor on a Sugar Plantation, 1913–1977* (Boston: Brill, 2015).

4 Suzanne Miers, *Slavery in the Twentieth Century: The Evolution of a Global Problem* (Walnut Creek: AltaMira Press, 2003), p. 135; Julia Seibert, 'More Continuity than Change? New Forms of Unfree Labour in the Belgian Congo, 1908–1960', in Marcel van der Linden (ed.), *Humanitarian Intervention and Changing Labor Relations: The Long-Term Consequences of the Abolition of the Slave Trade* (Leiden: Brill, 2011), pp. 369–86.

5 For a different view, see Miguel Bandeira Jerónimo and José Pedro Monteiro, 'Colonial Labour Internationalized: Portugal and the Decolonization Momentum (1945–1975)', *International History Review*, 42:3 (2020), 485–504, at p. 491.

6 Babacar Fall and Richard L. Roberts, 'Forced Labour', in Stefano Bellucci and Andreas Eckert (eds), *General Labour History of Africa: Workers, Employers and Governments, 20th–21st Centuries* (Woodbridge: James Currey, 2019), pp. 77–115, at p. 77.

7 Frederick Cooper, *Decolonization and African Society: The Labor Question in French and British Africa* (Cambridge: Cambridge University Press, 1996), pp. 26–9; Daniel Roger Maul, 'The International Labour Organization and the Struggle against Forced Labour from 1919 to the Present', *Labor History*, 48:4 (2007), 477–500.

8 Fall and Roberts, 'Forced Labour', pp. 88–96; Miers, *Slavery*, pp. 135–41.

Since administrators used these forms of compulsory labour to recruit for coffee plantations and other private enterprise, they were illegal not just according to the Forced Labour Convention – which Portugal ratified only in 1956 – but also under Portuguese law. Article 293 of the 1928 Native Labour Code defined forced labour as 'work that a native is coerced to do by threat or violence or by government order'.[9] The labour code only allowed the use of compulsory labour for specific public purposes, such as roadwork. In strictly legal terms, therefore, forced-labour practices were a corruption of the contract system, the main subject of the 1928 labour code.

Since introducing the notion of the contract to reconfigure labour relations in the colonies after the abolition of servitude in 1875, Portugal had defined contract labour as essentially free. In official parlance, African labour could be freely contracted in two ways: with and without state intervention.[10] In the first case, workers signed their contracts in the presence of an official from the Department of Labour (*Curadoria Geral*), which was necessary if they were recruited for work outside their home district. These contracts were counted in months or years and had a maximum length of two years. The labourers were known as *contratados*, and Africans often referred with anguish to this arrangement as 'the contract'. In the second case, workers negotiated labour contracts directly with employers. These could be written or verbal agreements. They were counted in days, weeks, or months, with a maximum length of one year, and were only allowed when the workplace was in the worker's home district or when a worker offered their labour spontaneously in a district different from their own. While the state did not mediate in these contracts, employers had to send details of contracted workers to the local administration for approval, except when day labour was considered 'occasional' (*eventual*). Workers in this second scenario were officially known as *voluntários*, a term that denoted free will but inadvertently suggested that unfreedom defined recruitment 'with state intervention'.[11]

By law, colonial officials could not interfere directly in recruitment, as workers were supposed to enter labour contracts freely. However, the labour code also prescribed that the state had a 'duty to facilitate' the work of recruitment agents.[12] Theoretically, facilitation meant directing recruiters to places the government designated as areas with a labour surplus and encouraging Africans to

9 Portugal, *Código de Trabalho dos Indígenas nas colónias portuguesas de África* (Luanda: Imprensa Nacional da Colónia de Angola, 1936), art. 293.

10 Portugal, *Código de Trabalho dos Indígenas*, art. 120-34. For a comparable discussion of the labour law, see René Pélissier, *La colonie du minotaure: Nationalismes et révoltes en Angola (1926–1961)* (Orgeval: Pélissier, 1978), pp. 136–52.

11 Arquivo Histórico Ultramarino (Lisbon, henceforth AHU), Ministério do Ultramar (MU), Inspecção Superior da Administração Ultramarina (ISAU), A2.01.002/012.00067, 'Inspecção Geral á Colónia de Angola, 1944: Relatório do Inspector Superior Nunes de Oliveira', p. 205.

12 Portugal, *Código de Trabalho dos Indígenas*, art. 36, art. 37, art. 97.

take up paid work, reminding them where necessary of their legal obligation to work and pay colonial taxes. In practice, low-ranked administrators often coerced chiefs to supply labour by intimation, threat, or violence. The result was a dissolution of the legal distinction between forced labour and contract labour.

Since state coercion was often so blatant, the Angolan historiography has largely equated the contract system with forced labour. But this comparison is problematic for several reasons. First, it implies that most contract labour was recruited by the state, which was not always the case. Second, it ignores that contract labour and forced labour were legally separate categories, a distinction that, even if blurred in practice, had a bearing on how government officials defined acceptable levels of coercion. Third, an emphasis on physical force obfuscates the different ways in which coercion crept into the contract system. Indeed, it assumes that forced recruitment was the antitype of free labour, while in practice the line between coercion and freedom in the labour market was never clearly drawn, either in Angola or elsewhere.[13]

According to labour historian Marcel van der Linden, all work that people do for others is coerced to one degree or another. Van der Linden identifies three general ways through which people have historically entered so-called heteronomous labour relations: physical compulsion, constrained choice, and free choice. Mechanisms of physical compulsion in colonial Angola included payment of debt (incurred voluntarily or involuntarily), abduction (such as police raids), kinship or community pressures, and prestation (labour tax). Examples of constrained choice were self-sale (such as indenture), money taxes, and 'free' wage labour. Free choice only existed when there were no pecuniary or non-pecuniary consequences to a decision not to work, for example when an agrarian household produced enough to sustain itself and cover all its financial obligations, but one or more members decided to seek employment to earn extra income.[14]

Several qualifications are in order. First, in the Angolan context, categories of physical compulsion and constrained choice often overlapped. For instance, labour requisitioning often involved chiefly authority, tax obligations, and police threats all at once. Furthermore, as a form of wage labour, contracts might appear relatively 'free' at the point of entry but could be extremely harsh

13 Madhavi Kale, *Fragments of Empire: Capital, Slavery, and Indian Indentured Labor Migration in the British Caribbean* (Philadelphia: University of Pennsylvania Press, 1998); Robert J. Steinfeld, *Coercion, Contract, and Free Labor in the Nineteenth Century* (Cambridge: Cambridge University Press, 2001); Alessandro Stanziani, 'Serfs, Slaves, or Wage Earners? The Legal Status of Labour in Russia from a Comparative Perspective, from the Sixteenth to the Nineteenth Century', *JGH*, 3:2 (2008), 183–202.

14 Marcel van der Linden, 'Dissecting Coerced Labor', in Marcel van der Linden and Magaly Rodriguez Garcia (eds), *On Coerced Labor: Work and Compulsion after Chattel Slavery* (Leiden: Brill, 2016), pp. 293–322.

when governed by master-servant regulations or criminal law, as was the case with contract labour.[15] In some regions, moreover, recruitment onto wage contracts happened under extreme physical duress.[16] Nevertheless, the categorization of coerced labour proposed by van der Linden permits a revision of the Angolan forced labour debate, recognizing the role of constrained choice in colonial labour recruitment and even allowing the possibility that some Africans accepted wage employment out of free choice.

This chapter examines forms of labour coercion in northern Angola by reading a series of government inspection reports completed after the Second World War on behalf of the Ministry of the Colonies. These inspections reviewed the general state of district administrations in Portuguese Africa, but labour recruitment was often their main subject. Other archival materials, data from the Angolan government's statistical yearbooks, and evidence supplied by eyewitnesses to the ILO in 1961 complement the contents of the inspection reports.[17] The chapter analyses the data for each of the main coffee-producing districts (*concelhos*) of northern Angola – Cazengo, Dembos, Ambaca, Uíge, and Negage – thereby revealing important differences and similarities between regional labour practices. Regarding the available statistical evidence, there are sometimes significant variations between the inspection reports and official government publications in the number of plantations and workers, and their outputs. While numerical data are important to understand the scale of settler expansion and contract labour in Angola, these discrepancies call for caution in the use of government statistics.[18] It is clear, for instance, that the yearbooks listed only the number of legally demarcated concessions in each district, excluding settler estates that were not properly legalized. Moreover, governments systematically undercounted plantation workers, as administrators registered workers with written contracts, but not necessarily those with verbal agreements, let alone the ones randomly recruited during the harvest season.[19]

15 Miers, *Slavery*, p. 107; Jan Lucassen, *The Story of Work: A New History of Humankind* (New Haven: Yale University Press, 2021), p. 357.

16 'Inspecção Geral á Colónia de Angola, 1944', p. 218, referring to Alto Cunene and Ganguelas.

17 International Labour Office (ILO), 'Report of the Commission Appointed under Article 26 of the Constitution of the International Labour Organisation to Examine the Complaint Filed by the Government of Ghana concerning the Observance by the Government of Portugal of the Abolition of Forced Labour Convention, 1957 (No. 105)', *Official Bulletin*, 45:2, supplement 2 (1962), pp. 1–253.

18 Alfredo de Sousa, *Ensaio de análise económica do café* (Lisbon: Junta de Investigação do Ultramar, 1958), p. 12.

19 AHU, MU, 2243/1, Angola, 'Relatório do ano de 1936 do Curador Geral dos Indígenas' (Luanda, 30 June 1937), p. 14.

Contratados and *voluntários* in Cazengo

The main change for workers on the coffee plantations in northern Angola during the early twentieth century was the effective installation of the contract system, which ended the practice of token contracts and automatic rehiring that kept them permanently trapped on the estates. It is difficult to trace this transformation in detail, but evidence from Cazengo allows for a schematic reconstruction. Archival documentation shows that, after planters were forced to replace their enslaved workers around 1915, the estates became an important destination for destitute wageworkers from regions near and far. Some had fixed-term contracts that were largely concluded outside their control, while others managed to arrange more flexible labour agreements.

By the 1930s, most Cazengo plantations employed a mixture of *contratados* and *voluntários*. Workers contracted 'with government intervention', as the 1928 labour code euphemistically described their recruitment, hailed from inside and outside the district. Many were bound to an employer for a fixed period that could be as short as four and as long as eighteen months, though migrant labourers from the Central Plateau typically arrived on 24-month contracts.[20] The law permitted re-contracting as well as short contract extensions, which planters occasionally made use of, either with or without the consent of their workers.[21] The contracts of *voluntários* differed from those of *contratados* mainly in length. *Voluntários* included workers on written contracts lasting up to six months as well as day labourers, whose employment was agreed verbally. Demand for the latter was highest during the harvest season from June to September. Most day labourers came from Cazengo, although several arrived from further afield. Indeed, some hailed from regions as far away as Pombo and Puri, about 300km northeast of Cazengo. With few cash-earning opportunities at home, they travelled to the coffee districts to gain wages and avoid being drafted as tax defaulters by their local governments, which likely resulted in a long stint on a cocoa plantation in São Tomé.[22]

20 ANA, códice 7873, Agência da curadoria de Cazengo, 'Registo de contratos indígenas com intervenção da autoridade, 1936–38'; ANA, códice 8701, Agência da curadoria de Cazengo, 'Registo de grupos de trabalhadores contratados para os agricultores do concelho de Cazengo, 1935–37'; ANA, códice 11918, 'Registo geral de trabalhadores indígenas que prestam serviço na área da Agência da Curadoria de Cazengo, 1937–39'.

21 ANA, códice 6176, Agência da curadoria do concelho de Cazengo, 'Registo de entrada de requerimentos, 1941'.

22 ANA, códice 7875, Agência da curadoria de Cazengo, 'Registo de trabalho eventual prestado na área do concelho, 1936–37'; ANA, códice 11919, Agência da curadoria de Cazengo, 'Registo de contratos sem intervenção da autoridade, 1936–45'; AHU, MU, 1661/1, Colónia de Angola, Repartição Central dos Negócios Indígenas, 'Relatório de 1942', pp. 309–14.

Wages for *contratados* and *voluntários* were largely the same, although there were small differences in pay between plantations, as some were able to increase wages to attract 'voluntary' workers.[23] Minimum rates were tied to local tax rates, to the effect that contract labourers generally needed to work three to four months per year to pay their taxes.[24] This helps explain why most Angolan workers preferred short-term contracts on a voluntary basis to fixed long-term contracts, when the option existed. In fact, workers who lived close to a coffee plantation often chose to hire out their labour for only part of the month, thereby spreading the tax burden and leaving time for their own crops and other responsibilities. This practice had existed for decades, and arguably longer, as labour shortages on coffee estates had pressed upon local populations from the mid-nineteenth century.[25] The arrangement suited some employers better than it did others. Large, well-endowed planters preferred long contracts, which were expensive but provided them with a stable workforce that was more securely bound to the plantations.[26] For many settlers, however, hiring workers informally was cheaper than recruiting them on written, fixed-term contracts, which came with government taxes, recruitment fees, and potentially high transportation costs. Furthermore, informal labour agreements still imposed contractual obligations on the worker, which employers were ready to exploit. As one witness explained, voluntary workers were 'easily cheated ... over wages and time of employment, which may be extended after the agreed term is finished or may be renewed ... without the workers' consent'. Administrators could classify absconding day labourers as 'vagrants' and punish them with forced labour.[27]

After the Second World War, the Cazengo estates increasingly relied on *contratados*, as local hiring stagnated and more workers were brought in from afar. There appeared to be two obstacles to local recruitment. One was the growing number of smallholders in the region who fulfilled their 'moral duty' to work by achieving specific production standards that made them 'independent' in the

23 Arquivo Nacional da Torre do Tombo (Lisbon), PT/TT/AOS/D-N/6/1/1, Relatório da Companhia do Cazengo do anno de 1926 (Lisbon, 1927).

24 ANA, caixa 796, Diretor interino dos Serviços e Negócios Indígenas, Exposição acerca do trabalho indígena na colónia de Angola, Luanda, 12 Feb. 1929; 'Inspecção Geral á Colónia de Angola, 1944', doc. 5; ILO, 'Report', p. 174. For comparison, see Ewout Frankema and Marlous van Waijenburg, 'Metropolitan Blueprints of Colonial Taxation? Lessons from Fiscal Capacity Building in British and French Africa, c. 1880–1940', *JAH*, 55:3 (2014), 371–400, at p. 390.

25 ANA, códice 1927, Circumscrição de Cazengo, Registo de trabalhadores voluntários em serviço agrícola, Dalatando, 1914.

26 AHU, MU, 2243/1, Angola, Curadoria Geral dos Indígenas, 'Relatório do ano de 1938', p. 23; The National Archives (Kew, henceforth TNA), CO371/90313, S. P. House to Nigel Ronald, confidential, Luanda, 16 Oct. 1951.

27 ILO, 'Report', pp. 148, 209 (quote).

eyes of the government, such as producing more than a ton of dried coffee in a year or cultivating more than three thousand coffee stands. There were over a thousand such relatively well-off farmers in the sub-districts of N'dalatando and Lucala alone, adding to a legion of stonemasons, carpenters, basket makers, and tailors whom the government considered 'self-employed' and, therefore, unavailable to European employers.[28] Second, many workers who were eligible for recruitment decided to find employment in cities like Luanda and Léopoldville (Kinshasa), where wages were higher than at home.[29] They were not alone. In the 1950s, thousands of adult men from northern Angola migrated on their own or with their families to the Belgian Congo in search of jobs, shrinking the regional labour pool.[30] Unless administrators were willing to increase levels of coercion locally – as happened in the Congo district – growing labour shortages forced planters to source more workers from elsewhere.

This increased reliance on migrant workers showed especially on the larger estates, which could more easily afford the high recruitment fees that came with out-of-district hiring. For instance, in 1956, the Companhia Agrícola Santos Diniz, a major export firm that owned seven coffee plantations with a combined area of five thousand hectares in Cazengo, employed six hundred *contratados*. They predominantly hailed from Bailundo, Huambo, and Bié, on the Central Plateau, while others came from regions east and northeast of Cazengo, like Ambaca, Malange, and Sanza Pombo. In contrast, within the district, Santos Diniz had recruited only fifty *voluntários* on monthly contracts and an indefinite number of female day labourers to help with the post-harvest sorting of dried coffee. Similarly, Fazenda Quigia, an 18,000-hectare estate owned by Paiva, Marcelo & Companhia in the Lucala region in the eastern corner of the district, employed 220 contract workers from central and southern Angola and only fifty people from Cazengo.[31] Nevertheless, voluntary labour supplies remained significant in the district, especially for smaller plantations that lacked the financial resources to recruit expensive migrant labour.[32]

The Bailundo people of the Central Plateau were a notable presence among the labour migrants to Cazengo when the contract system started in the late

28 AHU, MU, ISAU, A2.050.02/016.00100, 'Relatório da Inspecção ao Concelho de Cazengo, postos de Séde e Lucala, pelo Inspector Administrativo interino António do Nascimento Rodrigues, ano de 1956', pp. 123, 126.

29 AHU, MU, ISAU, A2.0001.02/012.00062, 'Relatório do Governador do Distrito do Cuanza Norte, António Francisco Neto Parra, respeitante ao período de 25 de outubro 1955 a 31 de dezembro 1956', p. 105; *ibid.*, A2.050.05/034.00203, 'Relatório do Governo da Província do Congo no ano de 1953', p. 125.

30 ILO, 'Report', p. 180. Outward migration decreased when coffee prices rose. See Afonso Mendes, 'A promoção das massas rurais indigenas', *Estudos Ultramarinos*, 7 (1957–8), 9–29, at p. 15.

31 'Relatório da Inspecção ao Concelho de Cazengo' (1956), p. 127.

32 'Relatório do Governo da Província do Congo' (1953), p. 137.

1870s.[33] Because of their continued prominence in interregional migration flows, *bailundos* became the generic term for workers from central Angola on the coffee estates. The Central Plateau was densely populated. Commercial maize cultivation flourished under colonial rule, providing cash incomes to many households. However, the colonial government raised taxes to levels that few households could pay by producing maize alone. Furthermore, the government imposed strict criteria on maize producers to be recognized as 'independent' cultivators freed from compulsory labour. Many adult men from Bailundo, Huambo, Bié, and around were thus compelled to migrate to earn cash wages, leaving maize production largely in female hands. Most of them travelled to the coffee zones north and south of the Cuanza River where, by the late 1950s, migrants from central Angola constituted more than half of the labour force employed on the plantations.[34] Debts to local traders were another motive to take up contract labour. 'The bush trader is a recruiter's best agent', inspector José Diogo Ferreira Martins wrote about the Huambo district in 1961. Local commerce largely thrived on incomes generated by labour migration, with returnees using their wages to pay for goods that traders had sold them on credit. Traders and administrators often connived to hook consumers onto contracts, while some traders even provided the trucks to transport workers to and from the plantations.[35] Although long-term contracts certified by the government were standard, many migrants travelled northward 'voluntarily' in the dry months between June and September. They perpetuated a nineteenth-century Bailundo tradition of taking on wage labour during the agricultural offseason. For these workers, earning cash to spend on consumer goods, such as cloth for wedding ceremonies, was an important motive to hire out their labour, besides the pressure of colonial taxation.[36]

33 ANA, códice 3399, 'Registo de contratos de serviçais e colonos contratados, Cazengo 1881–86'.

34 Fernando Diogo da Silva, *O Huambo: Mão-de-obra rural no mercado de trabalho de Angola* (Luanda: Fundo de Acção Social no Trabalho em Angola, 1968), pp. 186, 213; AHU, MU, ISAU, A2.050.04/027.00167, 'Relatório do Governador do Distrito do Quanza Norte, António Francisco Neto Parra, 1957', p. 120; William Gervase Clarence-Smith, 'Capital Accumulation and Class Formation in Angola', in David Birmingham and Phyllis M. Martin (eds), *History of Central Africa, Volume Two* (London: Longman, 1983), pp. 163–99, at pp. 185–6; Maria da Conceição Neto, 'In Town and Out of Town: A Social History of Huambo (Angola), 1902–1961' (Unpublished PhD dissertation, University of London, 2012), <http://eprints.soas.ac.uk/13822>, pp. 156, 252.

35 AHU, MU, ISAU, A2.01.02.008/00038, José Diogo Ferreira Martins, 'Relatório parcial no. 8, distrito do Huambo, 1961', pp. 26–7; *ibid.*, A2.49.004/51.00368, Lapido Loureiro, 'Relatório da Inspecção Ordinária ao Concelho do Bailundo, 1959', pp. 85, 119, 159, 175–6.

36 Afonso Mendes, 'O trabalho assalariado em Angola' (Unpublished PhD dissertation, Instituto Superior de Ciências Sociais e Política Ultramarina, 1966), pp. 84–94; José

Direct and indirect coercion in Dembos

Situated north of Cazengo, the mountainous Dembos region was home to extensive reserves of forest coffee that settlers gained access to only after the Portuguese defeat of the Dembo chiefs in 1919.[37] Until then, Dembo authorities had resisted white settlement in the region, allowing only a few Portuguese traders to open stores for the purchase of coffee from local producers. Colonial occupation, road improvements, and the arrival of motorized transport in the 1920s gradually opened the district to foreign investment. The number of settler estates increased from one in 1925 to thirty-eight in 1934, which immediately demanded help from the government with labour recruitment. By the time inspector Américo Baptista de Sousa visited the district, in 1949, there were at least eighty European plantations, most of which were illegal occupations.[38]

According to de Sousa's report, the foreign plantations together employed 5,576 workers. Two things about this labour force stand out. First, about 80 per cent of the workers were contracted inside the Dembos district. Most planters relied fully on regional labour supplies, while only a dozen of the larger, better-capitalized estates had capacity to recruit outside the district. Extensive local recruitment seemed to restrict African coffee production, which was surprisingly underdeveloped given the region's long familiarity with the coffee crop.[39] Second, most plantation workers (58 per cent) were on voluntary contracts, hiring out their labour on a daily, weekly, or monthly basis. Some had written contracts, but most had informal agreements with employers. De Sousa looked upon this situation positively, as voluntary contracts reduced the workload of local administrations and eased political discomfort about government contracting. He nevertheless acknowledged the contorted meaning of 'freedom' in

---

Augusto da Cunha Morais, *Africa occidental: Album photographico e descriptivo* (4 vols, Lisbon: David Corazzi, 1885–88), vol. 2; AHU, MU, ISAU, A2.01.001/02.00010, 'Relatório do governo do distrito do Bié-Cuando Cubango referente ao ano de 1958', p. 17; Yonah Ngalaba Seleti, 'Portuguese Colonialism, Capitalism and the Angolan Coffee Industry: 1850–1950' (Unpublished PhD dissertation, Dalhousie University, 1987), p. 109.

37 René Pélissier, *História das campanhas de Angola: Resistência e revoltas 1845–1941* (Lisbon: Editorial Estampa, 1997), pp. 44–8, 145–59, 321–49.

38 ANA, caixa 1767, 'Relatório anual referido ao ano económico de 1925–1926'; ANA, caixa 3658, Autos de processo disciplinar instaurado contra o chefe do posto João Pires Antunes, Camabatela, 18 Nov. 1935; AHU, MU, 1665/1, Colónia de Angola, Inspector administrativo Oscar Freire de Vasconcelos Ruas, 'Relatório de Inspecção Administrativa, 1937', p. 31; AHU, MU, ISAU, A2.050.02/016.00094, 'Inspecção feita ao concelho dos Dembos pelo Inspector Administrativo, Américo Baptista de Sousa, 1949', p. 10.

39 Angola, Repartição Central de Estatística Geral, *Anuário estatístico de Angola, ano de 1949* (Luanda: Imprensa Nacional, 1952).

the labour market. A district report from 1947 showed that workers accepted voluntary arrangements mainly to avoid government drafting onto long-term contracts. Some were the victims of treacherous labour touts, but many decided to 'volunteer' when local authorities scanned villages for men considered vagrants or tax delinquents. People therefore chose to work in the European coffee sector because the alternative would have been worse. There was some evidence of workers requesting extensions to their contracts, but this was likely an outcome of constrained, rather than free, choice.[40]

Coffee plantations housed workers arriving under widely varying conditions. A predominantly male workforce, recruited on long-term contracts, lived on the estates throughout the year, taking care of tilling, planting, and plantation upkeep. Women and children often followed husbands, fathers, uncles, or brothers to the plantations, especially during the harvest season starting in June, when planters needed extra hands to help with picking and sorting coffee. For example, in 1949, the 900-hectare Fazenda Santa Cruz, owned by Cabral Seabra, informally recruited 105 female relatives of men already on the plantation to help with the harvest. While some seasonal workers arrived on the plantations 'voluntarily', the coffee harvest also prompted forced conscription, as the government ramped up recruitment by requisitioning and raids.[41] An American Methodist, Ralph Dodge, witnessed such a moment of 'crisis' in 1949:

> It was coffee harvest time and all available laborers were conscripted by the European farmers, who were increasing yearly in numbers. In fact, it was at this time of the year that the Portuguese labor system was seen at its worst. Not only able-bodied men were taken from their own gardens to harvest the crop of the Europeans, but also trucks would drive into a village and pick up all the women, even those heavily pregnant or nursing small babies, to sort the dried coffee beans by hand. As the pressures grew, older school children were taken from their studies for two or three months just at the time when they should be preparing for exams. All activities of the villages were set aside until the coffee was harvested, the beans dried, sorted, and sacked for market.[42]

40 'Inspecção feita ao concelho dos Dembos' (1949), pp. 9–10 and docs 31 and 33. On swindle by recruitment agents, see Armando Castro, *O sistema colonial português em África (meados do século XX)*, 2nd edn (Lisbon: Editorial Caminho, 1980), p. 198; Henrique Martino, '"Panya": Economies of Deception and the Discontinuities of Indentured Labour Recruitment and the Slave Trade, Nigeria and Fernando Pó, 1890s–1940s', *AEH*, 44:1 (2016), 91–129. On weighing alternatives, see Stanley L. Engerman, 'Introduction', in Stanley L. Engerman (ed.), *Terms of Labor: Slavery, Serfdom, and Free Labor* (Stanford: Stanford University Press, 1999), pp. 1–23.

41 Castro, *Sistema*, pp. 196–7.

42 Ralph E. Dodge, *The Revolutionary Bishop Who Saw God at Work in Africa: An Autobiography* (Pasadena: William Carey Library, 1986), p. 93.

As other testimony suggests, administrators across northern Angola habitually used police raids to address urgent labour needs.[43]

Complaints from African communities recorded by de Sousa focused on settler expansion, labour demands, and illegal recruitment. Chiefs typically protested that labour contracting undermined African food production and the opportunity of farmers to grow coffee on their own. Chief Anzage in the Bula Atumba area reported that nine of his ten children were forced to work on European estates, which for him was labour stolen from his own coffee farm. Another example was the case of Quimbande Andale, a successful coffee grower who was called up for labour service and therefore had to abandon his own plantation (*tonga*). In 1956, the headmen of N'dalatando, in Cazengo, levied similar complaints about the negative impact of contract labour on African coffee production.[44]

Although an increasing number of smallholders in northern Angola were exempt from labour duties by growing more trees, cultivating more hectares, or producing more coffee than the legally required minimum to be counted as 'self-employed', most African farms were too small to meet these standards – although they got by just fine growing food crops and coffee. Moreover, because of a shortage of agricultural inspectors, many growers were unable to obtain an official certificate that recognized their independent status. According to the Methodist missionary, Malcom McVeigh, African smallholders were trapped in 'a vicious cycle in which they serve as unwilling and poverty-stricken servants, contributing to the growing wealth of a white man whose riches are made possible by both their land and their labor'.[45]

There were also complaints from extremely vulnerable contract workers. Near Dange, for instance, de Sousa met a local resident named Manuel Costa, who explained that after completing twenty years of compulsory labour in São Tomé, the government had placed him on a contract with a coffee estate in Cazengo. Costa decided to seek refuge in his hometown, reasoning that after two decades of hard and low-paid plantation labour he had a right to go home. Imposing new contracts on repatriated *santomistas* was one trick in the book of unscrupulous administrators desperate to satisfy the labour needs of nearby coffee estates. On a plantation in Pango Aluquém, owned by João Batista de Gois, de Sousa found a camp of forty-six workers who had completed fourteen years of compulsory labour in São Tomé. They said the truck that was supposed to bring them to their homes in Cuango and Maquela do Zombo, in the northeastern part of the Congo district, instead delivered them to the estate of de

43 ILO, 'Report', pp. 176, 179; Malcolm McVeigh, 'Labor in Chains', *Africa Today*, 8:8 (1961), 9–11; Castro, *Sistema*, pp. 196–7.

44 'Relatório da Inspecção ao Concelho de Cazengo' (1956), p. 135.

45 McVeigh, 'Labor in Chains', p. 10; A. E., 'A demarcação de terrenos de estado no distrito do Congo', *BGU*, 35:405 (1959), 63–70; ILO, 'Report', pp. 148–9.

Gois.[46] As settler estates mushroomed in the 1950s, administrators and planters across northern Angola increasingly used forced rehiring of contract workers as a strategy to combat growing labour shortages, ignoring the legal requirement of at least one year's rest between contracts.[47]

Occasional visits from labour inspectors aside, the Angolan peasantry had few formal channels to protest. People therefore generally resisted contract labour by voting with their feet. Several families left their homes in Dembos for the relatively safe surroundings of Luanda. They often settled in the suburbs, where a growing informal economy provided alternative wage-earning opportunities to plantation labour. De Sousa related the case of João Mainga, an elected chief in the Dange area, who moved to Luanda after the colonial authorities tried to use taxation to press him into contract labour. In Luanda, Mainga worked as a vendor, registered himself with the local government, and from 1944 to 1949 paid his taxes there. For Mainga and others, taxation was negotiable, but compulsory labour was not.[48]

In 1957, the Colonial Office sent António do Nascimento Rodrigues to Dembos for an inspection. His report shows that, in less than a decade, the number of settler estates had mushroomed from eighty to more than three hundred, an expansion that frequently involved the illegal incorporation of African farms. European planters employed between ten and thirteen thousand workers on both short- and long-term contracts. About five thousand of them came from the region and these were mostly day labourers. The remainder were from outside the district and hired for longer periods. To earn the wages they needed, local populations had learned to negotiate informal labour agreements with large coffee planters. These flexible arrangements, while still unpopular, allowed households to combine wage labour with their own agricultural activities, including coffee cultivation. Moreover, they knew the risk of long-term contracts: some workers remained stuck on a plantation for decades.

Planters exhausted virtually all locally available labour through informal contracts. Like their counterparts in Cazengo, they increasingly relied on migrant workers from outside the district, shifting the burden of recruitment to economies elsewhere.[49] The Department of Native Affairs made it appear as if the Angolan labour pool was sufficiently large to cover shortages in specific areas. Despite increasing demand, however, the total number of contract workers in Angola remained relatively stable after the Second World War.[50] In fact, as early

46 'Inspecção feita ao concelho dos Dembos' (1949), pp. 20–1.

47 ILO, 'Report', pp. 149–50, 189, 210.

48 'Inspecção feita ao concelho dos Dembos' (1949), doc. 25.

49 TNA, CO371/80861, G. W. Scott, Minute, 15 Nov. 1950, enclosed in J. R. Colville to Research Department at FO, confidential, Lisbon, 16 Nov. 1950.

50 ILO, 'Report', pp. 181–2; TNA, CO371/125912, Grant Purves to FO, Luanda, 9 March 1957.

as the 1930s, government officials knew that supplies of *contratados* were limited, creating competition between economic sectors and making workers generally expensive to recruit.[51] Indeed, many settlers could ill afford them. The average workforce on the Dembos plantations fell in size from approximately seventy workers in 1949 to forty in 1957, showing that labour shortages seriously hampered settler expansion in northern Angola.[52]

False voluntary contracts in Ambaca

In Ambaca, east of Cazengo, coffee cultivation was a predominantly African affair until settlers were given land to develop the crop around 1930.[53] Like elsewhere, the post-1945 commodity boom accelerated the growth of estate production, which soon outpaced smallholder efforts. By 1950, there were sixty-three European coffee plantations in Ambaca, producing about double what local African farmers harvested. White settlers occupied an area of nearly 100,000 hectares, but labour scarcity caused widespread underuse of land. As the inspection report for that year by Eduardo Lapido Loureiro makes clear, the vast majority of available *contratados* in Ambaca were trucked to other parts of Angola deemed in greater need of workers. Most settlers therefore relied on local *voluntários*, often recruited from communities of coffee growers. However, expanding African production strained local labour supplies.[54]

At the time of Loureiro's inspection, approximately five thousand people in Ambaca were on voluntary contracts with local coffee planters. As in Dembos, the voluntary worker label disguised the various forms of coercion under which people signed up for plantation labour. For example, workers at Roça Maria Beatriz, in Samba Cajú, claimed that despite the apparent voluntary nature of their contracts, they had signed the agreements under pressure from the local authorities. Other *voluntários* were small coffee farmers who were not exempt

51 'Relatório do ano de 1936 do Curador Geral dos Indígenas', p. 11; 'Inspecção Geral á Colónia de Angola, 1944', p. 218.

52 AHU, MU, ISAU, A2.49.005/59.00458, 'Relatório da Inspecção ao Concelho dos Dembos, pelo Inspector Administrativo António do Nascimento Rodrigues, 1957', pp. 159, 166, 168; AHU, Governo Geral de Angola, Repartição do Gabinete, D2.172.6/06, Chefe de gabinete to US consul, no. 3616, Luanda, 18 Sep. 1952; Angola, Repartição Central de Estatística Geral, *Anuário estatístico de Angola, ano de 1957* (Luanda: Imprensa Nacional, 1958).

53 'Mapas de produção agrícola, referente ao ano de 1930', *BAA*, 5:16–19 (1932), 102. In 1918, John Gossweiler, 'Um reconhecimento fitogeográfico à região produtora do café Encoje', *Relatórios e Informações*, 1:2 (1918), 19–40, at p. 32, saw some plantations along the road from Lucala to Uíge.

54 AHU, MU, ISAU, A2.050.02/016.00106, 'Relatório da Inspecção ao Concelho de Ambaca, pelo Inspector Administrativo, Eduardo B. Lapido Loureiro' (1950); 'Relatório do Governo da Província do Congo' (1953), p. 137.

from labour duties and had decided to hire out their labour to nearby estates, mainly to avoid being recruited on a long-term contract to an unknown region. Near the government post of Caculo Cabaça, a sixteen-year-old male named Manuel Curioria escaped on his bicycle after the chief of his community selected him for labour duty at a nearby coffee plantation. Picked up in a neighbouring village, Curioria managed to negotiate a fixed-term 'voluntary' contract based on daily pay, which allowed him to spend some time away from the plantation every month.[55]

Some people avoided contract labour altogether by fleeing to Luanda or by going into hiding on a large African farm or a white settler estate, as some planters were prepared to hire fugitives as day labourers without notifying the authorities. Repatriated workers, facing the threat of forced re-contracting, often felt compelled to escape as well. Desertion, while punishable by law, was also common. Loureiro learned that, in 1949, almost four hundred workers had abandoned their contracts in Ambaca, which was about 5 per cent of the plantation labour force that year. Similar ratios applied in Cazengo and Ambaca during the early 1940s.[56] In 1951, of the three hundred 'voluntary' plantation workers recruited by Diogo & Companhia in Cariamba, a small town near Caculo Cabaça, many never showed up or left before the end of their contract. Similarly, in 1952, several families contracted by Mattos, Vaz & Companhia to settle as workers on their coffee estate desisted before long.[57] A Danish planter in the nearby Dembos region said he generally expected half his labour force to escape within the first week.[58] These responses indicate how much contract labour was disliked in northern Angola, especially among coffee-cultivating peasant households. Few people found wage labour to be a matter of free choice.

While plantation labour was generally unpopular, working and living conditions on the estates could vary significantly. On some plantations, work was task-based, giving labourers some control of time; on others, it was time-based, causing complaints about excessive working hours. Task-based labour was most common in the harvest season, when working days consisted of clear, measurable targets.[59] Furthermore, pay for *contratados* was calculated monthly and based on a system of deferred wages, where part of the salary was paid on the spot and part through the Labour Office at the end of the contract. Pay for *voluntários* could be monthly or daily, with daily rates potentially resulting in higher monthly totals. In Ambaca, high coffee prices and labour shortages drove up wages in the 1950s, showing that voluntary workers had some bargaining power even if their choices were highly constrained.

55 ANA, caixa 2170, Agência da Curadoria de Ambaca.

56 'Relatório de 1942', pp. 284, 290–1.

57 ANA, caixa 2170, Agência da Curadoria de Ambaca.

58 TNA, CO371/125912, Grant Purves to FO, Luanda, 9 March 1957.

59 Jeffery M. Paige, *Agrarian Revolution: Social Movements and Export Agriculture in the Underdeveloped World* (New York: Free Press, 1975), p. 251.

There were differences, too, in the way African workers lived on the plantations. Several estates had begun the construction of brick or concrete lodgings for their workers. Loureiro mentioned Roça Canzela, a German-owned 1,200-hectare estate near Quiculungo, which employed more than 250 workers and was allegedly building three new accommodation blocks every other week.[60] It also had a small infirmary, containing a residence for a permanent nurse and a medical post that women and children visited twice a week. Nevertheless, on most plantations there was only a rudimentary infirmary, and workers saw a medical officer once per month at best, reflecting the generally inadequate provision of healthcare in the northern coffee sector.[61] Most settlers lacked either the capital or incentive to provide housing for incoming workers. Many labourers instead built their own wattle-and-daub homes, while some had their own homes and farms nearby to which they frequently returned. There were also workers who settled permanently with their families on the plantation, alternating wage labour with food cultivation on provision grounds of their own. However, the large influx of workers during harvest time often caused acute housing shortages, forcing men, women, and children to sleep in the open.[62]

Male contract workers were often accompanied by wives, children, younger brothers, or nephews. The 1928 labour code prescribed that it was illegal to employ children under the age of fourteen. Children fourteen to eighteen years old could be contracted, but only with the permission of their father, mother, or legal guardian.[63] Administrators everywhere tended to ignore these laws. In the 1930s, a conflict between two officials at the Dembos headquarters in Quibaxe revealed that armed police officers systematically recruited boys and girls under fourteen to pick and sort coffee.[64] In Ambaca, many plantations hired underaged children for four months or longer during the harvest season. One example was André Guma Capita, a twelve-year-old boy sent by his parents to work for Joaquim Aguiar de Oliveira, a Portuguese settler in Caculo Cabaça.[65] The five

60 Concession requested by Nikolaus von Larisch in Quiculungo, 1941, in Angola, Repartição Central dos Serviços de Cadastro, *Relação geral dos processos organizados para a concessão de terrenos do estado, desde 1912 até 31 de dezembro de 1943* (Luanda: Imprensa Nacional, 1944), p. 25.

61 'Relatório do ano de 1938', p. 26; 'Inspecção Geral á Colónia de Angola, 1944', doc. 7; AHU, MU, ISAU, A2.49.002/39.00251, 'Relatório da Inspecção Administrativa ao Concelho do Uíge, pelo Inspector Administrativo António do Nascimento Rodrigues, 1959', p. 180; ILO, 'Report', p. 209.

62 Castro, *Sistema*, pp. 197–8; 'Relatório da Inspecção ao Concelho dos Dembos' (1957), doc. 23.

63 Portugal, *Código de Trabalho dos Indígenas*, art. 99.

64 ANA, caixa 3658, Autos de processo disciplinar instaurado contra o chefe do posto João Pires Antunes, Camabatela, 18 Nov. 1935.

65 ANA, cx. 2170, Agência da Curadoria de Ambaca.

hundred-hectare Alto Minho estate near Uíge recruited fifty boys of about that same age to help with picking and sorting during the school holidays.[66] The practice of hiring minors was widespread in northern Angola. For planters, the economic benefits were obvious, as picking and sorting were tasks that children could perform as efficiently as adults, but for half the cost in wages.[67]

Forced labour in the Congo

In few places was state intervention in labour recruitment as systematic and brutal as in the Congo district during the 1950s, especially for the booming plantation sector around the city of Uíge (renamed Carmona in 1955). For reasons that seemed purely political, this sector came to rely almost exclusively on local government supplies of fieldhands. Before the Second World War, planters in the area generally attracted workers themselves, sometimes going into villages to negotiate wages and hours. Many workers were hired as day labourers who needed wages to pay taxes. But as African and European coffee production increased after the war and competition for labour intensified, district governors began to intervene directly in the labour market, using the police to round up workers to distribute to white settlers and some of the larger African farms. By 1953, according to official records, most plantation workers in the Uíge township (then called Bembe) were contracted through government mediation.[68]

An infamous case of labour coercion was the system of 'clustering' (*concentração*) implemented by the governor Hélio Esteves Felgas in 1956, supposedly to stamp out arbitrary police violence in recruitment.[69] This system required chiefs to bring monthly from their villages all able-bodied men deemed available for contract labour to the nearest administrative post, where the men were forced to sign contracts with local companies. The brutality of the system was recorded

66 Richard J. Houk, 'Recent Developments in the Portuguese Congo', *Geographical Review*, 48:2 (1958), 201–21, at p. 209.

67 'Inspecção feita ao concelho dos Dembos' (1949), pp. 11, 20–1, doc. 38; 'Relatório da Inspecção Administrativa ao Concelho do Uíge' (1959), pp. 167–71; AHU, MU, ISAU, A2.49.003/44.00300, 'Relatório da Inspecção ao Concelho do Negage, pelo Inspector Joaquim Henriques, 1960', pp. 79, 94, 104–7. See also McVeigh, 'Labor in Chains', p. 10; ILO, 'Report', pp. 199, 206.

68 Angola, Repartição Central de Estatística Geral, *Anuário estatístico de Angola* (Luanda: Imprensa Nacional, 1934–9); 'Relatório do Governo da Província do Congo' (1953), p. 137; Houk, 'Recent Developments', 209.

69 For background, see Alexander Keese, 'The Constraints of Late Colonial Reform Policy: Forced Labour Scandals in the Portuguese Congo (Angola) and the Limits of Reform under Authoritarian Colonial Rule, 1955–61', *Portuguese Studies*, 28:2 (2012), 186–200; José Pedro Monteiro, *Portugal e a questão do trabalho forçado: Um império sob escrutínio (1944–62)* (Lisbon: Edições 70, 2018), pp. 261–72.

by government inspectors as well as the ILO.[70] The most damning evidence came from the township of Negage, a burgeoning coffee zone southeast of Uíge. Here, local functionaries tortured non-compliant village chiefs, punished them with indentured servitude, and held family members of runaways for ransom. They also recruited men over sixty, officially exempt from tax and labour duties because of their age, as well as employees and apprentices of shopkeepers and artisans, which showed that the exigencies of coffee production overrode the legal protections provided by an existing job or old age.[71]

The intention of 'clustering' was to reduce recruitment costs by channelling local labour supplies to nearby plantations, cutting the need for planters to employ private recruitment agents or to hire expensive migrant workers through the state. Felgas admitted that labour requisitioning in Congo was not 'voluntary' but refused to call his methods coercive. Instead, he described them as 'directed' labour. He argued that voluntary recruitment as defined by the labour code of 1928 was always an illusion as Africans would not freely choose to work for Europeans. This was especially so in Congo, where many had their own coffee farms that gave them 'greater rewards for less work' – and on this point he was right. Significantly, in other contexts, Felgas was a reformist who defended the rights of plantation workers and small farmers and even supported the extension of political rights to black Africans.[72] But the interests of the settler population were clearly his primary concern, even if this complicated his advocacy for colonial reform. Opposing the efforts of the Department of Native Affairs to guarantee workers the 'freedom to contract', Felgas issued a circular in 1957 ordering local administrators to actively recruit for planters, invoking vagrancy laws if necessary. As he explained, the concerns of Native Affairs about free choice in the labour market were commendable, but 'it is also important to know the labour needs of employers ... which [are] the priority of the administrative authorities'.[73]

Government conscription of plantation workers not only diminished the importance of informal labour recruitment in the Congo district, but also lessened the dependence of the coffee estates on migrant labour from the south. In 1957, coffee planters in the Uíge area officially employed about seventeen thou-

70 'Relatório da Inspecção Administrativa ao Concelho do Uíge' (1959), pp. 166–71; ILO 'Report', pp. 178–9.

71 'Relatório da Inspecção ao Concelho do Negage' (1960), pp. 54, 79–107, 153–5, 303–12.

72 Alexander Keese, *Living with Ambiguity: Integrating an African Elite in French and Portuguese Africa, 1930–61* (Stuttgart: Franz Steiner Verlag, 2007), pp. 171–2.

73 AHU, MU, ISAU, A2.050.05/034.00207, Hélio Esteves Felgas, 'Relatório do Governo do Distrito do Congo referente a 1957 (Confidencial)', pp. 243–8, 256–63, quotes at pp. 244 and 259–61.

sand African workers, of whom only three thousand were *bailundos*.[74] In 1959, some 340 planters in Uíge together received close to thirteen thousand local recruits whom the government had placed on one-year contracts, while another four thousand were migrant workers from other regions.[75] The situation in Uíge provided a stark contrast with other coffee regions in northern Angola, where planters drew on nearby populations for day labourers and contracted migrant workers from the Central Plateau when local supplies proved insufficient. Thus, by 1960, *bailundos* constituted roughly half the population of forty thousand workers on the coffee plantations in Cuanza Norte province, comprising the districts of Quiculungo, Ambaca, Dembos, Cazengo, and Golungo Alto.[76]

While government inspectors were under no illusion about the nature of voluntary labour in northern Angola, as they recognized the various forms of coercion lurking behind ostensibly free contracts, to them the situation in the Congo district was of a different order. In his report of 1960, inspector José Diogo Ferreira Martins expressed dismay at how in Congo the contract had become a hollow concept, as recruitment had completely lost its grounding in consent. 'A black man was something you caught, moved, and employed without any concerns other than the formality of the "contract", which in Congo became synonymous with forced labour', he said.[77] Martins did not accept the argument espoused by Felgas and others that colonial plantations in Congo depended for labour on the district government because most of them were relatively small and undercapitalized, and therefore unable to pay high recruitment fees. If anything, coffee estates in Cuanza Norte were on average even smaller; but the intensive recruitment campaigns during the harvest season aside, they relied far less on direct government intervention to hire workers.

The incidence of labour resistance in the Congo district mirrored the intensity of coercion. In 1959, chiefs in Bembe informed inspector Rodrigues that many of their subjects sought refuge from forced labour in large urban centres, like Carmona and Luanda. Two years earlier, governor Felgas acknowledged

74 Angola, Repartição Central de Estatística Geral, *Anuário estatístico de Angola, ano de 1957* (Luanda: Imprensa Nacional, 1958); 'Relatório do Governo do Distrito do Congo' (1957), pp. 273–7.

75 'Relatório da Inspecção Administrativa ao Concelho do Uíge' (1959), p. 170; Angola, Repartição Central de Estatística Geral, *Anuário estatístico de Angola, ano de 1959* (Luanda: Imprensa Nacional, 1960).

76 Angola, Repartição Central de Estatística Geral, *Anuário estatístico de Angola, ano de 1959* (Luanda: Imprensa Nacional, 1960); 'Relatório do Governo da Província do Congo' (1953), p. 137; AHU, MU, ISAU, A2.050.05/033.00202, José Diogo Ferreira Martins, 'Relatório da Inspecção aos Distritos de Cuanza Norte, Cuanza Sul, 1960–1961', pp. 106, 120–1.

77 AHU, MU, ISAU, A2.49.002/39.00247, José Diogo Ferreira Martins, 'Parecer e relatório do distrito do Congo, 1960', pp. 41–2.

that in Bembe and São Salvador, the heartland of the old Kongo kingdom, people avoided recruitment by escaping in nearby forests or migrating to the Belgian Congo, where many had family to rely on. In 1956, as news about Portugal's ratification of the ILO Forced Labour Convention spread inland, many workers deserted the coffee plantations in protest at underpayment, illegal contract extensions, and corporal punishment. These mass departures were a clear signal that plantation labour was underpaid, leading the central government to increase the African minimum wage to 200 *angolar* per month, a significant improvement from the going rate of 120. The higher wages seemed to attract some poverty-stricken migrants from Pombo and Damba, but for most people in the coffee-growing regions plantation labour remained an unappealing proposition, and workers continued to leave the estates.[78] Salaries in the settler economy were generally not high enough to attract labour in all but some commercially disadvantaged regions.[79] Regarding northern Angola, one government inspector speculated – not wrongly – that many small coffee farmers could earn more in one year from their own cultivations than from five years toiling on a settler estate.[80] Gang-based labour, physical abuse, poor nutrition, and inadequate medical and housing provisions were conditions that further discouraged Africans from working on the plantations.[81]

Panyarring in Negage

Convict labour, prestation, and requisitioning were forms of forced labour that were regularly used to recruit workers for the government farms (*granjas*) that were attached to administrative posts in northern Angola. These farms, instituted in 1936, were designed as experimental stations with the intention of cultivating a variety of crops, distributing seeds to farmers, and teaching African trainees supposedly new and useful agricultural techniques.[82] In the mid-1950s, there were nine of them in the Cuanza Norte district and nineteen in Congo.

78 'Relatório do Governo do Distrito do Congo' (1957), pp. 238, 243–4, 258, 266–7, 273–8; Ronald Chilcote, *Emerging Nationalism in Portuguese Africa: Documents* (Stanford: Hoover Institution Press, 1972), p. 46; ILO, 'Report', p. 149. On coordination between Felgas and the Luanda government in the field of labour policy, see Horácio de Sá Viana Rebelo, *Angola na África deste tempo* (Lisbon: edição do autor, 1961), pp. 62–4.

79 Mendes, 'O trabalho assalariado', pp. 43–6, cited in Paige, *Agrarian Revolution*, p. 250.

80 'Relatório da Inspecção ao Concelho de Ambaca' (1950), p. 124.

81 'Relatório da Inspecção Administrativa ao Concelho do Uíge' (1959), pp. 166–80; 'Relatório da Inspecção ao Concelho dos Dembos' (1957), pp. 158–69.

82 AHU, MU, 2243/2, Direcção dos Serviços de Adminsitração Civil, Curadoria Geral, 'Relatório do Curador Geral dos Indígenas da Colónia de Angola, Ano de 1937' (Luanda, 15 May 1938), p. 15.

From botanical gardens, however, most had turned into provision grounds or commercial coffee farms, often using unpaid labour under conditions 'worse than slavery', as one government inspector put it. Their yields, while generally modest compared to what most coffee plantations produced, generated revenue for the government and handsome commissions for administrators.[83]

Most government farms employed a small number of permanent staff in skilled-labour positions and as overseers. To this they added a large number of convicts, *contratados*, people arrested as 'vagrants', and workers of different ages requisitioned through chiefs.[84] For instance, the *granja* in Bula Atumba, Dembos, in 1949 used fifty boys – conveniently labelled 'apprentices' – and twenty contract workers to collect the coffee harvest, prune stands, and plant new shade trees.[85] In 1950, at the 400-hectare *granja* in Quiculungo, Ambaca, one European manager and six African headmen oversaw the work of sixty poorly paid *contratados* and sixty young apprentices. Additionally, every other week, the administrator called up sixty women from the community to help with farm upkeep, labour for which they only received food rations in return. This relatively large farm produced a hundred tons of unhusked coffee (*café mabuba*), which the government sold to Paiva, Marcelo & Companhia, a local plantation, processing, and export firm. At the nearby government post of Dimuca, the administrator coerced repatriated contract workers to labour on the local *granja* before allowing them to return home.[86] Everywhere, pay was either extremely low or non-existent, which was a clear violation of the law on forced labour, which stipulated wage parity with contract labour. Using forced labour to transform *granjas* into cash-crop ventures was legally dubious to begin with.[87]

Reports of abuses committed by José de Figueiredo Veloso, a *chefe de posto* (head of post) in the Negage district, reflect both the sense of ownership over African labour that corrupted settler lives, and the extreme vulnerability of the victims of forced labour. When these abuses came to light in 1960, Negage had existed as an independent township for only a few years. It owed its new status to its growing coffee sector, which consisted of thirty-six fully demarcated estates in 1959, requiring the distribution of thousands of contract workers for plantation upkeep and coffee picking, and hundreds of minors for post-harvest selection. Recruitment for these jobs was mostly involuntary and often violent, prompting several African residents and sometimes whole villages to seek refuge in other

83 'Relatório da Inspecção ao Concelho de Ambaca' (1950), p. 127; 'Relatório do Governador do Distrito do Cuanza Norte' (1956), p. 9; 'Relatório da Inspecção aos Distritos de Cuanza Norte, Cuanza Sul' (1960–1), pp. 82, 86 (quote).

84 'Relatório da Inspecção ao Concelho dos Dembos' (1957), pp. 40, 159; 'Relatório da Inspecção Administrativa ao Concelho do Uíge' (1959), pp. 168, 171.

85 'Inspecção feita ao concelho dos Dembos' (1949), docs. 43 and 45.

86 'Relatório da Inspecção ao Concelho de Ambaca' (1950), pp. 94, 101.

87 Portugal, *Código de Trabalho dos Indígenas*, art. 296-9.

regions and nearby cities. The evidence gathered against Veloso was notable for its graphic detail. Veloso was the administrator of Puri, a small town 50km east of Negage. One of his most notorious crimes was the seizure of relatives of labour absconders and forcing them to work in the local *granja*, a practice reminiscent of the *panyarring* of Africans by European slave traders in previous centuries – except now the state was the assailant.[88]

Veloso was an experienced colonial administrator. He had entered the colonial service in 1923, was promoted to the rank of *chefe de posto* in 1935 and became head of the Puri post in 1950. Statements by several African witnesses before government inspector Joaquim Henriques in 1960 show that Veloso, his subordinates, and his family brutally exploited his administrative position for personal gain. For instance, chief Salomão of Quiximbo said that his wife was imprisoned in Puri when their son escaped from contract duties. Veloso's wife then forced her to work in the government garden and demanded a pig for her release. A woman named Zua, from the village of Quibaba, said she was imprisoned for the same reason and had to pay Veloso's wife 250 escudos to be freed. Similarly, three women, Mussari, Muquembi, and Joaquina, claimed they were held captive at the government post for twelve months in retaliation for their sons' escape from contract labour. Veloso forced them to work, unpaid, at the *granja* and at the farm of his son, Nuno. Guialo Malundo, from Quizemba, informed Henriques that Veloso captured five women after his son ran away from a coffee plantation. He put them to work at Nuno's farm for five months, after which Malundo paid Nuno five hundred escudos for their release.

Chief Pacheco of Quimuinga told Henriques that women from his village were treated like 'slaves' at the government farm in Puri, where they worked without pay and were sexually exploited by police officers and Veloso's cook. Although women appeared to suffer the most, there were plenty of other victims of forced labour. The chief of Quimexone stated that one of his sons had worked at the *granja* for eight years without pay. Panzo Matondo, from Quizemba, said he had worked at Nuno's farm for five years and at the *granja* in Puri for four months without receiving any form of compensation. Dala, a boy from Cahenda, had worked as Veloso's domestic servant for three years, also without pay, when Veloso handed him over to a female acquaintance to become her servant in Malange. The same happened to four other men, as Veloso forced them to work for relations of his in Sanza Pombo. Morais Zuco, a man from Dala-Quiangala, said that after completing a term of labour service in São Tomé, he was forced to work in the houses of Veloso and of his daughter, Arminda. During Zuco's absence, the *granja* had annexed the coffee farm of his father, confiscating its harvest for six years in a row.

88 'Relatório da Inspecção ao Concelho do Negage' (1960), pp. 77, 83, 93, 100, 143. On panyarring, see Paul E. Lovejoy and David Richardson, 'The Business of Slaving: Pawnship in Western Africa, c. 1600–1810', *JAH*, 42:1 (2001), 67–89; Jennifer Lofkrantz and Olatunji Ojo, 'Slavery, Freedom, and Failed Ransom Negotiations in West Africa, 1730–1900', *JAH*, 53:1 (2012), 25–44.

These were only some of the illegalities recorded in Negage. The list continued, cataloguing other forms of unpaid labour and abuse by policemen, overseers, and administrative assistants. It showed how low-ranked administrators in Negage transformed their posts into fiefdoms, exploiting the contract labour system to illegally extract labour and sexual services from powerless subjects. These practices continued until they were investigated, at which point the culprits were removed from office or transferred to other districts. It is difficult to determine whether the situation in Negage was exemplary of the contract system in general or represented the extreme end of a broad spectrum of coercive practices. For people in northern Angola, government inspections were often the only opportunity to voice their concerns, but not all inspectors were as scrupulous as Joaquim Henriques, nor did people always trust them.[89]

Unrewarding labour

Sá da Bandeira had said it in the 1870s, Ferreira Diniz in the 1910s, and economist Armando Castro repeated the message in the 1950s: settlers failed to attract labour because the colonial system they relied on paid below the reservation wage.[90] This was particularly evident in the coffee zones of northern Angola. There, as the agronomist Artur Eduardo Rocha de Medina explained, small farming units easily earned more from growing coffee independently than from plantation labour. He calculated that a husband-and-wife team could cultivate three thousand coffee trees, covering about three hectares, if they worked all year round on their own land. Many tasks in the production cycle, including the harvest, were carried out jointly, but clearing, replanting, shading, and pruning were typically male jobs, whereas hulling and sorting were characteristically female activities. In general, the husband devoted most of his time to coffee production, while the wife combined coffee labour with subsistence farming. Three thousand stands produced approximately 1,000kg dried coffee, and yields were obviously higher if more labour could be added from family and village networks. With the high coffee prices of 1954, such proceeds amounted to approximately thirty thousand escudos. In contrast, plantation workers were paid about eighteen hundred escudos annually. Even if coffee prices were lower, work on a settler estate was clearly unrewarding compared to independent coffee farming.[91]

As Medina explained, there were approximately twenty-four thousand African coffee growers in northern Angola in 1954 – up from fourteen thousand in 1945 – some of whom produced more than ten tons, others less than 100kg. A coffee harvest of only a few hundred kilograms earned a small family more than

89 ILO, 'Report', pp. 221–2.

90 Castro, *Sistema*, pp. 110, 131, 196.

91 AHU, Governo Geral de Angola, Repartição do Gabinete, D2.172.6/06, Artur Medina to Junta de Exportação do Café, Informação no. 17-D/54-ST, Luanda, 5 Aug. 1954. For 1945, see Seleti, 'Portuguese Colonialism', p. 331.

settlers paid a father or son to work on a plantation all year round. To be excused from labour service, however, a farmer had to produce at least 1,000kg, according to a 1948 decree, which perhaps only one in ten managed.[92] New regulations issued in 1956 required farmers to cultivate more than three thousand stands to be exempt, although exemptions were never fully guaranteed. Most farmers therefore worked on a settler estate for part of the year, which for them was economically and socially degrading labour.

These calculations explain why contract labour was so unpopular in northern Angola. From a planter's perspective, paying recruitment fees on top of the legal minimum wage was cheaper than paying market rates for labour, which most could not afford. Recruiting among local populations for the coffee plantations therefore took place with varying levels of coercion, as this chapter has shown. There was physical compulsion in the form of requisitioning, abduction, police raids, forced rehiring, corvée, and conscript labour. So-called voluntary labour was often borne out of a desire to avoid lengthy compulsory contracts. Countrywide, colonial taxation forced many workers to seek paid employment, making wage labour generally a case of constrained choice.[93] Furthermore, the option to choose between employers was limited when there were few cash-earning opportunities and recruitment agents directed contract labourers to specific plantations. Debts to petty traders sometimes forced workers to accept contracts offered by labour touts, which was another instance of compulsion. The only potential case of free choice in the labour market seen so far was that of *bailundos* who migrated north to earn money so they could buy luxury items like textiles, although the extent to which these purchases were based on credit, turning labour migration into a form of indenture, remains unclear.[94]

The creation of a labour-hungry settler economy in the coffee districts of northern Angola changed the daily lives of local populations profoundly, as every year tens of thousands of residents were forced to leave their homes to labour on a white colonist's estate. Recruitment for the plantations could affect anyone, even those who had coffee farms of their own or had other means to sustain themselves and pay their debts to the colonial state. Because of the settler presence, in the words of one eyewitness, people in the north 'became slaves

92 TNA, CO371/97264, 'Summary of 3 articles by E. V. Pena', enclosed in House to FO, Luanda, 13 March 1952.

93 'Relatório do Curador Geral dos Indígenas da Colónia de Angola, Ano de 1937', p. 35.

94 Todd Cleveland, *Diamonds in the Rough: Corporate Paternalism and African Professionalism on the Mines of Colonial Angola, 1917–1975* (Athens: Ohio University Press, 2015), pp. 42–79, 191–211; Henrique Martino, '*Dash*-Peonage: The Contradictions of Debt Bondage in the Colonial Plantations of Fernando Pó', *Africa*, 87:1 (2017), 53–78.

on their own land'.[95] In addition to international condemnation of contract labour in the Portuguese colonies, there were internal critics. Inspectors sent by the Ministry of the Colonies, while not there to question the system, often disapproved of the chosen recruitment methods. Some district governors tried to curtail abuses committed by their subordinates but, like most inspectors, they stopped short of criticizing the colonial model of subsidized settler agriculture.

Supporting European coffee planters with coerced labour was not only politically contentious, but also economically irrational. It channelled labour to an inefficient production system that, under equal conditions, could not compete with local smallholders. Portugal's decision to cling to a model that other colonial powers were giving up on was rooted in a fundamental belief in economic development through white-owned, estate-based agriculture. This conviction underlay the proposal of the governor of the Congo province, Otelo Henriques da Fonseca, in 1953 to relocate African coffee growers to designated reserves to make room for allegedly more productive European planters. Before 1961, forced removals only happened on a small scale, although many growers lost their land to colonists in other ways, as Chapter 4 has shown.[96] Fonseca's successor, Hélio Felgas, was more appreciative of smallholder production, but at the same time a principled defender of the plantation model, which in his view warranted radical intervention in African labour markets. In 1957, he dismissed proposals by some government officials to give Africans more autonomy in their choice of work.

> If Africans could declare their preference [to be employed or self-employed], then the Angolan economy would become dependent, in fertile regions, on African farms of one hectare ... And poor regions would be abandoned as everyone would seek employment elsewhere. If that happened, Europeans would no longer be able to live in these fertile regions and the Angolan economy would collapse, as no modern economy is sustainably based on one-hectare cultures.

Felgas was imagining a counterfactual scenario of Angola as a peasant colony, in which African farmers dominated production and labour migration was no longer controlled by the government. The result: economic ruin and the end of settler enterprise. He was probably right about the latter, but almost certainly wrong about the former. Previously, Felgas had admitted that a smallholder economy would not necessarily be disastrous. Yet like many Portuguese men of empire, he could not envision Angola as a colony without white settlers. 'What if the economic output of 80,000 African farms of one hectare each

95 ILO, 'Report', p. 225.

96 'Relatório do Governo da Província do Congo no ano de 1953', p. 179; Paige, *Agrarian Revolution*, pp. 241–2; Miguel Bandeira Jerónimo, 'A Robust Operation: Resettling, Security, and Development in Late Colonial Angola (1960s–1970s)', *Itinerario*, 44:1 (2020), 55–79.

were comparable to current production', he asked. It was a rhetorical question. Felgas knew that a free peasantry would undermine the viability of European agriculture and cause an exodus of planters from Angola. 'Is this the policy we want to follow? Is it not to promote European settlement, the necessary condition to our survival?'[97] Ideologically, as in practice, white settlement and labour coercion were inseparable.

97 'Relatório do Governo do Distrito do Congo' (1957), pp. 251, 254 (quoting from his own Confidencial no. 226 to Negócios Indígenas, 8 Aug. 1956).

7

What Angolans Got for Their Coffee

It is time to return to the African smallholders who developed the Angolan coffee economy during the nineteenth century and carry their story forward into the late colonial period. This group lost their position as the country's dominant cash-crop producers during the 1920s, as colonists took hold of most of the land, labour, capital, and entrepreneurship available for coffee growing. State-sponsored settler expansion narrowed opportunities for material progress for thousands of farmers in northern Angola. It did not, however, destroy independent peasant production. In response to rising world coffee prices, smallholders in the north significantly increased their output. In 1928, they brought approximately 2,700 tons of coffee to market, but three decades later their contribution had grown to 22,500 tons, based mainly on expansion in the Congo district.[1] 'It so happens', the Portuguese agronomist Jorge Trancoso Vaz observed, 'that the native Kongo, taken by the increase in value of coffee, has amplified his plantations, making use of every bush available, just like the Europeans'.[2]

This chapter uses qualitative – occasionally anecdotal – evidence to argue that coffee production improved the living standards of small-scale farmers in Angola, especially during periods of favourable commodity prices.[3] The history of these farmers, poorly documented in colonial archives, is an example of African involvement in cash-crop production by grower initiative.[4] This provides a contrast not only with known cases of coffee culture development

1 'Mapa da produção de café referente ao ano de 1928', *BAA*, 2:7 (1929), 341; Angola, Repartição Central de Estatística Geral, *Anuário estatístico de Angola, ano de 1958* (Luanda: Imprensa Nacional, 1959).

2 Jorge Trancoso Vaz, 'Problemas da cafeicultua no Congo e a mão de obra', *RCP*, 3:11 (1956), 26–32.

3 Michiel de Haas, 'Measuring Rural Welfare in Colonial Africa: Did Uganda's Smallholders Thrive?', *Economic History Review*, 70:2 (2017), 605–31, reaches the same conclusion in Uganda using quantitative evidence. De Haas shows that, until around 1960, cash-crop farming was more remunerative than unskilled wage labour.

4 Gareth Austin, 'Capitalism and the Colonies', in Larry Neal and Jeffrey G. Williamson (eds), *The Cambridge History of Capitalism*, vol. 2 (Cambridge: Cambridge University Press, 2014), pp. 301–47, at p. 330.

in colonial Africa by state intervention – via taxation, propagation, or forced cultivation – but also with recent reformulations of classic dependency approaches to tropical crop production that relate it to colonial coercion and extraction.[5] With the exception of plantation workers, Angolan growers did not experience coffee cultivation as a burden. Rather, they saw it as a business. They were driven by material gain, channelling external price stimuli into local cultures of consumption and their associated political economies.[6]

The expansion of African cultivation, especially after the Second World War, led to substantial commerce in consumer goods, with white-owned retail trade in some regions becoming wholly dependent on indigenous coffee production.[7] Illuminating the connection between production and consumption, this chapter specifically asks 'what Africans got' for their coffee.[8] While textiles consistently topped the list of imported consumer items, purchasing patterns became increasingly globalized during the twentieth century, as common industrial commodities entered the lives of coffee-growing families.[9] Discussions about

5 Kris Manjapra, 'Plantation Dispossessions: The Global Travel of Agricultural Racial Capitalism', in Sven Beckert and Christine Desan (eds), *American Capitalism: New Histories* (New York: Columbia University Press, 2018), pp. 361–88. For examples of coffee growing by colonial intervention, see Kenneth Curtis, 'Smaller Is Better: A Consensus of Peasants and Bureaucrats in Colonial Tanganyika', in William Gervase Clarence-Smith and Steven Topik (eds), *The Global Coffee Economy in Africa, Asia, and Latin America, 1500–1989* (Cambridge: Cambridge University Press, 2003), pp. 312–34, at p. 314; Andreas Eckert, 'Comparing Coffee Production in Cameroon and Tanganyika, c.1900–1960s: Land, Labor, and Politics', *ibid.*, pp. 286–311, at p. 305; Sven Van Melkebeke, *Dissimilar Coffee Frontiers: Mobilizing Labor and Land in the Lake Kivu Region, Congo and Rwanda (1918–1960/62)* (Leiden: Brill, 2020), p. 41.

6 For cash-crop agriculture as business, see Polly Hill, *Studies in Rural Capitalism in West Africa* (Cambridge: Cambridge University Press, 1970), p. 23. For the distinction between opportunities and motives, or 'external' and 'internal' causes, see A. G. Hopkins, 'Innovation in a Colonial Context: African Origins of the Nigerian Cocoa-Farming Industry, 1880–1920', in Clive Dewey and A. G. Hopkins (eds), *The Imperial Impact: Studies in the Economic History of Africa and India* (London: Athlone Press, 1978), pp. 83–96.

7 Arquivo Histórico Ultramarino (Lisbon, henceforth AHU), Ministério do Ultramar (MU), Inspecção Superior da Administração Ultramarina (ISAU), A2.49.003/44.00300, 'Relatório da Inspecção ao Concelho do Negage, pelo Inspector Joaquim Henriques, 1960', p. 47; *ibid.*, A2.050.05/033.00202, José Diogo Ferreira Martins, 'Relatório da Inspecção aos Distritos de Cuanza Norte, Cuanza Sul, 1960–1961', p. 37.

8 Stanley B. Alpern, 'What Africans Got for Their Slaves: A Master List of European Trade Goods', *History in Africa*, 22 (1995), 5–43.

9 For comparison, see Robert Ross, *Things Change: Black Material Culture and the Development of a Consumer Society in South Africa, 1800–2020* (Leiden: Brill, 2023).

the gains of African cash-crop production have recently turned to the phenomenon of conspicuous consumption, the argument being that long-established ideas about wealth, honour, and social status stimulated the purchase of goods, thereby forming an impediment to capital accumulation and economic development.[10] In the Angolan context, you could ask which avenues, besides extending one's farm, were open to Africans to build up capital when, for example, colonial rule restricted the acquisition of private property and trade licences. But the point advanced here is more straightforward: revenue from coffee sales raised living standards and created chances for upward mobility. Increasing prosperity, in addition to social power, was a fundamental aim of farmer enterprise. To succeed, however, coffee growers needed to invest in labour. Based on Sara Berry's concept of entrepreneurial work, the chapter suggests that the spending habits of African farmers were part of smallholder strategies to gain access to family, village, and migrant labour.[11]

Production and consumption

Colonial agronomists estimated there were approximately thirty thousand independent African coffee growers in northern Angola in 1958, producing an average yield of 750kg. It is therefore likely that about one in four men over the age of nineteen within the main coffee areas in the Uíge and Cuanza Norte districts had a coffee farm.[12] Most of them used household labour to cultivate plots of one-half to two hectares in size. Coffee trees and their produce were typically owned by men, but women helped their husbands with planting, weeding, and harvesting and used part of their time to grow food crops on plots of their own. 'It is the woman's task to provide the food for her family while the man supplies the clothing', was how two protestant missionaries explained this process of female exclusion from agricultural capital.[13] Several thousand farmers

10 Ayodeji Olukoju, 'Accumulation and Conspicuous Consumption: The Poverty of Entrepreneurship in Western Nigeria, ca. 1850–1930', in Emmanuel Akyeampong *et al.* (eds), *Africa's Development in Historical Perspective* (Cambridge: Cambridge University Press, 2014), pp. 208–30.

11 Sara S. Berry, 'Entrepreneurial Labour', in Stefano Bellucci and Andreas Eckert (eds), *General Labour History of Africa: Workers, Employers and Governments, 20th–21st Centuries* (Woodbridge: James Currey, 2019), pp. 457–74.

12 In 1960, the male population over nineteen in Uíge, Songo, Bembe, Negage, Damba, Cazengo, Golungo Alto, Ambaca, Quiculungo, and Dembos was approximately 115,000. In Uíge, in total, there were 34,050 smallholders, 95 per cent being male; in Cuanza Norte, there were 12,565 smallholders, 98 per cent being male. See Angola, Direcção dos Serviços de Estatística, *3º Recenseamento geral da população, 1960*, vol. 4, *População residente segundo as condições perante o trabalho* (Luanda: Direcção dos Serviços de Estatística, 1964), pp. 14, 42, 46, 48.

13 The Angus Library and Archive, Regent's Park College (Oxford, henceforth ALA), A/124, Clifford & Lottie Parsons to Friends, S. Salvador, 10 March 1941.

managed to convert small plots into larger plantations, even into small estates. This allowed them to cultivate more than three thousand coffee stands and thus be freed from colonial labour obligations. These farms attracted workers who had hitherto toiled on European plantations to pay their taxes, underscoring the comparative strength of smallholder production.[14]

From a visit to Angola in 1957, the French coffee researcher René Coste concluded that African growers achieved the same yield per hectare as European planters, only they did so more efficiently.[15] Smallholders had a competitive advantage as their farms required fewer labour inputs per hectare than larger European plantations. In addition, they were not burdened by the costs of coercion and could offer workers more attractive compensation and conditions than European settlers provided.[16] By law, officially registered smallholders had

14 Armando Castro, *O sistema colonial português em África (meados do século XX)*, 2nd edn (Lisbon: Editorial Caminho, 1980), pp. 118, 129–30, 178–9, 196, 202; 'Relatório da Inspecção ao Concelho do Negage' (1960), doc. 16. For an indication of the number of large smallholders, see AHU, MU, ISAU, A2.050.02/016.00106, 'Relatório da Inspecção ao Concelho de Ambaca, pelo Inspector Administrativo, Eduardo B. Lapido Loureiro' (1950), p. 98 (forty farmers producing over 1,000kg in Quisseque, Dimuca); 'Relatório da Inspecção aos Distritos de Cuanza Norte, Cuanza Sul, 1960–1961', p. 47 (two thousand sales licenses issued in Quiculungo, Ambaca, 1960); AHU, Governo Geral de Angola (GANG), Repartição do Gabinete, D2.172.6/06, Artur Eduardo Rocha de Medina, Informação no. 6/GG/58, Luanda, 19 June 1958 (eight hundred farmers near Uíge producing on average 5,625kg); *ibid.*, Administrador dos Dembos, Quibaxe, 14 May 1952 (fifty-seven farmers in Dembos producing over 1,000kg); *ibid.*, Governo do Congo to Chefe do gabinete, Uíge, 30 May 1952 (922 farmers in Bembe and 124 farmers in Ambaca producing over 1,000kg); *ibid.*, Governador do Uíge to GG, telegram 28 Feb. 1951 (145 farmers producing more than 5,000kg unhusked). About three thousand stands, or three hectares, were needed to produce 1,000kg of hulled coffee; this required 351 man-days, including sixty-six days for hulling and sorting (considered female labour). See AHU, GANG, Repartição do Gabinete, D2.172.6/06, Artur Medina to Junta de Exportação do Café, Informação no. 17-D/54-ST, Luanda, 5 Aug. 1954. According to Paul Janssens, *Le café robusta dans l'Angola* (Brussels: Imprimerie Industrielle et Financière, 1930), pp. 82, 84, 101–2, new shaded plantations produced 600–1,000kg of dried coffee per hectare, whereas the yield of older plantations was 200kg per hectare. Castro, *O sistema*, p. 129, suggests average yields of 300–400kg per hectare for African farms. In Uganda, de Haas, 'Measuring', pp. 615, 621, 623, suggests an average yield of 800lbs of unhulled berries per acre (900kg per hectare) with a labour input of eighty man-days (198 days per hectare); a third of smallholders employed migrant wage labour.

15 René Coste, 'Impressões de uma viagem às regiões cafeeiras de Angola', *RCP*, 5:19 (1958), 5–11. See also René Coste, *Les caféiers et les cafés dans le monde* (2 vols, Paris: Larose, 1955–61), vol. 2, p. 452.

16 Sara S. Berry, *No Condition Is Permanent: The Social Dynamics of Agrarian Change in Sub-Saharan Africa* (Madison: University of Wisconsin Press, 1993), pp. 135–48;

access to contract labour. One publication put the number of such smallholders at fifteen thousand in 1960. However, despite their relative wealth, most of them could not afford the recruitment fees. Reliance on family and neighbourhood labour was therefore widespread. In general, recruitment occurred informally, with household and village heads invoking the power of dependency and the promise of material and non-material rewards.[17]

African coffee production stimulated a vigorous trade in consumer goods north of the Cuanza River, as farmers sold their product to European middlemen who were often coffee planters themselves. Junta engineer Artur Eduardo Rocha de Medina estimated the size of this trade in 1958 at about four hundred million escudos, or five million pounds sterling, which amounted to approximately 10 per cent of all imports in Angola.[18] There were different ways in which coffee from small farms moved up the supply chain. Growers were supposed to sell their coffee for cash in licensed plantation shops or at official regional markets, and many did. Consequently, several European plantations acquired more coffee through purchase than they produced on their own.[19] But outside these formal channels there was a substantial informal goods-for-coffee trade conducted by shopkeepers and itinerant traders. The latter operated from local stores or came all the way from Luanda, filling trucks with merchandise and buying directly in the villages. Although the truck trade was difficult to avoid as most African growers did not have their own means of transportation, it worried Portuguese officials for different reasons. Much of this trade was illicit, unregulated, and untaxed. Furthermore, it was often based on the provision of credit, paid off with coffee during the harvest season, which exposed African farmers to the risk of expropriation if they had a bad crop. In this regard, the seasonal-

Gareth Austin, 'Mode of Production or Mode of Cultivation: Explaining the Failure of European Cocoa Planters in Competition with African Farmers in Colonial Ghana', in William Gervase Clarence-Smith (ed.), *Cocoa Pioneer Fronts since 1800: The Role of Smallholders, Planters and Merchants* (London: Macmillan, 1996), pp. 154–75.

17 Agência Geral do Ultramar, *Notas económicas: A agricultura em Angola* (Lisbon: Agência Geral do Ultramar, 1960); AHU, MU, ISAU, A2.050.05/034.00207, Hélio Esteves Felgas, 'Relatório do Governo do Distrito do Congo referente a 1957 (Confidencial)', p. 269; *ibid.*, A2.49.002/39.00251, 'Relatório da Inspecção Administrativa ao Concelho do Uíge, pelo Inspector Administrativo António do Nascimento Rodrigues, 1959', p. 169.

18 Angola, Repartição Central de Estatística Geral, *Anuário estatístico de Angola, ano de 1958* (Luanda: Imprensa Nacional, 1959); Werner Antweiler, 'Foreign Currency Units per 1 British Pound, 1950–2023' (2024) <https://fx.sauder.ubc.ca/etc/GBPpages.pdf> [accessed 22 May 2024].

19 AHU, MU, ISAU, A2.050.02/016.00094, Colónia de Angola, Inspecção dos Serviços Administrativos e dos Negócios Indígenas, 'Inspecção feita ao concelho dos Dembos pelo Inspector Administrativo, Américo Baptista de Sousa' (1949), p. 10.

ity of cash crops differentiated coffee growers from pastoralists on the higher plateaus, who could sell livestock year-round when they needed cash and thus took on fewer debts. Finally, itinerant traders encouraged farmers to harvest early and cut short the drying, which resulted in lower-quality coffee.[20] Many farmers sold dried but unhusked berries (*café mabuba*), which gave them half the price of hulled coffee but freed household labour for other activities.[21] In the Uíge sub-district alone, there were about two-hundred licensed retailers at the time, and many more unauthorized village stores (*cantinas*) buying coffee.[22] The feverish trade of the 1950s infiltrated the remotest corners of the Congo district, including places where arid soils did not favour cultivation but people could reap the benefits of collecting wild coffee from isolated forest reserves.[23]

Throughout the modern colonial period, coloured (dyed or printed) cottons for African consumption were the most important Angolan import. Their value increased from an average of 34 million escudos in 1926–30 (£314,000 in 1930) to 217 million escudos in 1951–55 (£2.7m in 1955). Until 1960, they continuously constituted between 10 and 20 per cent of Angola's total imports.[24] A significant

20 AHU, GANG, Repartição do Gabinete, D2.172.6/06, Artur Eduardo Rocha de Medina, Informação no. 6/GG/58, Luanda, 19 June 1958; *ibid.*, Governador do Congo to Chefe de gabinete, no. 5, confidential circular, Carmona, 5 May 1956; *ibid.*, Governador do Congo, no. 30/1ª/31, confidential circular, Carmona, 29 May 1956; 'Relatório do Governo do Distrito do Congo referente a 1957', pp. 190, 199. On coffee, cattle, and credit, see 'Relatório da Inspecção aos Distritos de Cuanza Norte, Cuanza Sul, 1960–1961', p. 65.

21 AHU, GANG, Repartição do Gabinete, D2.165.1/11, Inspector de fomento, mapas do movimento de compras de café (1952–4); AHU, MU, ISAU, A2.050.02/018.00122, Província de Angola, Inspecção dos Serviços Administrativos, 'Relatório sobre a inspecção ordinária à Camara Municipal de Negage, pelo Inspector Administrativo António Emílio Maria Rodrigues da Silva' (1968), pp. 5, 160.

22 'Relatório da Inspecção Administrativa ao Concelho do Uíge' (1959), pp. 19–20; 'Relatório da Inspecção ao Concelho do Negage' (1960), doc. 26; 'Relatório da Inspecção aos Distritos de Cuanza Norte, Cuanza Sul, 1960–1961', pp. 38, 50, 56; Castro, *Sistema*, p. 128.

23 AHU, GANG, Repartição do Gabinete, D2.165.1/11, Administrador do Pombo, 17 Oct. 1952; *ibid.*, Administrador do Cuango, Quimbele, 4 Oct. 1952; Eurico de Azevedo Noronha, 'O "café Cuango": Relatório de uma viagem às regiões de Mococola e Quimbele', *RCP*, 1:4 (1954), 37–41. The smallholder practice of selling unprocessed coffee to larger estates also existed in Puerto Rico. See Fernando Picó, 'Coffee and the Rise of Commercial Agriculture in Puerto Rico's Highlands: The Occupation and Loss of Land in Guaonico and Roncador (Utuado), 1833–1900', in William Roseberry *et al.* (eds), *Coffee, Society, and Power in Latin America* (Baltimore: Johns Hopkins University Press, 1995), pp. 94–111.

24 Rodney Edvinsson, 'Historical Currency Converter (test version 1.0)' (2016) <https://www.historicalstatistics.org/Currencyconverter.html> [accessed 22 May 2024]; Angola, Repartição Central de Estatística Geral, *Anuário estatístico*

part of these cottons was traded in northern Angola for coffee, continuing the age-old dominance of textiles in the coastal barter trade. In the late nineteenth and early twentieth centuries, European merchants in Luanda and Ambriz bought coffee mainly with textiles, especially striped cottons (*riscados*) and printed calicos, also known as chintz. In addition, so-called trade blankets were an important currency.[25] White and blue, or white cloth with blue or red stripes, were popular colours. However, unbleached cottons were also in demand; some craftsmen treated them with resin oils to make rain covers. While imported textiles were sometimes used as garments (Plate 7.1), for most buyers they were a form of capital, a currency they could invest in other things.[26]

Before the First World War, most textiles consumed in Angola came from Manchester, which besides striped and chequered calicos also supplied finer goods like satins, muslins, and silks. But a significant devaluation of the escudo after 1920 boosted the Portuguese textile industry, which further benefited from preferential import duties in Luanda. Local retailers, including the 'bush traders' in the coffee zones, were often dependencies of Portuguese import houses, which through their agents in Lisbon were closely linked to metropolitan manufacturers. Very soon, Portuguese textile manufacturers cornered the market for bleached and unbleached, as well as dyed and printed, cottons in

de Angola (Luanda: Imprensa Nacional, 1934–61). The values exclude imports of other cotton piece goods, like bleached and unbleached cottons, and cotton thread, cotton blankets, used clothing, and worked-up textiles. In the 1950s, alcohol, consumed by a growing urban population, overtook textiles as the dominant import group. See Augusto L. Ferreira dos Santos and V. M. Rabaça Gaspar, *Estrutura do comércio externo de Angola* (Lisbon: Junta de Investigações do Ultramar, 1959), p. 68.

25 AHU, Secretaria de Estado da Marinha e Ultramar (SEMU), Direcção Geral do Ultramar (DGU), Angola, no. 641, Mapa estatístico das mercadorias importadas e reexportadas na alfândega do Ambriz, durante 1869; *ibid.*, no. 640-2, Mapa dos principais géneros importados na alfândega de Loanda, 1869; António José Valente, *Novo projecto da pauta aduaneira da Alfândega do Ambriz* (Lisbon: Typografia Franco-Portugueza, 1889), p. 26; Portugal, *Relatório do Ministério e Secretário d'Estado dos Negócios da Marinha e Ultramar* (Lisbon: Imprensa Nacional, 1898), 194–203; Portugal, Ministério das Colónias, Direcção Geral de Fazenda das Colónias, *Estatística das alfândegas da Província de Angola: Importação, exportação e reexportação no ano de 1912* (Lisbon: Tip. Casa Portuguesa, 1914), 3–15. Blankets remained a significant import as employers were legally obliged to provide them to contract workers. See Maurício Loureiro de Almeida e Cruz, 'O café de Angola: Ligeiros apontamentos de um caderno', *Revista do Ultramar*, 1:10 (1948), 21–6.

26 Fernando Pimentel, *Investigação commercial na província de Angola* (Porto: Typographia a Vapor da Empreza Guedes, 1903), pp. 145–6, 149; Great Britain, Foreign Office, *Report for the Year 1908 on the Trade of the Province of Angola* (London: HMSO, 1909), p. 49.

Plate 7.1 Woman in Sunday dress, Luanda, 1886. Source: José Augusto da Cunha Morais, *Africa occidental: Album photographico e descriptivo* (4 vols, Lisbon: David Corazzi, 1885–8), vol. 2, PT/AHM/FE/010/B02/PQ/06. Image provided by Arquivo Histórico Militar.

Angola.[27] Controlled by their suppliers, traders in the coffee zones often stimulated textile purchases, even when African producers preferred the flexibility of payments in cash.[28]

As imported textiles became more widely available in the twentieth century, their use for clothing increased. Plates 7.2 and 7.3 show a woman dressed in striped cotton wrappers picking coffee and emptying her basket on cleared ground to sun-dry the berries. These pictures were taken by photographer Elmano da Cunha e Costa near Calandula, in the Malange district, in the late 1930s.[29] Located east of the Angolan montane forest, this was not a major coffee-producing region; nevertheless, in the 1920s and 1930s, African and European farmers had started cultivating coffee, partly by exploiting small forest reserves.[30] The trees pictured here were probably planted. The proximity of the house to the coffee bush and Costa's labelling of the two individuals as 'Calandulas' suggest this was a small African farm, the two persons possibly being husband and wife. The young man is barefoot but wearing trousers and a jacket, which look like

27 Great Britain, Foreign Office, *Report for the Year 1904 on the Trade and Commerce of Angola* (London: HMSO, 1905); *Report for the Year 1906 on the Trade and Commerce of Angola* (London: HMSO, 1907); *Report for the Year 1908*, p. 49; Great Britain, Department of Overseas Trade, *Report on the Economic Conditions in Angola (Portuguese West Africa), Dated March, 1923* (London: HMSO, 1923), p. 27; *Economic Conditions in Angola (Portuguese West Africa), Dated February, 1929* (London: HMSO, 1929), p. 25; *Economic Conditions in Angola (Portuguese West Africa)* (London: HMSO, 1932), p. 22; *Economic Conditions in Angola (Portuguese West Africa) (March, 1934)* (London: HMSO, 1934), pp. 15, 18; *Report on the Economic and Commercial Conditions in Angola (Portuguese West Africa), February, 1937* (London: HMSO, 1937), pp. 12–13; D. O. Fynes-Clinton, *Portuguese West Africa: Economic and Commercial Conditions in Portuguese West Africa (Angola), June, 1949* (London: HMSO, 1949), pp. 17, 23; T. C. Sharman, *Portuguese West Africa: Economic and Commercial Conditions in Portuguese West Africa (Angola), June, 1953* (London: HMSO, 1954), p. 30.

28 Ronald Chilcote, *Emerging Nationalism in Portuguese Africa: Documents* (Stanford: Hoover Institution Press, 1972), p. 46.

29 On the photography of Elmano da Cunha e Costa, see Cláudia Castelo and Catarina Mateus, '"Etnografia Angolana" (1935–1939): Histórias da coleção fotográfica de Elmano Cunha e Costa', in Filipa Lowndes Vicente (ed.), *O império da visão: Fotografia no contexto colonial português (1860–1960)* (Lisbon: Edições 70, 2014), pp. 85–106; João de Castro Maia Veiga Figueiredo, 'Heimlich/unheimlich: Outlining the Influence of Spiritan Worldviews in the Work of Angolan Pioneer Photographers José Moraes and Elmano Costa', *Social Sciences and Missions*, 30:3–4 (2017), 366–87.

30 'Mapa da produção de café referente ao ano de 1928', *BAA*, 2:7 (1929), 341; John Gossweiler, 'Reconhecimento agronómico no Distrito de Malanje', *BAA*, ser. 6, 5:16–19 (1932), 19–52; J. Costa Rosa, 'Relatório annual da 6ª Delegação Regional dos Serviços Agrícolas', *BAA*, ser. 6, 6:20–3 (1933), 85–104.

Plate 7.2 Woman picking coffee, Calandula, c.1935–9. Source: Agência Geral do Ultramar, Elmano Cunha e Costa, no. 9346, ECC/NC1975. Image provided by Arquivo Histórico Ultramarino.

imported second-hand clothing. In addition to her cotton wrappers, the woman wears a beaded necklace and a headcover with sewn-on buttons. The pictures convey a connection between small-scale producers and a world of imported consumer goods, although apart from the thatched house, there is little indication of extraordinary affluence.

By contrast, the woman and child in Plate 7.4 show signs of greater material welfare. This picture was taken by Costa close to Uíge in the same series. He labelled the woman and child 'Mahungos', an ethnic designation of populations that historically inhabited the region west and east of Encoge. The setting is unclear. At first glance, the buildings in the background are reminiscent of European settlement, but it was very likely an African village. In this region,

Plate 7.3 Woman drying coffee, Calandula, c.1935–9. Source: Agência Geral do Ultramar, Elmano Cunha e Costa, no. 9352, ECC/NC1981. Image provided by Arquivo Histórico Ultramarino.

according to José Diniz, director of Native Affairs, 'all houses are gabled'.[31] The woman is cleaning and separating husked coffee. Her clothing suggests she is not an ordinary farmhand, but rather the wife or daughter of a successful African farmer. Striking elements are the woman's one-piece dress made of bright cotton checks and her multi-stringed beaded collar, held together by pins. The little girl, dressed in a jersey, also wears a beaded necklace. Whoever they were, their picture communicates relative prosperity.

Until around 1900, besides European textiles, common barter goods in the coastal trade were liquor, rifles, gunpowder, beads, and African cloth (*panos*

31 José de Oliveira Ferreira Diniz, *Populações indígenas de Angola* (Coimbra: Imprensa da Universidade, 1918), pp. 165–86, quote at p. 171.

Plate 7.4 Woman sorting dried coffee, Uíge, c.1935–9. Source: Agência Geral do Ultramar, Elmano Cunha e Costa, no. 15362, ECC/NC8256. Image provided by Arquivo Histórico Ultramarino.

da costa). Over the course of the twentieth century, these traditional means of exchange gradually gave way to a more varied range of consumer goods, although, as the Anglican missionary Edgar Cooper observed in 1942, income from coffee sales and other crops was still mainly spent on 'better wearing apparel'.[32] For instance, in the Ambaca district, trade houses in 1950 bought coffee and other produce, such as manioc flour, beans, peanuts, and raffia fibre, from local producers. In exchange, they sold second-hand clothes, British and Japanese bicycles, gramophones, imported food items, wine, beer, furniture, and tableware. In the textile department, quilts and African cloth remained popular, but people were also buying Tobralco, a relatively new crease-resistant fabric made by the British company Tootal. In several places, men and women used income from coffee sales to buy ready-made clothes or employ a tailor to help them

32 North Angola Mission, Archibald Patterson Papers, Cooper to Patterson, Uíge, 31 Dec. 1942.

dress 'European style', although women typically still wore cotton wrappers.[33] Similarly, in São Salvador (Mbanza Kongo), where coffee cultivation expanded during the 1950s, sales to rural producers consisted mainly of textiles, but also included books, sewing machines, enamelled iron dishes, and zinc roofing for homes.[34] Textile imports created work for seamsters, which in turn created demand for sewing equipment.

Motives

The overwhelming impression from the archives for this period is that coffee cultivation allowed smallholders to raise their standard of living. This mainly applied to those who managed to avoid government conscription and 'live at ease', as one government inspector put it; but there were many of them.[35] Revenue from coffee sales allowed people to partake in a rapidly globalizing consumer culture. 'It is a very poor marriage feast these days if there is no "Canada Dry" "Pepsi Cola" or "Coka Cola" to be had', the Baptist missionary David Grenfell reported from the Congo district in 1960.[36] During the 'big euphoria' of the 1950s, coffee growers in Uíge spent money on items like refrigerators, typewriters, fountain pens, and sunglasses. According to one Portuguese eyewitness, the purpose of such purchases was in part to show wealth.[37] Grenfell related the story of a coffee-growing catechist, who bought a moped for £75 although he barely knew

33 'Relatório da Inspecção ao Concelho de Ambaca' (1950), pp. 23–32, 59–64, 72–6, 83, 98–9. On Western dress codes, see Jean Allman (ed.), *Fashioning Africa: Power and Politics of Dress* (Bloomington: Indiana University Press, 2004). On second-hand clothes, see Karen Tranberg Hansen, *Salaula: The World of Secondhand Clothing and Zambia* (Chicago: University of Chicago Press, 2000). Bicycles are mentioned in Gabriel Lefebvre, *L'Angola: Son histoire, son économie* (Liège: Georges Thone, 1947), p. 229. In the 1930s, Japan made inroads in the Angolan textile trade, leading Portugal to increase tariffs on khaki and linen imports. See Great Britain, Department of Overseas Trade, *Report* (1937), pp. 11–13; Kweku Ampiah, *The Dynamics of Japan's Relations with Africa: South Africa, Tanzania and Nigeria* (London: Routledge, 1997), pp. 34–66.

34 AHU, MU, ISAU, A2.49.002/40.00266, 'Relatório da Inspecção ao Concelho de S. Salvador do Congo, pelo inspector administrativo António do Nascimento Rodrigues, 1959', Table 5.

35 'Relatório da Inspecção ao Concelho de Ambaca' (1950), p. 53.

36 ALA, A/44/8b, W. D. Grenfell, David Grenfell to 'Daphne & Arthur' [Annual report to former workers, 1960].

37 'Relatório da Inspecção aos Distritos de Cuanza Norte, Cuanza Sul, 1960–1961', p. 60. On refrigerators (and the lack of electricity to power them), see also Sharman, *Portuguese West Africa*, p. 28; Jeffery M. Paige, *Agrarian Revolution: Social Movements and Export Agriculture in the Underdeveloped World* (New York: Free Press, 1975), p. 236.

how to drive it. Similar accusations of conspicuous consumption were levelled at the African coffee producers of N'dalatando, 'the land of black millionaires', as a visitor put it. 'Wealth has no limits here and is glorified … in some comic scenes – empty American beer cans piled up in villages; blacks traveling on motorbikes with side-car and chauffeur, because while rich, being illiterate they cannot drive; big brand cars – Plymouths and Dodges – parked under thatched roofs.'[38] While there was much racial bias in these European observations of African consumer behaviour, they provide a snapshot of the changing material culture in northern Angola during the post-war commodity boom.

Spending on imported foodstuffs also increased. In Ambaca, colonial inspector Eduardo Loureiro reported in 1950 that Africans were living 'reasonably well, feeding themselves not just with the products of the land, but also buying, in the shops, flour, spaghetti, olive oil, lard, chorizo, etc.'[39] Many of these items were new additions to local diets. In Uíge, growing incomes from coffee stimulated the consumption of chicken and beef, another nutritional novelty. Beef was imported from the highland regions of northern Angola, with supply apparently unable to keep up with demand.[40] There were fears that rising coffee prices led many households to give up on subsistence farming. In 1957, according to inspector António do Nascimento Rodrigues, Ambaca was 'importing almost all products that it needs, like manioc flour, maize, rice, potato, groundnuts, beans, fish, meat, fruit, cement, etc. The local people produce hardly anything because coffee gives enough to satisfy their limited needs.'[41] In the Dembos district, Rodrigues observed the same pattern, adding that 'apart from coffee and some manioc flour, the [African farmer] grows almost nothing anymore and … the European planter dedicates himself almost exclusively to coffee culture, buying at quite high prices what he needs for himself and to feed his workers'.[42]

Colonial inspection reports from the 1940s and 1950s often warned of the effect of the growing coffee economy on local food production, whether through forced labour or small-scale cultivation. African community leaders shared the concerns about the impact of labour recruitment. But they argued that recruitment for settler farms affected household production generally, thus food and coffee cultivation

38 Almerindo Lessa, 'Angola e Moçambique: Panorama da terra e dos homens', *BGU*, 28:326–7 (1952), 89–156, at pp. 120–1.

39 'Relatório da Inspecção ao Concelho de Ambaca' (1950), p. 32.

40 The National Archives (Kew), CO371/97249, House to FO, Luanda, 12 Feb. 1952; AHU, MU, ISAU, A2.050.05/034.00203, 'Relatório do Governo da Província do Congo no ano de 1953', p. 153.

41 AHU, MU, ISAU, A2.49.005/59.00457, 'Relatório da Inspecção ao Concelho de Ambaca, pelo Inspector Administrativo interino António do Nascimento Rodrigues, 1957', p. 24.

42 AHU, MU, ISAU, A2.49.005/59.00458, 'Relatório da Inspecção ao Concelho dos Dembos, pelo Inspector Administrativo António do Nascimento Rodrigues, 1957', p. 20.

in equal measure. In 1956, the governor of Cuanza Norte, António Francisco Neto Parra, warned that African growers were prioritizing coffee over crops like peanuts, potatoes, beans, maize, and manioc.[43] In São Salvador, the government tried to combat coffee monocropping by distributing seeds for peanut cultivation, but the campaign was stranded by the minimal interest of local farmers (who anyway did not need government help to grow peanuts).[44] Fears about food shortages were often misplaced, however. In principle, coffee growing was compatible with existing subsistence patterns, as only the harvest required intensive labour inputs, and this was during the dry season from June to September when other crops demanded less attention. Moreover, food crops like plantain could be intercropped with coffee, providing shade to the latter. In Uganda, where coffee was predominantly a peasant crop, farm structures remained largely the same during the post-war cash-crop boom, with coffee typically occupying only about half of the smallholding.[45]

Generally, African outputs of food and coffee seemed to be moving in the same direction. In the Congo district, for instance, the production of local staples like peanuts, rice, sweet potato, beans, and manioc decreased slightly between 1954 and 1957, but so did African coffee production as world market prices dropped.[46] By contrast, in the Ambaca subdistrict, agricultural outputs grew from 20,000 tons in 1943 to 28,000 tons in 1949, with coffee accounting for only 10 per cent of this increase. As inspector Loureiro observed, farmers saw most of their crops as cash generating – refuting the definition of food crops as subsistence crops – and took strategic decisions on which to prioritize according to the possibilities of the land and changing prices.[47] The result may have been that growers in coffee-rich areas such as Uíge focused more on this crop during the 1950s, boosting demand for foodstuffs from neighbouring regions such as Damba and Pombo, which were less well-endowed for coffee cultivation.[48] But they would not have easily dismissed the possibilities and benefits of crop diversification. As Gareth Austin has pointed out, the fact that cash-crop zones in colonial Africa often became net importers of food could have been caused as much by increased levels of consumption as by a decline in food production.[49]

43 'Relatório do Governador do Distrito do Cuanza Norte', pp. 7, 99, 104.

44 'Relatório da Inspecção ao Concelho de S. Salvador' (1959), p. 20.

45 Ralph Austen, *African Economic History: Internal Development and External Dependency* (Oxford: James Currey, 1987), p. 139; de Haas, 'Measuring', pp. 612, 614 fn. 45.

46 'Relatório do Governo do Distrito do Congo referente a 1957', pp. 182, 188. The figures for coffee outputs in this report show a different trend (upward) than those in the *Anuário estatístico* for 1954–57.

47 'Relatório da Inspecção ao Concelho de Ambaca' (1950), pp. 107–8.

48 'Relatório da Inspecção Administrativa ao Concelho do Uíge' (1959), p. 15.

49 Gareth Austin, 'Explaining and Evaluating the Cash Crop Revolution in the "Peasant" Colonies of Tropical Africa, ca. 1890–ca.1930: Beyond "Vent for Surplus"', in Akyeampong *et al.*, *Africa's Development in Historical Perspective*, pp. 295–320, at p. 302.

Successful farmers also invested in human capital. First, they used coffee money to pay for their children's education at local mission schools. Both the Baptist Missionary Society and the North Angola Mission (affiliated with the Church of England and the Swiss Reformed Church) had a strong presence in the coffee-growing areas of Uíge and Bembe.[50] Furthermore, some farmers were wealthy enough to marry more than one wife, thereby expanding the productive and reproductive capacity of their households. As a Baptist missionary in Bembe observed in 1954,

> coffee-growing is a very remunerative job in this area, so that those who have a large number of trees can become quite wealthy in a comparatively short time provided they have enough 'hands' to pick the berries for them! This economic factor is making men keener than ever to have several wives with the hope of correspondingly large families.[51]

Finally, what Europeans considered conspicuous consumption was often part of entrepreneurial strategies aimed to display social status and extend relations of patronage. Based on this kind of 'social work', as Sara Berry has coined these strategies, smallholders managed to compete for labour, generally providing a more attractive package of remuneration and working conditions than the European plantation sector offered.[52]

Writing on African agrarian entrepreneurship, Berry has argued that successful farmers invested a lot in social relationships 'because of the continued importance of social networks as channels of access to the means of production', especially land and labour.[53] Social work included spending on ceremonies, community projects, and the career advancement of dependents and clients, among other things. In terms of start-up costs, coffee farms in Angola were not very different from the cocoa plantations Berry studied in West Africa. Coffee required little capital as mechanization played no role in cultivation. Transforming wild coffee bushes into a healthy farm and expanding production by adding new trees required mainly labour. As alternative commercial opportunities – in crafts, petty trade, and urban economies – widened after the Second World War, household heads could rarely rely on authority alone to control the labour of their dependents. Loyalty was bought, Berry explains, through 'gifts, extra household consumption, and future assistance in starting farms or businesses of their own', to which can be added the promise of upward mobility through education.[54]

50 'Relatório da Inspecção Administrativa ao Concelho do Uíge' (1959), pp. 174–6.

51 ALA, A/94, Bembe, Women's Report, 1954.

52 Berry, 'Entrepreneurial Labour'.

53 Berry, *No Condition*, p. 159; see also pp. 160–6.

54 Berry, 'Entrepreneurial Labour', pp. 463–4; Austen, *African Economic History*, pp. 145–6.

Caveats

Cash-crop production provided small farmers in Angola opportunities to improve their living standards. This was especially so when they grew coffee, although producers of food crops like beans and manioc also appeared to enjoy higher incomes.[55] The experience of Angolan coffee farmers resembled that of growers in other African colonies, like Uganda, Tanzania, the Congo, Rwanda, and Cameroon, where substantial gains were made from coffee cultivation, especially after 1945.[56] These African cases provide a contrast with coffee economies in Latin America, where Steven Topik and others have seen a closer relation of coffee with poverty and sheer survival than with prosperity.[57] The Latin American coffee landscape has always been very diverse in land and labour regimes, but there was one fundamental difference with the African continent: in colonial Africa, indigenous farmers generally retained ownership of the land and could, as a result, reap the fruits of their own labour, whereas in twentieth-century Latin America coffee workers were often tenants, sharecroppers, or impoverished wage labourers with less control over their economic affairs.[58] As studies of forced cotton cultivation regimes in Africa have shown, when Africans lost control over production, pauperization was often the result.[59]

In Angola, too, smallholder success was always relative. More people worked for repressed wages on foreign coffee plantations than as owners, dependents, or migrant labourers on African coffee farms. In regions where coffee was not widespread, people complained about a shortage of cash-earning opportunities, as a free labour market was virtually non-existent.[60] According to the British consul

55 Fynes-Clinton, *Portuguese West Africa*, p. 22.

56 De Haas, 'Measuring'; Catherine Baroin, 'L'impact social de la caféiculture en Tanzanie du Nord', *Études rurales*, 180 (2007), 85–100; Curtis, 'Smaller is Better', pp. 316, 319; Eckert, 'Comparing Coffee Production', p. 306; Van Melkebeke, *Dissimilar Coffee Frontiers*, pp. 192, 210, 229, 241.

57 Steven C. Topik, 'Coffee', in Steven C. Topik and Allen Wells (eds), *The Second Conquest of Latin America: Coffee, Henequen, and Oil during the Export Boom, 1850–1930* (Austin: University of Texas Press, 1998), pp. 37–84.

58 See the contributions in Clarence-Smith and Topik, *Global Coffee Economy*.

59 Allen F. Isaacman, *Cotton is the Mother of Poverty: Peasants, Work, and Rural Struggle in Colonial Mozambique, 1938–1961* (Cape Town: Heinemann, 1996); Osumaka Likaka, *Rural Society and Cotton in Colonial Zaire* (Madison: University of Wisconsin Press, 1997). Robert E. Elson, *Village Java under the Cultivation System, 1830–1870* (Sydney: ASAA Southeast Asia Publication Series, 1994) argues that there was an uptick in rural trade and consumption in Java during the nineteenth century, even though smallholders laboured under a forced cultivation system. For a critique, see Jan Breman, *Mobilizing Labour for the Global Coffee Market: Profits from an Unfree Work Regime in Colonial Java* (Amsterdam: Amsterdam University Press, 2015).

60 Chilcote, *Emerging Nationalism*, p. 46.

in Luanda, Thomas Sharman, in 1953, African purchasing power was generally low in Angola, and most additional income was spent on textiles.[61]

Unilever agents visiting Angola came to similar conclusions. The company sold a range of consumer goods in the country through Robert Hudson & Sons, who distributed these products to approximately five hundred retail outlets across Angola. In 1956, the value of these imports was £53,616. A smashing third of this consisted of margarine, which was used for everyday consumption and in biscuit and pastry manufacture. Other products included detergents (Surf and Omo) and their popular Lifebuoy soap.[62] However, their customers lived mainly in urban areas and were predominantly white, while African buyers in the countryside proved difficult to reach. This was partly because many were too poor, as one company official noted:

> it must be assumed that a very high percentage of our sales is concentrated in the cities, with a total population of some 800.000 [*sic*] ... The problem is not that the remaining 3.700.000 [*sic*] are buying competitive products, they do not buy this sort of product at all ... to a large extend they probably cannot because their income does not allow them to do so.[63]

In addition, Unilever found it difficult to reach the better-off rural producers through the retail trade. Markets were poorly developed in the interior. As mentioned earlier, producers often sold directly to shopkeepers, either by truck, in villages stores, or in plantation shops, and these transactions involved very little cash. The continuing barter trade complicated business for Hudson, which did not accept coffee as payment. The solution for Hudson was to sell more through textile-toting wholesalers, as they had the capacity to transform coffee purchases from local retailers into cash. In other words, to reach more African consumers, Unilever had to adapt to prevailing commercial structures, which were dominated by Portuguese import and wholesale companies and their shopkeeping clients.

These observations underline the uneven impact of economic development in northern Angola. This manifested in the dominance of settler plantations over smallholders, the vastly different levels of purchasing power between plantation workers and independent coffee growers, and the inequalities within farming units between male heads, their dependents, and any extra-familial labour. It was also displayed in African consumption patterns, which were constrained by the continued prevalence of barter, the ascendency of Portuguese imports, and

61 Sharman, *Portuguese West Africa*, p. 28.

62 Unilever Archives (Port Sunlight), GB1752.UNI/RM/OC/2/2/2/1, R. D. Camplin, 'Angola (March/April, 1957)'. On Lifebuoy in Africa, see Timothy Burke, *Lifebuoy Men, Lux Women: Commodification, Consumption, and Cleanliness in Modern Zimbabwe* (Durham: Duke University Press, 1996).

63 Unilever Archives, GB1752.UNI/RM/OC/2/2/2/2, E. W. Pera, 'Visit to Angola and Discussions at Lisbon (November 1963)'.

the dominance of textiles over other consumer goods – which, it turns out, was not merely the result of African cultural preferences.

As with the goods that came in, there were asymmetries in the movement of coffee upstream. This question goes beyond well-known colonial export controls. An understudied paradox in the commercialization of coffee in Angola was that only a small part of the crop remained in the country, although domestic consumption increased significantly during the colonial period. Coffee-growing countries worldwide have generally consumed little of their own product. Dependency on exports has made producers vulnerable to international price shocks and underlined the popular image of the Global South as a raw-material supplier to the Global North.[64] In Angola, coffee consumption was mainly associated with the European settler population, while coffee planters also provided coffee as a drink to their workers.[65] Although local populations knew the coffee tree, there is little evidence of African consumption before its exploitation for trade. According to the nineteenth-century botanist Friedrich Welwitsch, Kimbundu speakers in northern Angola used the name *muriambambe* for the tree, referring to an antelope species that ate the leaves.[66] Botanist John Gossweiler recorded similar names in the first half of the twentieth century, but also found that people used a European loanword, *café*, to name the tree, which suggests they did not use coffee before they started growing it for export.[67]

A culture of coffee drinking developed first among the nineteenth-century settler population of Luanda. Concentrated in local taverns, this culture depended until the 1850s on imported beans, although Angola already produced more coffee for export than it bought from Brazil and Portugal.[68] As immigrant

64 Bryan Lewin *et al.*, 'Coffee Markets: New Paradigms in Global Supply and Demand', World Bank Agriculture and Rural Development Discussion Paper No. 3 (2004), <http://dx.doi.org/10.2139/ssrn.996111>.

65 Cruz, 'Café de Angola'; 'Relatório da Inspecção ao Concelho de Ambaca' (1950), pp. 59–64. From 1947, African workers were legally entitled to 15g of coffee per day. See Ruy de Sá Carneiro, *O trabalho do engenheiro em África* (Lisbon: Agência Geral do Ultramar, 1951).

66 Friedrich Welwitsch, *Synopse explicativa das amostras de madeiras e drogas medicinaes e de outros objectos mormente ethnographicos colligidos na Provincia de Angola enviados á Exposição Internacional de Londres em 1862* (Lisbon: Imprensa Nacional, 1862), p. 9; William Hiern, *Catalogue of the African Plants Collected by Dr. Friedrich Welwitsch in 1853–61* (2 vols, London: British Museum, 1896–1901), vol. 1, pt 2, p. 489.

67 John Gossweiler, 'Um reconhecimento fitogeográfico à região produtora do café Encoje', Relatórios e Informações, 1:2 (1918), 19–40, at p. 39; 'Informação sobre cafeicultura na fazenda "Monte Belo" – Cazengo', *BAA*, ser. 6, 5:16–19 (1932), 73–85, at p. 78; *Nomes indígenas de plantas de Angola*, reprint of *Agronomia Angolana*, 7 (Luanda: Imprensa Nacional, 1953).

68 AHU, SEMU-DGU, Angola, no. 827, 'Papeis e vários documentos sobre Angola'; Gerardo A. Pery, *Geographia e estatistica geral de Portugal e colónias com um atlas*

populations built up in the interior after the First World War, the consumption of locally produced coffee increased.[69] By 1951, government officials estimated that Angola consumed a thousand tons of its own coffee, amounting to roughly 2 per cent of the country's production. African consumption was highest in the Congo province, where independent smallholder cultivation was also substantial.[70] As the European population in Angola more than doubled from 79,000 to 172,000 inhabitants during the 1950s, and the number of contract workers employed on the coffee plantations grew from 40,000 to 90,000 in the same period, the amount of coffee drunk in the country also increased. Around 1960, domestic consumption stood at three to four thousand tons per year, which was about 4 per cent of Angola's total production.[71] This amounted to an intake per head of nearly 1kg, which was still significantly below consumption levels in the Netherlands or the United States, but not much below Portugal during the 1960s. By that time, Portuguese coffeeshop culture was well established in towns across Angola.[72] A question for future research is to what extent colonialism has led African populations to adopt the habit of coffee drinking.

(Lisbon: Imprensa Nacional, 1875), p. 357. See figures for the period 1812–49 in Alan de Carvalho Souza, 'Do Brasil para África: o café na viragem do império português (1807–1850)' (Unpublished PhD dissertation, University of Lisbon, 2020), <http://hdl.handle.net/10451/45282> [accessed 10 May 2023], pp. 49, 112; AHM, 2ª Divisão, 2ª Secção, Angola, caixa 1, doc. 12, 'Relação das fazendas, generos e mais objectos de importação que entraram no reino de Angola em 1820'; AHU, LR 33/1, Relatório do Ministério da Marinha e Ultramar em 1849. On taverns, see José de Almeida Santos, *Vinte anos decisivos da vida de uma cidade (1845/1864)* (Luanda: Câmara Municipal, 1970), docs. 428, 431, 433; *A alma de uma cidade* (Luanda: Câmara Municipal, 1973), doc. 261.

69 John Gossweiler, 'Reconhecimento agronómico no Distrito de Malanje', *BAA*, ser. 6, 5:16–19 (1932), 19–52, at p. 28.

70 AHU, GANG, Repartição do Gabinete, D2.172.6/06, Chefe de Gabinete to US Consul, Luanda, 7 Nov. 1951; *ibid.*, Chefe de Gabinete to US Consul, no. 3616, Luanda, 18 Sep. 1952.

71 Coste, *Les caféiers*, vol. 2, p. 455; Cláudia Castelo, *Passagens para África: O povoamento de Angola e Moçambique com naturais da metrópole (1920–1974)* (Lisbon: Edições Afrontamento, 2007), p. 143; Angola, *Anuário estatístico*, 1950–51, 1959.

72 Universidade Católica Portuguesa (Lisbon), Biblioteca Universitária João Paulo II, Espólio Ruy Cinatti, RC.1.2/19, caixa 18, Ruy Cinatti, 'Itinerário Angolano' (Lisbon, 1972), pp. 24–5. Cláudia Castelo kindly shared her notes on this source.

Epilogue

NEW HISTORIES of empire, colonialism, and commodity production show a particular concern with the impact of 'global capitalism' – concretely the commodification of land and labour – on the Global South. With few exceptions, commodification is associated with social and ecological disruption and the defensive strategies that local communities put up against world economic forces. These critical studies find easy targets in historical settler colonies and plantation economies because of the devastation they often wrought on resident and migrant labour populations, and sometimes on landscapes too. But they struggle to explain the growth of independent peasant production in Africa, Asia, and Latin America during the nineteenth and twentieth centuries. The general assumption is that small farmers were, if not coerced, at least duped into cash-crop production for global markets. Their choices were either to resist market pressures in the hope of maintaining their autonomy, or to adapt and become poor as a result.[1]

This book has offered a counter-narrative to such overly pessimistic views on commodity production in the Global South, albeit a story with a tragic twist.[2] In Angola, no empire, colonial state, or capitalist enterprise coaxed peasant households into coffee cultivation. The extension of the Angolan coffee frontier during the second half of the nineteenth century was mainly the work of small-scale farmers outside the proto-colonial enclaves of Portuguese Angola. Their entrepreneurship has not yet been sufficiently recognized in the historical literature, which has often likened African coffee production to foraging 'wild' coffee or improving spontaneous stands – not dissimilar to the arguments of colonial settlers, who, to boost their own image, depicted African producers as hopelessly inefficient. In fact, by 1900, much of Angola's natural coffee landscape was no

1 Kris Manjapra, *Colonialism in Global Perspective* (Cambridge: Cambridge University Press, 2020); Kehinde Andrews, *The New Age of Empire: How Racism and Colonialism Still Rule the World* (Dublin: Penguin, 2021), pp. 89–92; Sandip Hazareesingh and Haro Maat, 'Anti-Commodities Revisited: Food, Culture, and Resistance', in Jonathan Curry-Machado *et al.* (eds), *The Oxford Handbook of Commodity History* (Oxford: Oxford University Press, 2024), pp. 65–83; Ulbe Bosma and Eric Vanhaute, 'Commodity Frontiers: Linking Global Capitalism and Local Resilience', *ibid.*, pp. 85–101.

2 For a similar position, see Tariq Omar Ali, *A Local History of Global Capital: Jute and Peasant Life in the Bengal Delta* (Princeton: Princeton University Press, 2018).

longer wild but sub-spontaneous, such had been the impact of human intervention. Besides amelioration, farmers increased cultivation by planting seeds, seedlings, or cuts from healthy trees, sometimes travelling long distances to import plant material and exchange knowledge of growing techniques. By doing so, they created the environment within which coffee production expanded on a much larger scale during the twentieth century. This was a classic African 'cash-crop revolution', built on indigenous, rather than colonial, expertise and initiative.[3]

This coffee frontier was markedly sustainable. Deforestation scarcely happened in plantation building before white settlers invaded northern Angola in the 1920s. Farmers generally removed underbrush to create space for coffee but used the natural forest canopy for shading. The lifespan of some early plantations – with fruit-bearing trees growing up to a hundred years old, albeit with diminishing yields – and the continued expansion of production within the frontier were signs of the forest's regenerative capacity. Preservation of this ability was a growing concern of twentieth-century colonial agronomists.[4] By 1960, the Angolan coffee frontier had barely advanced beyond regions developed by African farmers fifty to a hundred years earlier, although production had exponentially grown in the meantime. There even appeared to be room for further expansion, especially since labour shortages on the settler estates left many forest reserves untapped.[5]

To understand the involvement of small farmers in export production, it helps to step away from the world-system perspective adopted in Chapter 1 and much of the anti-colonial literature, in which Africa features as 'raw-material' supplier to the Global North. Such a view risks neglecting historical examples of commodity processing in Africa and creating an image of African producers as people lacking agency and economic motives of their own.[6] In contrast, looking at the world of production from the vantage point of farmers, and asking what they got in return for their cash crops, it becomes clear that consumption played an important role in their economic lives.[7]

3 Paul Richards, *Indigenous Agricultural Revolution: Ecology and Food Production in West Africa* (London: Hutchinson, 1985); Polly Hill, *Migrant Cocoa-Farmers of Southern Ghana: A Study in Rural Capitalism*, 2nd edn (Oxford: James Currey, 1997).

4 On this point, see Helen Tilley, *Africa as a Living Laboratory: Empire, Development, and the Problem of Scientific Knowledge, 1870–1950* (Chicago: University of Chicago Press, 2011), p. 117.

5 Agência Geral do Ultramar, *Notas economicas: A agricultura em Angola* (Lisbon: Agência Geral do Ultramar, 1960).

6 William Gervase Clarence-Smith, 'The Textile Industry of Eastern Africa in the *Longue Durée*', in Emmanuel Akyeampong *et al.* (eds), *Africa's Development in Historical Perspective* (Cambridge: Cambridge University Press, 2014), pp. 264–94.

7 Jelmer Vos, 'What Angolans Got for Their Coffee: Connecting Histories of Labour and Consumption in Colonial Africa, c.1860–1960', in Devyani Gupta and Purba

Historians of consumption have long argued that people in early modern Europe and elsewhere became involved in market production because they had a desire to purchase goods.[8] Africanists, especially those working in the 'dependency' tradition, failed to reach similar conclusions about the people they studied. If Africans consumed, during the slave trade or after, it was because colonizers used the continent as a dumping ground for European manufactures.[9] In the 1990s, however, scholars who looked beyond the narrow framework of colonial exploitation to understand the continent's external relationships began to recognize consumption as an important motive for trade, work, and migration.[10] Against this background, the agrarian transition during the nineteenth century can be redefined as an 'industrious revolution', with small farmers adopting the consumer habits of their slave-trading predecessors.[11]

The long timeframe applied in this book has foregrounded the agency of African smallholders in Angolan coffee production, the benefits they gained from growing coffee, and their fancy for textiles in this context. Even after the imposition of colonial rule, the desire to earn 'cash' – often goods rather than coins or paper money – remained the most important driver of agrarian enterprise. Cash was needed to pay taxes, certainly, but an equally significant motive to earn cash was growing purchasing power: the capacity to buy consumer goods, food products, and educational and medical services, things that contributed to people's comfort, wellbeing, and social standing.

The tragedy of the Angolan experience with coffee was that the colonial government never fully supported the burgeoning smallholder economy. During

---

Hossain (eds), *Across Colonial Lines: Commodities, Networks and Empire Building* (London: Bloomsbury Academic, 2023), pp. 157–77.

8 Frank Trentmann, 'Introduction', in Frank Trentmann (ed.), *The Oxford Handbook of the History of Consumption* (Oxford: Oxford University Press, 2012), pp. 1–19.

9 The classic text is Walter Rodney, *How Europe Underdeveloped Africa* (London: Verso, 2018). A more recent statement is Toby Green, *A Fistful of Shells: West Africa from the Rise of the Slave Trade to the Age of Revolution* (Chicago: University of Chicago Press, 2019).

10 Patrick Harries, *Work, Culture and Identity: Migrant Laborers in Mozambique and South Africa, c. 1860–1910* (Johannesburg: Witwatersrand University Press, 1994); Phyllis M. Martin, *Leisure and Society in Colonial Brazzaville* (Cambridge: Cambridge University Press, 1995). More recently, Jeremy Prestholdt, *Domesticating the World: African Consumerism and the Genealogies of Globalization* (Berkeley: University of California Press, 2008); Pedro Machado, *Ocean of Trade: South Asian Merchants, Africa and the Indian Ocean, c.1750–1850* (Cambridge: Cambridge University Press, 2014).

11 Jan de Vries, *The Industrious Revolution: Consumer Behavior and the Household Economy, 1650 to the Present* (Cambridge: Cambridge University Press, 2008); Jeremy Prestholdt, 'Africa and the Global Lives of Things', in Trentmann, *Oxford Handbook*, pp. 85–108; Bronwen Everill, 'All the Baubles That They Needed: "Industriousness" and Slavery in Saint-Louis and Gorée', *Early American Studies*, 15:4 (2017), 714–39.

the twentieth century, it tried in vain to balance two agricultural models – peasant production on the one hand, and settler expansion on the other – resulting in a significant loss of African land and labour to white colonists. From a metropolitan viewpoint, helping settlers was economically unnecessary and even counterproductive, as a peasant economy would have been compatible with Portugal's imperial strategy of using the colonies as protected markets for domestic industries and a source of foreign exchange.[12] If anything, small coffee growers were more efficient users of land than estates were, so supporting them, instead of the white planter class, would very likely have generated greater exports and, consequently, higher revenues for the state. To understand why the colonial state allowed settler expansion to continue, a new look at empire is required, one that is less concerned with metropolitan debates and more focused on the interaction between settler initiative and government policy.

From an African angle, meanwhile, the history of coffee becomes a story of what-might-have-been.[13] If Portugal had stopped settlers in their tracks, as France and Britain did in their African coffee colonies after the Second World War, Angola would very likely have produced more coffee than it already did. More African growers would have been involved, raising general welfare levels. Many farmers would have grown substantially richer, and (free) migrant wage labour would have been more common. These were real possibilities sadly foreclosed by a lack of imperial imagination.

12 Gervase Clarence-Smith, *The Third Portuguese Empire, 1825–1975: A Study in Economic Imperialism* (Manchester: Manchester University Press, 1985).

13 On the use of counterfactuals, see Gavriel D. Rosenfeld, 'Whither "What If" History?', *History and Theory*, 53 (2014), 451–67; Adriano Vinale, '(Hi)story-Telling: An Introduction to Italian Alternate and Counterfactual History', *History*, 108:382 (2023), 355–64.

Bibliography

Archives

Angola

Arquivo Nacional de Angola, Luanda

Brazil

Arquivo do Instituto Histórico e Geográfico Brasileiro, Rio de Janeiro

France

Archives Nationales d'Outre-Mer, Aix-en-Provence

Netherlands

Maritiem Museum Rotterdam
Nationaal Archief, The Hague
Stadsarchief Amsterdam
Stadsarchief Rotterdam
Tresoar, Leeuwarden

Portugal

Arquivo Histórico Diplomático, Lisbon
Arquivo Histórico Militar, Lisbon
Arquivo Histórico Ultramarino, Lisbon
Arquivo Nacional da Torre do Tombo, Lisbon
Banco de Portugal, Arquivo Histórico, Lisbon
Sociedade de Geografia de Lisboa
Universidade Católica Portuguesa, Biblioteca Universitária João Paulo II, Lisbon

United Kingdom

Cadbury Research Library, University of Birmingham
Liverpool Record Office
North Angola Mission, Archibald Patterson Papers (privately held)
Rhodes House Library, Oxford

Royal Botanic Gardens Library, Kew
The Angus Library and Archive, Regent's Park College, Oxford
The National Archives, Kew
Unilever Archives, Port Sunlight

United States

Phillips Library, Peabody Essex Museum, Salem

Printed primary sources

'A inauguração da fábrica de Luanda da Junta de Exportação do Café', *RCP*, 1:1 (1954), 33–6.

Afonso, Francisco Gonçalves, *Um colono e coisas do Golungo* (2 vols, Porto: Tipografia Modesta, 1958).

'Africa Coffee Trade Had Good Year in 1953', *TCTJ*, 106:4 (1954), 22–3, 52.

Agência Geral do Ultramar, *Notas económicas: A agricultura em Angola* (Lisbon: Agência Geral do Ultramar, 1960).

Almeida, João de, *Operações militares nos Dembos em 1907* (Lisbon: Typographia Universal, 1909).

Almeida, José Joaquim de, 'Na Provincia de Angola: Administração colonial debaixo do ponte de vista agrícola', *Revista Agronomica*, 2 (1904), 97–110, 137–48, 161–75, 193–205.

Alves, José Bento, 'Produção e comércio de café', *Actividade Económica de Angola*, 1 (1936), 59–75.

Amaral, Abelardo Pompeu do, *Cultura prática e racional do cafeeiro* (São Paulo: CMG Editora, 1925).

Angola, *Negócios Indígenas: Relatório do ano de 1913* (Luanda: Imprensa Nacional de Angola, 1914).

——, *Negócios Indígenas: Relatório do ano de 1914* (Luanda: Imprensa Nacional, 1915).

——, *Negócios Indígenas: Relatório do ano de 1916* (Lisbon: Typ. do Annuario Commercial, 1917).

——, *Negócios Indígenas: Relatório do ano de 1915* (Lisbon: Tipografia Universal, 1918).

——, Direcção dos Serviços de Estatística, *3º Recenseamento geral da população, 1960*, vol. 4, *População residente segundo as condições perante o trabalho* (Luanda: Direcção dos Serviços de Estatística, 1964).

——, Concelho de Coordenação Técnica e Económica, *Planos de trabalho para 1943 dos serviços técnicos e organismos de coordenação económica* (Luanda: Imprensa Nacional de Angola, 1943).

——, Repartição Central de Estatística Geral, *Anuário estatístico de Angola*, 1933–60 (Luanda: Imprensa Nacional, 1935–61).

——, Repartição Central dos Serviços de Cadastro, *Relação geral dos processos organizados para a concessão de terrenos do estado, desde 1912 até 31 de dezembro de 1943* (Luanda: Imprensa Nacional, 1944).

——, Serviços de Agricultura e Comércio, *Algumas considerações sobre a cultura do café em Angola e regulamento da exportação* (Luanda: Empreza Gráfica de Angola, 1932).

'Angola e o café', *RCP*, 1:3 (1954), 42–5.

'Angola Writes New Chapter in the Production of Coffee', *TCTJ*, 73:1 (1937), 11, 36.

Arnold, Edwin Lester, *Coffee: Its Cultivation and Profit* (London: W. B. Whittingham & Co., 1886).

Bandeira, Bernardo de Sá Nogueira de Figueiredo Sá da, *O trabalho rural africano e a administração colonial* (Lisbon: Imprensa Nacional, 1873).

Barbosa, João Guilherme Pereira, 'Cazengo: Descripção d'este districto', *Annaes do Conselho Ultramarino*, parte não official, ser. 1 (1858), 470–74.

Bastos, Fernando Pereira, 'Angola Is Winning "The Battle of Quality"', 113:4 (1957), 28, 68–9.

——, 'How the Angolan Coffee Board Operates', *TCTJ*, 114:1 (1958), 70, 124.

Beça, Gonçalo de Oliveira, 'Presídio de Encoge', *Annaes do Conselho Ultramarino*, parte não official, ser. 2 (1860), 90–3.

Boletim de agricultura, pecuária e fomento (1908–09); *Boletim de agricultura da província de Angola* (1912, 1915–16); *Boletim de agricultura, pecuária e fomento*, ser. 3 (1919); *Boletim de agricultura da província de Angola*, ser. 4 (1920); *Boletim da secretaria de agricultura*, ser. 5 (1923–26); *Boletim da direcção dos serviços de agricultura e comércio*, ser. 6 (1928–33); *Boletim dos serviços de agricultura, comércio, colonização e florestas*, ser. 7 (1934–37).

Boletim oficial do Governo Geral da Provincia de Angola (1851–1911).

Boletim da Agência Geral das Colónias (1925–31); *Boletim Geral das Colónias* (1932–51); *Boletim Geral do Ultramar* (1951–70).

Capelo, Guilherme Augusto de Brito, *Relatório do Governador Geral da Província de Angola em 1887* (Lisbon: Imprensa Nacional, 1889).

Cardoso, José, *No Congo Português: Viagem ao Bembe e Damba, considerações relacionadas, setembro a outubro de 1912* (Luanda: Imprensa Nacional de Angola, 1914).

Carneiro, Ruy de Sá, *O trabalho do engenheiro em África* (Lisbon: Agência Geral do Ultramar, 1951).

Carreira, Amílcar, 'Estação agronómica de Cazengo: Relatório', *BAA*, ser. 3, 4 (1919), 132–56.

'Cartilha do cafeicultor', *RCP*, 1:4 (1954), 57–65.

Carvalho, Tito Augusto de, *Les colonies portugaises* (Paris: Aillaud, 1900).

Carvalho, Henrique Augusto Dias de, *Descripção da viagem á Mussumba do Muatiânvua* (4 vols, Lisbon: Imprensa Nacional, 1890–94).

Casimiro, Augusto, 'O nosso Congo: Esboço dum relatório', *BGC*, 2:17 (1926), 23–56.

Chevalier, Auguste, *Les caféiers du globe* (3 vols, Paris: Paul Lechevalier, 1929–47).

Chilcote, Ronald, *Emerging Nationalism in Portuguese Africa: Documents* (Stanford: Hoover Institution Press, 1972).

'Classificação e exportação dos cafés angolanos', *RCP*, 2:8 (1955), 51–67.

Coelho, Laurentino Pereira, 'Relatório sobre o ataque do Stephanodores Coffea, Hagd. às bagas de café na região do Uige', *BAA*, ser. 6, 1:4 (1929), 3–13.

'Coffee Propaganda Is Begun in Spain and Portugal', *TCTJ*, 57:4 (1929), 489–90.

Companhia Agrícola de Cazengo, *Relatório da Companhia Agricola de Cazengo do anno de 1908* (Lisbon: Typ. A.M. Antunes, 1909).

——, *Relatório da Companhia Agricola de Cazengo do anno de 1909* (Lisbon: Typ. Sport, 1910).

Contreiras, Manuel José Martins, *A província de Angola* (Lisbon: La Bécarre, 1894).

Cortezão, Maia, 'Breve ensaio sobre o café', *Boletim do Instituto de Angola*, 11 (1958), 135–47.

Costa, Cândido Augusto Fortunato da, 'Apontamentos de um agricultor' (Fazenda d'Aguas doces, 16 Nov. 1854), *BOA*, 485 (13 Jan. 1855).

Coste, René, 'Impressões de uma viagem às regiões cafeeiras de Angola', *RCP*, 5:19 (1958), 5–11.

Cruz, Maurício Loureiro de Almeida e, 'O café de Angola: Ligeiros apontamentos de um caderno', *Revista do Ultramar*, 1:10 (1948), 21–6.

Davidson, Basil. 'Africa's Modern Slavery', *Harper's Magazine*, 209:1250 (1954), 56–63.

Delegação do Governo Geral de Angola à Primeira Exposição Colonial Portuguesa, *Angola, café, exportação* (Luanda: Imprensa Nacional, 1934).

Diniz, José de Oliveira Ferreira, *Populações indígenas de Angola* (Coimbra: Imprensa da Universidade, 1918).

Dodge, Ralph E., *The Revolutionary Bishop Who Saw God at Work in Africa: An Autobiography* (Pasadena: William Carey Library, 1986).

'Dutch Tea, Coffee and Cocoa Trades Seek to Regain Pre-War Importance', *TCTJ*, 91:1 (1946), 16.

E., A., 'A demarcação de terrenos de estado no distrito do Congo', *BGU*, 35:405 (1959), 63–70.

Ebale, E., '"Office du Cafe" a Boon to Congo Coffee', *TCTJ*, 107:6 (1954), 28.

'Elaboração do café soluvel', *RCP*, 4:13 (1957), 58–66.

Ellis, John, *An Historical Account of Coffee, with an Engraving and Botanical Description of the Tree* (Cambridge: Cambridge University Press, 2013 [1774]).

'Exportação e melhoria do café de Angola', *BGC*, 24:275 (1948), 212–13.

Falush, Paul, 'History of Angola Robustas Enters New Phase in World Coffee Market', *TCTJ*, 107:6 (1954), 43.

Ferrão, António Pais dos Santos da Fonseca, 'Os principais problemas da cafeicultura na Costa do Marfim', *RCP*, offprint no. 4 (Lisbon: Junta de Exportação do Café, 1955).

——, 'Sobre a lei do crescimento das exportações de café de Angola', *RCP*, 5:17 (1958), 45–52.

Ferreira, Vicente, *A situação de Angola* (Luanda: Imprensa Nacional, 1927).

——, *Estudos Ultramarinos* (3 vols, Lisbon: Agência do Ultramar, 1953–55).

Ferreira, Pedro Cintra, *O café no commercio* (Brussels: Generaux, 1908).

Ferreira, Francisco de Salles, 'Diário da viagem para S. José de Encoge, feita em dezembro de 1854', *Annaes do Conselho Ultramarino*, parte não official, ser. 2 (1859), 51–4.

Fonseca, Francisco Teixeira da, *Á volta da falência da minha firma Teixeira da Fonseca & Cia, Lda (Angola)* (Luanda: Lusitana, [1933]).

Fragateiro, Bernardo de Oliveira, 'O districto do Congo debaixo do ponto de vista agrícola', *Revista Agronomica*, 2 (1904), 240–7, 273–80, 308–14, 339–42.

Francina, Manuel Alves de Castro, 'Viagem a Cazengo pelo Quanza, e regresso por terra', *Annaes do Conselho Ultramarino*, parte não official, ser. 1 (1858), 452–64.

Fynes-Clinton, D. O., *Portuguese West Africa: Economic and Commercial Conditions in Portuguese West Africa (Angola), June, 1949* (London: HMSO, 1949).

Galvão, A., 'Relatório duma viagem ao Congo em agosto e setembro de 1915', *Boletim da Sociedade de Geografia de Lisboa*, 36:4–6 (1918), 81–155.

Galvão, Henrique, *Dembos* (3 vols, Lisbon: Agência Geral das Colónias, 1935).

——, *Santa Maria: My Crusade for Portugal* (Cleveland: World Publishing Company, 1961).

Gossweiler, John, 'O horto experimental de Cazengo', *BAA*, 1:1 (1908), 16–21.

——, 'Carpodinus Chylorrhiza: A principal productora da borracha de Angola', *BAA*, 1:4 (1908), 150–61.

——, 'Um reconhecimento fitogeográfico à região produtora do café Encoje', *Relatórios e Informações*, 1:2 (1918), 19–40.

——, 'Contribuição para o estudo da flora dos Dembos', *BAA*, ser. 6, 3:8–12 (1930), 89–96.

——, 'Relatório sobre a viagem à região do Seles', *BAA*, ser. 6, 3:8–12 (1930), 211–21.

——, 'Informação sobre cafeicultura na fazenda "Monte Belo" – Cazengo', *BAA*, ser. 6, 5:16–19 (1932), 73–85.

——, 'Reconhecimento agronómico no Distrito de Malanje', *BAA*, ser. 6, 5:16–19 (1932), 19–52.

——, 'Relatório sobre as doenças do cafeeiro da região do Amboim', *BAA*, publicação extraordinária, 1 (1933), 5–31.

——, *Nomes indígenas de plantas de Angola*, reprint of *Agronomia Angolana*, 7 (Luanda: Imprensa Nacional, 1953).

——, and Francisco de Ascensão Mendonça, *Carta fitogeográfica de Angola* (Lisbon: Ministério das Colónias, Governo Geral de Angola, 1939).

Great Britain, Department of Overseas Trade, *Economic Conditions in Angola (Portuguese West Africa), Dated February, 1929* (London: HMSO, 1929).

——, *Economic Conditions in Angola (Portuguese West Africa)* (London: HMSO, 1932).

——, *Economic Conditions in Angola (Portuguese West Africa) (March, 1934)* (London: HMSO, 1934).

——, *Report on the Economic Conditions in Angola (Portuguese West Africa), Dated March, 1923* (London: HMSO, 1923).

——, *Report on the Economic and Commercial Conditions in Angola (Portuguese West Africa), February, 1937* (London, 1937).

——, Foreign Office, *Report for the Year 1904 on the Trade and Commerce of Angola* (London: HMSO, 1905).

——, *Report for the Year 1906 on the Trade and Commerce of Angola* (London: HMSO, 1907)

——, *Report for the Year 1908 on the Trade of the Province of Angola* (London: HMSO, 1909).

Guardado, Raul A. de S., 'Breve relatório sobre o Amboim florestal e algumas medidas de fomento florestal a adoptar', *BAA*, ser. 5, 1:5 (1925), 137–41.

Hewitt, Jr, Robert, *Coffee: Its History, Cultivation, and Uses* (New York: D. Appleton & Co., 1872).

Hiern, William, *Catalogue of the African Plants Collected by Dr. Friedrich Welwitsch in 1853–61* (2 vols, London: British Museum, 1896–1901).

International Institute of Agriculture, *Coffee in 1931 and 1932: Economic and Technical Aspects* (Rome: Printing Office of the Chamber of the Deputies, 1934).

International Labour Office, 'Report of the Commission Appointed under Article 26 of the Constitution of the International Labour Organisation to Examine the Complaint Filed by the Government of Ghana concerning the Observance by the Government of Portugal of the Abolition of Forced Labour Convention, 1957 (No. 105)', *Official Bulletin*, 45:2, supplement 2 (1962), pp. 1–253.

Jacinto, António, 'Monangamba', in Mário de Andrade, *Antologia da poesia negra de expressão portuguesa* (Paris: P. J. Oswald, 1958).

Janssens, Paul, *Le café robusta dans l'Angola* (Brussels: Imprimerie Industrielle et Financière, 1930).

Jeannest, Charles, *Quatre années au Congo* (Paris: G. Charpentier, 1883).

Jornal da Sociedade Agrícola do Porto, ser. 4, 10 (1861).

Júnior, António de Assis, *Relato dos acontecimentos de Dala Tando e Lucala* (Lisbon: Mercado de Letras Editores, 2014).

Júnior, Manoel do Nascimento Lopes da Silva (ed.), *Testemunos de José Cristovão Henriques (Engenheiro-Silvicultor)* (Lisbon: Junta de Investigações Científicas do Ultramar, 1981).

Junta de Exportação do Café, *Regulamento para a classificação dos cafés portugueses: Portaria no. 17330* (Lisbon: Junta de Exportação do Café, 1959).

——, *Quatro anos de propaganda do café português* (Lisbon: Junta de Exportação do Café, 1961).

——, Delegação de Angola, Serviços Técnicos, *Primeira Conferência Agronómica dos Serviços Técnicos: Programa de trabalhos para o ano de 1955/1956* (Luanda, 1955).

Kappenberg, William, 'Solubles Increase Total Coffee Consumption', *TCTJ*, 103:4 (1952), 28.

Keable, B. B., *Coffee: From Grower to Consumer* (London: Isaac Pitman and Sons, 1933 [1910]).

Kingsley, Mary, *Travels in West Africa: Congo Français, Corisco and Cameroons* (London: Macmillan, 1897).

'Koffieverbruik in Nederland met sprongen omhoog', *Allerhande*, 44 (April 1959), 1.

Laborie, Pierre Joseph, *The Coffee Planter of Santo Domingo* (London: T. Cadell & W. Davies, 1798).

Laerne, Cornelis Frederik van Delden, *Brazil and Java: Report on Coffee Culture in America, Asia and Africa* (The Hague: Martinus Nijhoff, 1885).

Lefebvre, Gabriel, *L'Angola: Son histoire, son économie* (Liège: Georges Thone, 1947).

Leitão, Alberto de Souza Maia, *Relatório da visita sanitária aos concelhos de leste de Loanda mais victimados pela doença de somno* (Porto: Typ. a vapor da Empreza Litteraria e Typographica, 1901).

Lessa, Almerindo, 'Angola e Moçambique: Panorama da terra e dos homens', *BGU*, 28:326–7 (1952), 89–156.

Lima, José Joaquim Lopes de, *Ensaios sobre a statística das possessões portuguezas na África occidental e oriental, na Ásia occidental, na China e na Oceania* (3 vols, Lisbon: Imprensa Nacional, 1844–46).

Livingstone, David, *Missionary Travels and Researches in South Africa* (New York: Harper and Brothers, 1858).

Lopes, José Quintella Pessoa, *Subsídios para o estudo dos cafés de Angola* (Porto: Tip. Sociedade Papelaria, 1934).

Lopes, António Teixeira, *Considerações acerca de alguns aspectos da produção em Angola* (Luanda: Imprensa Nacional, 1951).

Loureiro, Jaime de Almeida, 'A portaria no. 15.913, de 19 de Julho de 1956, e a classificação dos cafés portugueses', *RCP*, 3:11 (1956), 33–44.

——, 'Os cafés soluveis e a sua crescente expansão', *RCP*, 4:14 (1957), 17–23.

Magno, David, *Relatório dos serviços militares do Lombige* (Luanda: Governo Geral de Angola, 1910).

Martinez, Jr, Gregory L., 'African Coffees Are Now Firmly Established in the US Market Primarily Due to Solubles', *TCTJ*, 113:4 (1957), 20–1, 59–64.

——, 'Growing Importance of African Coffee', *TCTJ*, 101:1 (1951), 72, 74, 76–8.

Martins, José Roque, João Augusto Afonso, and Carlos Alves (eds), *Uige, Songo, Bembe: A circunscrição civil do Bembe, na primeira exposição portuguesa* (Luanda: Imprensa Nacional, 1934).

Mascarenhas, Filipe Martins Barbosa de, *O outro lado da escravatura: Repressão e abolição do serviço de carregadores e do tráfico de escravos* (Luanda: edição do Autor, 2012).

Massin, Pierre L., 'Ivory Coast Tops African Producers in Volume', *TCTJ*, 107:6 (1954), 30, 51.

Matias, Manuel António, 'Fábricas de rebenefício e homogeneização do Ambrizete e Ambriz', *RCP*, 2:6 (1955), 37–44.

Mattos, José de Almeida, *O Congo Português e as suas riquezas* (Lisbon: Simões, Marques, Santos & Cia, 1924).

McVeigh, Malcolm, 'Labor in Chains', *Africa Today*, 8:8 (1961), 9–11.

Medina, Artur Rocha de, *A tecnologia do café e o tamanho da propriedade* (Lisbon: Junta de Exportação do Café, 1950).

Mendes, António Leite, *Abolição da escravatura em Angola e organisação do trabalho* (Lisbon: Typographia Jornal de Lisboa, 1867).

Mendonça, Camilo Lemos de, 'Review of Angola Coffee Growing, Exports', *TCTJ*, 107:6 (1954), 26.

Menezes, Sebastião Lopes de Calheiros e, *Relatório do Governador Geral da Provincia de Angola, referido ao anno de 1861* (Lisbon: Imprensa Nacional, 1867).

Menezes, Joaquim António de Carvalho e, *Demonstração geográfica e politica do território portuguez na Guiné inferior* (Rio de Janeiro: Typ. Classica de F. A. de Almeida, 1848).

Mesquita, João, *Dados estatísticos para o estudo das pautas de Angola: Exportação pelas alfândegas do Círculo e do Congo nos anos de 1888 a 1913* (Luanda: Imprensa Nacional, 1918).

Mesquitela, João Carlos, 'Determinações do custo da produção do café numa propriedade de tipo médio em Angola', *RCP*, 3:9 (1956), 25–43.

——, 'Guia do cafeicultor de Angola', *Gazeta Agrícola de Angola*, 10:5 (1965), 212–15, 217.

Mezerik, A. G., 'World Coffee Consumption', *TCTJ*, 105:4 (1953), 18–19, 34.

Montalvão, Aníbal Coelho de, 'Cotações dos principais géneros de exportação de Angola', *BAA*, ser. 6, 1:3 (1928), 241–5.

Monteiro, Joachim John, *Angola and the River Congo* (2 vols, London: Frank Cass, 1968 [1875]).

Monteiro, José Firmo de Sousa, *Breve noticia das riquezas naturais de Angola: Possibilidade da sua produção e aspectos regionais agrícolas* (Luanda: Imprensa Nacional, 1921).

Morais, José Augusto da Cunha, *Africa occidental: Album photographico e descriptivo* (4 vols, Lisbon: David Corazzi, 1885–8).

Morna, Álvaro de Freitas, *Problemas económicos da colónia: Algodão, milho, café, trigo* (Luanda: Imprensa Nacional, 1943).

Negreiros, António Lobo de Almada, *La main-d'œuvre en Afrique: mémoire presenté au Congrès International de 1900* (Paris: s.l., 1900).

'Netherlands Is the Leading Coffee Market of Europe', *TCTJ*, 57:4 (1929), 456–60.

Neuparth, Augusto Eduardo, *Apontamentos para a história da Companhia Agrícola de Cazengo* (Lisbon: Typographia do Commercio, 1904).

Neves, José Acúrsio das, *Considerações políticas e comerciais sobre os descobrimentos e possessões portuguezes na África e na Ásia* (Lisbon: Impressão Regia, 1830).

Nevinson, Henry W., *A Modern Slavery* (New York: Harper Brothers Publishers, 1906).

'O café de Angola', *O Século*, 10 Oct. 1914.

Peck, L. Doyle, 'Product Consistency Key to Roaster's Success', *TCTJ*, 108:3 (1955), 28.

Pery, Gerardo A., *Geographia e estatística geral de Portugal e colónias com um atlas* (Lisbon: Imprensa Nacional, 1875).

Newbury, Colin W., *British Policy towards West Africa: Select Documents, 1786–1874* (Oxford: Clarendon Press, 1965).

Noronha, Eurico de Azevedo, 'O "café Cuango": Relatório de uma viagem às regiões de Mococola e Quimbele', *RCP*, 1:4 (1954), 37–41.

——, 'Plantação de cafezal em curvas de nivel e linhas cerradas', *RCP*, 2:7 (1955), 18–28.

Oliveira, Eduardo de, *Café (instruções e conselhos práticos): Plantação do café, técnica agrícola, 1961–2011* (Rio Tinto: Mosaico de Palavras, 2012).

Oliveira and Eduardo Santos, Oliviera, and Eduardo Santos (eds), *Angolana (documentação sobre Angola)* (4 vols, Lisbon: Instituto de Investigação Científica Tropical, 1968–95).

Pickersgill, W. Clayton, 'Coffee Cultivation in Angola', *Bulletin of Miscellaneous Information (Royal Botanic Gardens, Kew)*, 89 (1894), 161–3.

Pimentel, Fernando, *Investigação commercial na província de Angola* (Porto: Typographia a Vapor da Empreza Guedes, 1903).

Pina, Adolfo (ed.), *A Província de Angola: Número extraordinário dedicado à exposição colonial portuguesa e em honra da restauração de Angola* (Luanda: Empresa Gráfica de Angola, 1934).

Pinto, Francisco António, *Angola e Congo: Conferências* (Lisbon: Livraria Ferreira, Editora, 1888).

Pires, António, *Tonga: Epopeia do café* (Luanda: Edições Lello, 1959).

Portugal, *Relatórios do Ministro e Secretário de Estado dos Negócios da Marinha e do Ultramar apresentados às Cortes na sessão legislativa de 1870* (Lisbon: Ministério do Ultramar, 1969).

——, *Relatórios do Ministro e Secretário d'Estado dos Negócios da Marinha e Ultramar* (Lisbon: Imprensa Nacional, 1875).

——, *Relatório do Ministério e Secretário d'Estado dos Negócios da Marinha e Ultramar* (Lisbon: Imprensa Nacional, 1898).

——, Ministério das Colónias, Direcção Geral de Fazenda das Colónias, *Estatística das alfândegas da Província de Angola: Importação, exportação e reexportação no ano de 1912* (Lisbon: Tip. Casa Portuguesa, 1914).

——, *A agricultura em Angola: Breve resumo sobre os recursos agrícolas da província de Angola* (Lisbon: Agência Geral de Angola, 1922).

——, *Código de Trabalho dos Indígenas nas colónias portuguesas de África* (Luanda: Imprensa Nacional da Colónia de Angola, 1936).

——, 'Portaria 10835', *Diário de Governo*, Ser. 1, 9 (12 Jan. 1945), 30–2.

——, *Regulamento para a classificação dos cafés coloniais portugueses* (Porto: Oficinas de O Comércio do Porto, 1945).

Raoul, Edouard, *Culture du caféier: Semis, plantations, taille, dépulpation, décorticage, expédition, commerce, espèces et races* (Paris: Augustin Challamel, 1897).

Rebelo, Horácio de Sá Viana, *Angola na África deste tempo* (Lisbon: edição do autor, 1961).

Revista do Café Português (1954–61).

Revista do Ultramar, 1:10 (1948).

Richards, Elizabeth A., 'An analysis of the retail coffee market', *TCTJ*, 102:6 (1952), 18, 41–2.

Rosa, J. Costa, 'Relatório annual da 6ª Delegação Regional dos Serviços Agrícolas', *BAA*, ser. 6, 6:20–3 (1933), 85–104.

Ross, Edward Alsworth, *Report on Employment of Native Labour in Portuguese Africa* (New York: Abbott Press, 1925).

Rouvre, Charles de, 'La Guinée Méridionale Indépendante: Congo, Kacongo, N'Goyo, Loango, 1870–1877', *Bulletin de la Société de Géographie*, 20 (1880), 289–327, 401–34, at p. 420.

Rufenacht, Charles, 'A Review of European Coffee Option Markets', *TCTJ*, 112:3 (1957), 14, 94.

Santos, José de Almeida, *Vinte anos decisivos da vida de uma cidade (1845/1864)* (Luanda: Câmara Municipal, 1970).

——, *Apenas um punhado de bravos!* (Luanda: Câmara Municipal, 1971).

——, *A alma de uma cidade* (Luanda: Câmara Municipal, 1973).

Santos, Augusto L. Ferreira dos, and V.M. Rabaça Gaspar, *Estrutura do comércio externo de Angola* (Lisbon: Junta de Investigações do Ultramar, 1959).

Santos, António de Sousa, 'Aspectos económicos da cafeicultura angolana: O preço do custo de produção de 1 kg de café comercial', *RCP*, 4:13 (1957), 47–57.

Secretaria do governo geral da província de Angola, 'Nota demonstrativa do número de escravos registados na província de Angola, e suas dependências, nos termos do Decreto de 14 de Dezembro de 1854' (11 Feb. 1856), *Diário do Governo*, 145 (21 June 1856), 854.

Schepel, A. F. (ed.), *Reisjournaal van Lodewijk Kerdijk: West-Afrika 1857/1858* (Schiedam: Interbook International, 1978).

Sharman, T. C., *Portuguese West Africa: Economic and Commercial Conditions in Portuguese West Africa (Angola), June, 1953* (London: HMSO, 1954).

Silva, Hélder Lains e, 'Nota sobre o consumo do café na metrópole de 1900 a 1952', *RCP*, 1:1 (1954), 27–31.

——, 'A enxertia do Robusta, com garfos provenientes dos ramos horizontais (plagiotrópicos), na restauração de cafezais decrépitos', *RCP*, 1:4 (1954), 28–36.

——, 'Exports from Angola in 1954 Show Marked Decline from Previous Year', *TCTJ*, 109:6 (1955), 60.

——, 'Programa de selecção de café robusta em Angola', *RCP*, 3:9 (1956), 7–24.

——, 'Progressos técnicos da cafeicultura no Congo Belga e na Costa Rica', *RCP*, offprint no. 16 (Lisbon: Junta de Exportação do Café, 1959).

Silva, Francisco Teixeira da, 'Relatório da Estação Naval d'Angola acerca da questão do norte da província, especialmente Ambriz, Quicombo e rio Zaire, em 1880', *Arquivo das Colónias*, 5 (1930), 183–99.

Simmonds, P.L., *The Commercial Products of the Vegetable Kingdom* (London: T. F. A. Day, 1854).

——, *Tropical Agriculture* (London: E. and F. N. Spon, 1889).

Sousa, António de Figueiredo Gomes e, 'Relatório de uma missão de reconhecimento agronómico no Distrito do Cuanza-Sul', *BAA*, ser. 5, 1:4 (1925), 7–32.

Souza, Manuel Ramos de, *A Junta de Exportação do Café Colonial em Angola: 5 anos de actividade* (Luanda: Mondego, 1946).

Speke, John Hanning, *Journal of the Discovery of the Source of the Nile* (London: William Blackwood, 1863).

'Survey of Coffee Drinking Habits in U.K.', *TCTJ*, 94:3 (1948), 20.

Tea and Coffee Trade Journal (1927–60).

The Economist (1864–5).

Thurber, Francis B., *Coffee: From the Plantation to the Cup* (New York: American Grocer Publishing Association, 1881).

United Kingdom, Foreign Office, *Report on the Trade of Loanda, for the Year 1885* (London: Her Majesty's Stationery Office, 1886).

United States, Bureau of Foreign and Domestic Commerce, Department of Commerce, *Daily Consular and Trade Reports*, vol. 3 (Washington: Government Printing Office, 1915), pp. 1697–713, 'Commercial Study of Portuguese West Africa'.

Valente, António José, *Novo projeto da pauta aduaneira da alfândega do Ambriz* (Lisbon: Typgraphia Franco-Portugueza, 1889).

Vaz, Jorge Trancoso, 'Problemas da cafeicultua no Congo e a mão de obra', *RCP*, 3:11 (1956), 26–32.

Velloso, José Mariano da Conceição, *O fazendeiro do Brasil, cultivador* (Lisbon: Officina de Simão Thaddeo Ferreira, 1799).

'Vier-smaken-systeem', *Allerhande*, 34 (May 1958), 3.

Walsh, Joseph M., *Coffee: Its History, Classification, and Description* (Philadelphia: Henry T. Coates & Company, 1894).

Welwitsch, Friedrich, *Synopse explicativa das amostras de madeiras e drogas medicinaes e de outros objectos mormente ethnographicos colligidos na Provincia de Angola enviados á Exposicão Internacional de Londres em 1862* (Lisbon: Imprensa Nacional, 1862).

Secondary sources

Alexandre, Valentim, *Origens do colonialismo português moderno (1822–1891)* (Lisbon: Sá da Costa Editora, 1979).

——, *Velho Brasil, novas Áfricas: Portugal e o Império (1808–1975)* (Porto: Edições Afrontamento, 2000).

Ali, Tariq Omar, *A Local History of Global Capital: Jute and Peasant Life in the Bengal Delta* (Princeton: Princeton University Press, 2018).

Allina, Eric, *Slavery by Any Other Name: African Life under Company Rule in Colonial Mozambique* (Charlottesville: University of Virginia Press, 2012).

Allman, Jean (ed.), *Fashioning Africa: Power and Politics of Dress* (Bloomington: Indiana University Press, 2004).

Alpern, Stanley B., 'What Africans Got for Their Slaves: A Master List of European Trade Goods', *History in Africa*, 22 (1995), 5–43.

Ampiah, Kweku, *The Dynamics of Japan's Relations with Africa: South Africa, Tanzania and Nigeria* (London: Routledge, 1997).

Andrews, Kehinde, *The New Age of Empire: How Racism and Colonialism Still Rule the World* (Dublin: Penguin, 2021).

Antunes, Cátia, and Jelmer Vos, 'Port Cities and Commodities: Luanda in the Early-Modern Period', in Jonathan Curry-Machado, Jean Stubbs, William Gervase Clarence-Smith, and Jelmer Vos (eds), *The Oxford Handbook of Commodity History* (Oxford: Oxford University Press, 2024), pp. 127–43.

Arsan, Andrew, *Interlopers of Empire: The Lebanese Diaspora in Colonial French West Africa* (New York: Oxford University Press, 2014).

Austen, Ralph, *African Economic History: Internal Development and External Dependency* (Oxford: James Currey, 1987).

Austin, Gareth, 'Mode of Production or Mode of Cultivation: Explaining the Failure of European Cocoa Planters in Competition with African Farmers in Colonial Ghana', in William Gervase Clarence-Smith (ed.), *Cocoa Pioneer Fronts since 1800* (London: Palgrave Macmillan, 1996), pp. 154–75.

——, *Labour, Land and Capital in Ghana: From Slavery to Free Labour in Asante, 1807–1956* (Rochester: University of Rochester Press, 2005).

——, 'Capitalism and the Colonies', in Larry Neal and Jeffrey G. Williamson (eds), *The Cambridge History of Capitalism*, vol. 2 (Cambridge: Cambridge University Press, 2014), pp. 301–47.

——, 'Explaining and Evaluating the Cash Crop Revolution in the "Peasant" Colonies of Tropical Africa, ca. 1890–ca.1930: Beyond "Vent for Surplus"', in Emmanuel Akyeampong, Robert H. Bates, Nathan Nunn, and James Robinson (eds), *Africa's Development in Historical Perspective* (Cambridge: Cambridge University Press, 2014), pp. 295–320.

——, 'The Economics of Colonialism in Africa', in Célestin Monga and Justin Yifu Lin (eds), *The Oxford Handbook of Africa and Economics*, vol. 1 (Oxford: Oxford University Press, 2015), pp. 522–35.

Azevedo, João Maria Cerqueira de, *Angola, exemplo de trabalho* (Luanda: edição do autor, 1958).

Bales, Kevin, *Disposable People: New Slavery in the Global Economy*, rev. edn (Berkeley: University of California Press, 2012).

Ball, Jeremy, *Angola's Colossal Lie: Forced Labor on a Sugar Plantation, 1913–1977* (Boston: Brill, 2015).

Barbosa, L. A. Grandvaux, *Carta fitogeográfica de Angola* (Luanda: Instituto de Investigação Científica de Angola, 1970).

Bates, Robert H., *Markets and States in Tropical Africa* (Berkeley: University of California Press, 2014).

Beckert, Sven, 'American Danger: United States Empire, Eurafrica, and the Territorialization of Industrial Capitalism, 1870–1950', *American Historical Review*, 122:4 (2017), 1137–70.

Behrendt, Stephen D., Anthony J. H. Latham, and David Northrup, *The Diary of Antera Duke, an Eighteenth-Century African Slave Trader* (Oxford: Oxford University Press, 2010).

Beinart, William, and Karen Middleton, 'Plant Transfers in Historical Perspective: A Review Article', *Environment and History*, 10:1 (2004), 3–29.

Belich, James, *Replenishing the Earth: The Settler Revolution and the Rise of the Angloworld* (Oxford: Oxford University Press, 2009).

Berry, Sara S., *No Condition Is Permanent: The Social Dynamics of Agrarian Change in Sub-Saharan Africa* (Madison: University of Wisconsin Press, 1993).

——, 'Debating the Land Question in Africa', *Comparative Studies in Society and History*, 44:4 (2002), 638–68.

——, 'Entrepreneurial Labour', in Stefano Bellucci and Andreas Eckert (eds), *General Labour History of Africa: Workers, Employers and Governments, 20th–21st Centuries* (Woodbridge: James Currey, 2019), pp. 457–74.

Birmingham, David, 'The Coffee Barons of Cazengo', *JAH*, 19:4 (1978), 523–38.

——, 'A Question of Coffee: Black Enterprise in Angola', *Canadian Journal of African Studies*, 16:2 (1982), 343–6.

——, *A Short History of Modern Angola* (Oxford: Oxford University Press, 2015).

Boahen, A. Adu, *African Perspectives on Colonialism* (New York: Diasporic African Press, 2011).

Bosma, Ulbe, and Eric Vanhaute, 'Commodity Frontiers: Linking Global Capitalism and Local Resilience', in Jonathan Curry-Machado, Jean Stubbs, William Gervase Clarence-Smith, and Jelmer Vos (eds), *The Oxford Handbook of Commodity History* (Oxford: Oxford University Press, 2024), pp. 85–101.

Bowman, Joyce L., '"Legitimate" Commerce and Peanut Production in Portuguese Guinea, 1840s–1880s', *JAH*, 28:1 (1987), 87–106.

Breman, Jan, *Mobilizing Labour for the Global Coffee Market: Profits from an Unfree Work Regime in Colonial Java* (Amsterdam: Amsterdam University Press, 2015).

Brooks, George E., 'Peanuts and Colonialism: Consequences of the Commercialization of Peanuts in West Africa, 1830–70', *JAH*, 16:1 (1975), 29–54.

Brown, Christopher Leslie, *Moral Capital: Foundations of British Abolitionism* (Chapel Hill: University of North Carolina Press, 2006).

Burke, Timothy, *Lifebuoy Men, Lux Women: Commodification, Consumption, and Cleanliness in Modern Zimbabwe* (Durham: Duke University Press, 1996).

Butel, Paul, *The Atlantic* (London: Routledge, 1999).

Cahen, Michel, 'Seis teses sobre o trabalho forçado no império português continental em África', *África* (São Paulo), 35 (2015), 129–55.

Campbell, Gwyn, 'The Origins and Development of Coffee production in Réunion and Madagascar, 1711–1972', in William Gervase Clarence-Smith and Steven Topik (eds), *The Global Coffee Economy in Africa, Asia, and Latin America, 1500–1989* (Cambridge: Cambridge University Press, 2003), pp. 67–99.

Candido, Mariana Pinho, *An African Slaving Port and the Atlantic World: Benguela and Its Hinterland* (Cambridge: Cambridge University Press, 2013).

——, 'Conquest, Occupation, Colonialism and Exclusion: Land Disputes in Angola', in João Vicente Serrão, Bárbara Direito, Eugénia Rodrigues, and Susana Munch Miranda (eds), *Property Rights, Lands and Territory in the European Overseas Empires* (Lisbon: Imprensa de Ciências Sociais, 2014), pp. 223–33.

——, *Wealth, Land, and Property in Angola: A History of Dispossession, Slavery, and Inequality* (Cambridge: Cambridge University Press, 2022).

Carneiro, Armando, *Honra e glória ao fundador do Uige: Júlio Thomaz Berberan* (Rio Maior: Armando Carneiro, 1962).

Carreira, António, *Angola – da escravatura ao trabalho livre: Subsidios para a história demográfica do século XVI até à independência* (Lisbon: Arcadia 1977).

Castelo, Cláudia, *Passagens para África: O povoamento de Angola e Moçambique com naturais da metrópole (1920–1974)* (Lisbon: Edições Afrontamento, 2007).

——, 'Developing "Portuguese Africa" in Late Colonialism: Confronting Discourses', in Joseph M. Hodge, Gerald Hödl, and Martina Kopf (eds), *Developing Africa: Concepts and Practices in Twentieth-Century Colonialism* (Manchester: Manchester University Press, 2014), pp. 63–83.

——, '"Village Portugal" in Africa: Discourses of Differentiation and Hierarchisation of Settlers, 1950s–1974', in Duncan Money and Danelle van Zyl-Hermann (eds), *Rethinking White Societies in Southern Africa* (London: Routledge, 2020), pp. 115–33.

——, and Catarina Mateus, '"Etnografia Angolana" (1935–1939): Histórias da coleção fotográfica de Elmano Cunha e Costa', in Filipa Lowndes Vicente (ed.), *O império da visão: Fotografia no contexto colonial português (1860–1960)* (Lisboa: Edições 70, 2014).

Castro, Armando, *O sistema colonial português em África (meados do século XX)*, 2nd edn (Lisbon: Editorial Caminho, 1980).

Charlip, Julie A., 'Small Farmers and Coffee in Nicaragua', in William Gervase Clarence-Smith and Steven Topik (eds), *The Global Coffee Economy in Africa, Asia, and Latin America, 1500–1989* (Cambridge: Cambridge University Press, 2003), pp. 236–53.

Clarence-Smith, William Gervase, 'Capital Accumulation and Class Formation in Angola', in David Birmingham and Phyllis M. Martin (eds), *History of Central Africa, Volume Two* (London: Longman, 1983), pp. 163–99.

——, 'Business Empires in Angola under Salazar, 1930–1961', *AEH*, 14 (1985), 1–13.

——, *The Third Portuguese Empire, 1825–1975: A Study in Economic Imperialism* (Manchester: Manchester University Press, 1985).

——, 'Labour Conditions in the Plantations of São Tomé and Príncipe, 1875–1914', *Slavery & Abolition*, 14:1 (1993), 149–67.

——, *Cocoa and Chocolate, 1765–1914* (London: Routledge, 2000).

——, 'The Coffee Crisis in Asia, Africa, and the Pacific, 1870–1914', in William Gervase Clarence-Smith and Steven Topik (eds), *The Global Coffee Economy in Africa, Asia, and Latin America, 1500–1989* (Cambridge: Cambridge University Press, 2003), pp. 100–19.

——, 'The Textile Industry of Eastern Africa in the *Longue Durée*', in Emmanuel Akyeampong, Robert Bates, Nathan Nunn, and James A. Robinson (eds), *Africa's Development in Historical Perspective* (Cambridge: Cambridge University Press, 2014), pp. 264–94.

——, and Steven Topik (eds), *The Global Coffee Economy in Africa, Asia, and Latin America, 1500–1989* (Cambridge: Cambridge University Press, 2003).

Cleveland, Todd, *Diamonds in the Rough: Corporate Paternalism and African Professionalism on the Mines of Colonial Angola, 1917–1975* (Athens: Ohio University Press, 2015).

Coghe, Samuël, 'The Problem of Freedom in a Mid Nineteenth-Century Atlantic Slave Society: The Liberated Africans of the Anglo-Portuguese Mixed Commission in Luanda (1844–1870)', *Slavery & Abolition*, 33:3 (2012), 479–500.

Cooper, Frederick, *Decolonization and African Society: The Labor Question in French and British Africa* (Cambridge: Cambridge University Press, 1996).

Coste, René, *Les caféiers et les cafés dans le monde* (2 vols, Paris: Éditions Larose, 1955–61).

Cramer, P. J. S., *A Review of Literature of Coffee Research in Indonesia* (Turrialba: SIC Editorial, Inter-American Institute of Agricultural Sciences, 1957).

Curtis, Kenneth, 'Smaller Is Better: A Consensus of Peasants and Bureaucrats in Colonial Tanganyika', in William Gervase Clarence-Smith and Steven Topik (eds), *The Global Coffee Economy in Africa, Asia, and Latin America, 1500–1989* (Cambridge: Cambridge University Press, 2003), pp. 312–34.

Curto, José C., 'A família Fortunato da Costa: de Portugal a Angola, via São Tomé, c.1808 a 1859', *Afro-Ásia*, 67 (2023), 97–141.

Curto, Diogo Ramada, and Bernardo Pinto da Cruz, 'Cidades coloniais: Fomento ou controlo?', in Nuno Domingos and Else Peralta (eds), *Cidade e Império: Dinâmicas coloniais e reconfigurações pós-coloniais* (Lisbon: Edições 70, 2013), pp. 113–65.

Dalrymple-Smith, Angus, *Commercial Transitions and Abolition in West Africa 1630–1860* (Boston: Brill, 2020).

Daviron, Benoit, 'Small Farm Production and the Standardization of Tropical Products', *Journal of Agrarian Change*, 2:2 (2002), 162–84.

——, 'Mobilizing Labour in African Agriculture: The Role of the International Colonial Institute in the Elaboration of a Standard of Colonial Administration, 1895–1930', *JGH*, 5:3 (2010), 479–501.

——, and Stefano Ponte, *The Coffee Paradox: Global Markets, Commodity Trade and the Elusive Promise of Development* (London: Zed Books, 2005).

Davis, Aaron P., Rafael Govaerts, and Diane M. Bridson, 'Annotated Taxonomic Conspectus of the Genus *Coffea* (Rubiaceae)', *Botanical Journal of the Linnean Society*, 152:4 (2006), 465–512.

Dean, Warren, 'The Green Wave of Coffee: Beginnings of Tropical Agricultural Research in Brazil (1885–1900)', *Hispanic American Historical Review*, 69:1 (1989), 91–115.

——, *With Broadax and Firebrand: The Destruction of the Brazilian Atlantic Forest* (Berkeley: University of California Press, 1997).

Delle, James A., 'Women's Lives and Labour on Radnor, a Jamaican Coffee Plantation, 1822–1826', *Caribbean Quarterly*, 48:4 (2002), 27–40.

Desai, Manali, 'Colonial Legacies and Repertoires of "Ethnic" Violence: The Case of Western India, 1941–2002', *Journal of Historical Sociology*, 22:2 (2009), 147–79.

De Haas, Michiel, 'Measuring Rural Welfare in Colonial Africa: Did Uganda's Smallholders Thrive?', *Economic History Review*, 70:2 (2017), 605–31.

De Vries, Jan, *The Industrious Revolution: Consumer Behavior and the Household Economy, 1650 to the Present* (Cambridge: Cambridge University Press, 2008).

Dias, Jill R., 'Famine and Disease in the History of Angola, c. 1830–1930', *JAH*, 22:3 (1981), 349–78.

——, 'Changing Patterns of Power in the Luanda Hinterland: The Impact of Trade and Colonisation on the Mbundu ca. 1845–1920', *Paideuma: Mitteilungen zur Kulturkunde*, 32 (1986), 285–318.

——, 'Angola', in Valentim Alexandre and Jill Dias (eds), *O império africano, 1825–1890* (Lisbon: Editorial Estampa, 1998), pp. 319–556.

Direito, Bárbara, 'African Access to Land in Early 20th Century Portuguese Colonial Thought', in João Vicente Serrão, Bárbara Direito, Eugénia Rodrigues, and Susana Munch Miranda (eds), *Property Rights, Lands and Territory in the European Overseas Empires* (Lisbon: Imprensa de Ciências Sociais, 2014), pp. 255–63.

——, 'The Land Question in Early Twentieth-Century Portuguese Legal Colonial Thought', *Portuguese Journal of Social Science*, 16:2 (2017), 181–93.

Dore, Elizabeth, 'Patriarchy from Above, Patriarchy from Below: Debt Peonage on Nicaraguan Coffee Estates, 1870–1930', in William Gervase Clarence-Smith and Steven Topik (eds), *The Global Coffee Economy in Africa, Asia, and Latin America, 1500–1989* (Cambridge: Cambridge University Press, 2003), pp. 209–35.

Duffy, James, *A Question of Slavery* (Oxford: Clarendon Press, 1967).

Eckert, Andreas, 'Comparing Coffee Production in Cameroon and Tanganyika, c.1900–1960s: Land, Labor, and Politics', in William Gervase Clarence-Smith and Steven Topik (eds), *The Global Coffee Economy in Africa, Asia, and Latin America, 1500–1989* (Cambridge: Cambridge University Press, 2003), pp. 286–311.

Ellis, Stephen, *Season of Rains: Africa in the World* (Chicago: University of Chicago Press, 2011).

Elmore, Bartow J., *Citizen Coke: The Making of Coca-Cola Capitalism* (New York: W. W. Norton, 2016).

Elson, Robert E., *Village Java under the Cultivation System, 1830–1870* (Sydney: ASAA Southeast Asia Publication Series, 1994).

Eltis, David, *Economic Growth and the Ending of the Transatlantic Slave Trade* (Oxford: Oxford University Press, 1987).

——, and Stanley Engerman (eds), *The Cambridge World History of Slavery*, vol. 4, *ad 1804–ad 2016* (Cambridge: Cambridge University Press, 2017).

Engel, Alexander, 'Buying Time: Futures Trading and Telegraphy in Nineteenth-Century Global Commodity Markets', *JGH*, 10:2 (2015), 284–306.

——, 'Futures Trading and German Agricultural Markets', in Jonathan Curry-Machado, Jean Stubbs, William Gervase Clarence-Smith, and Jelmer Vos (eds), *The Oxford Handbook of Commodity History* (New York: Oxford University Press), pp. 167–85.

Engerman, Stanley L., 'Introduction', in Stanley L. Engerman (ed.), *Terms of Labor: Slavery, Serfdom, and Free Labor* (Stanford: Stanford University Press, 1999), pp. 1–23.

Esteves, A. Baião, and F. Santos Oliveira, *Contribuição para o estudo das características dos cafés de Angola* (Lisbon: Junta de Investigações do Ultramar, 1970).

Everill, Bronwen, 'All the Baubles That They Needed: "Industriousness" and Slavery in Saint-Louis and Gorée', *Early American Studies*, 15:4 (2017), 714–39.

——, *Not Made by Slaves: Ethical Capitalism in the Age of Abolition* (Cambridge: Harvard University Press, 2020).

Fall, Babacar, and Richard L. Roberts, 'Forced Labour', in Stefano Bellucci and Andreas Eckert (eds), *General Labour History of Africa: Workers, Employers and Governments, 20th–21st Centuries* (Woodbridge: James Currey, 2019), pp. 77–115.

Ferreira, Frederico Antonio, 'Augustus Archer, entre o passado e o future das relações entre o império do Brasil e a África portuguesa', *Transversos*, 15 (2019), 213–29.

Ferreira, Roquinaldo, 'The Suppression of the Slave Trade and Slave Departures from Angola, 1830s–1860s', in David Eltis and David Richardson (eds), *Extending the Frontiers: Essays on the New Transatlantic Slave Trade Database* (New Haven: Yale University Press, 2008), pp. 313–34.

——, *Cross-Cultural Exchange in the Atlantic World: Angola and Brazil during the Era of the Slave Trade* (Cambridge: Cambridge University Press, 2012).

——, *Dos sertões ao Atlântico: Tráfico ilegal de escravos e comércio lícito em Angola, 1830–1860* (Luanda: Kilombelombe, 2012).

——, 'Agricultural Enterprise and Unfree Labour in Nineteenth-Century Angola', in Robin Law, Suzanne Schwarz, and Silke Strickrodt (eds), *Commercial Agriculture, the Slave Trade and Slavery in Atlantic Africa* (Woodbridge: James Currey, 2013), pp. 225–42.

Figueiredo, João de Castro Maia Veiga, 'Heimlich/unheimlich: Outlining the Influence of Spiritan Worldviews in the Work of Angolan Pioneer Photographers José Moraes and Elmano Costa, *Social Sciences and Missions*, 30:3–4 (2017), 366–87.

Florentino, Manolo, *Em costas negras: uma história do tráfico de escravos entre a África e o Rio de Janeiro (séculos XVIII e XIX)* (São Paulo: Companhia das Letras, 1997).

Florescu, Mădălina, 'Post-Abolition Angola in a Post-Colonial Mission Archive: A Preliminary Contextualisation of a Photograph from the Spiritans' Mission in Malange, Northern Angola, 1904', *Social Dynamics*, 40:1 (2014), 66–84.

Follett, Richard, 'Legacies of Enslavement: Plantation Identities and the Problem of Freedom', in Richard Follett, Eric Foner, and Walter Jonson, *Slavery's Ghost: The Problem of Freedom in the Age of Emancipation* (Baltimore: Johns Hopkins University Press, 2011), pp. 50–84.

Font, Mauricio A., *Coffee and Transformation in São Paulo, Brazil* (Lanham: Lexington Books, 2010).

Fourie, Johan, *Our Long Walk to Economic Freedom: Lessons from 100,000 Years of Human History* (Cape Town: Tafelberg, 2021).

Frankema, Ewout, Erik Green, and Ellen Hillbom, 'Endogenous Processes of Colonial Settlement: The Success and Failure of European Settler Farming in Sub-Saharan Africa', *Revista de Historia Económica*, 34:2 (2016), 237–65.

——, and Marlous van Waijenburg, 'Metropolitan Blueprints of Colonial Taxation? Lessons from Fiscal Capacity Building in British and French Africa, c. 1880–1940', *JAH*, 55:3 (2014), 371–400.

——, Jeffrey Williamson, and Pieter Woltjer, 'An Economic Rationale for the West African Scramble? The Commercial Transition and the Commodity Price Boom of 1835–1885', *Journal of Economic History*, 78:1 (2018), 231–67.

Fréchou, Hubert, 'Les plantations européennes en Côte d'Ivoire', *Cahiers d'outre-mer*, 8:29 (1955), 56–83.

Freudenthal, Aida, 'Angola', in A. H. de Oliveira Marques (ed.), *O império africano, 1890–1930* (Lisbon: Editorial Estampa, 2001), pp. 259–467.

——, *Arimos e fazendas: A transição agrária em Angola* (Luanda: Chá de Caxinde, 2005).

Gago, Maria do Mar, 'How Green was Portuguese Colonialism? Agronomists and Coffee in Interwar Angola', in Ana Delicado, Nuno Domingos, and Luís de Sousa (eds), *Changing Societies: Legacies and Challenges*, vol. 3, *The Diverse Worlds of Sustainability* (Lisbon: Instituto de Ciências Sociais, 2018), pp. 229–46.

——, 'Moving Coffee from the Forests of Colonial Angola to the Breakfast Tables of Main Street America, 1940–1961', in John Krige (ed.), *Knowledge Flows in a Global Age: A Transnational Approach* (Chicago: Chicago University Press, 2022), pp. 231–52.

Garvin, Diana, 'The Italian Coffee Triangle: From Brazilian *Colonos* to Ethiopian *Colonialisti*', *Modern Italy*, 26:3 (2021), 291–312.

Gaspar, Abílio Mendes, *Programa de melhoramento do cafeeiro robusta em Angola* (Nova Lisbon: Instituto de Investigação Agronómica de Angola, 1969).

Giacomin, Valeria, 'The Transformation of the Global Palm Oil Cluster: Dynamics of Cluster Competition between Africa and Southeast Asia (c.1900–1970)', *JGH* 13:3 (2018), 374–98.

Gonçalves, Márcia, 'Of Peasants and Settlers: Ideals of Portugueseness, Imperial Nationalism and European Settlement in Africa, c.1930–c.1945', *European Review of History: Revue Européene d'Histoire*, 25:1 (2018), 166–86.

Gourgel, Aniceto, *A povoação de Zavula na época colonial: Província do Kwanza-Norte (principio do sec. XX até 1974)* (Luanda: Self-published, 2012).

Grabs, Janina, and Stefano Ponte, 'The Evolution of Power in the Global Coffee Value Chain and Production Network', *Journal of Economic Geography*, 19:4 (2019), 803–28.

Grant, Kevin, *A Civilised Savagery: Britain and the New Slaveries in Africa, 1884–1926* (New York: Routledge, 2005).

Green, Toby, 'Baculamento or Encomienda?', *Journal of Global Slavery*, 2:3 (2017), 310–36.

——, *A Fistful of Shells: West Africa from the Rise of the Slave Trade to the Age of Revolution* (Chicago: University of Chicago Press, 2019).

Gudmundson, Lowell W., 'On Paths Not Taken: Commercial Capital and Coffee Production in Costa Rica', in William Gervase Clarence-Smith and Steven Topik (eds), *The Global Coffee Economy in Africa, Asia, and Latin America, 1500–1989* (Cambridge: Cambridge University Press, 2003), pp. 335–59.

Guthrie, Zachary Kagan, *Bound for Work: Labor, Mobility, and Colonial Rule in Central Mozambique, 1940–1965* (Charlottesville: University of Virginia Press, 2018).

Haarer, Alec Ernest, *Modern Coffee Production* (London: Leonard Hill, 1958).

——, *Coffee Growing* (Oxford: Oxford University Press, 1963).

Hansen, Karen Tranberg, *Salaula: The World of Secondhand Clothing and Zambia* (Chicago: University of Chicago Press, 2000).

Harries, Patrick, *Work, Culture and Identity: Migrant Laborers in Mozambique and South Africa, c. 1860–1910* (Johannesburg: Witwatersrand University Press, 1994).

Harris, John, 'Circuits of Wealth, Circuits of Sorrow: Financing the Illegal Transatlantic Slave Trade in the Age of Suppression, 1850–66', *JGH*, 11:3 (2016), 409–29.

——, *The Last Slave Ships: New York and the End of the Middle Passage* (New Haven: Yale University Press, 2020).

Hazareesingh, Sandip, and Haro Maat, 'Anti-Commodities Revisited: Food, Culture, and Resistance', in Jonathan Curry-Machado, Jean Stubbs, William Gervase Clarence-Smith, and Jelmer Vos (eds), *The Oxford Handbook of Commodity History* (Oxford: Oxford University Press, 2024), pp. 65–83.

Herlin, Susan J., 'Brazil and the Commercialization of Kongo, 1840–1870', in José C. Curto and Paul E. Lovejoy (eds), *Enslaving Connections: Changing Cultures of Africa and Brazil during the Era of Slavery* (Amherst: Humanity Books, 2004), pp. 265–87.

Higgs, Catherine, *Chocolate Islands: Cocoa, Slavery, and Colonial Africa* (Athens: Ohio University Press, 2013).

Hill, Polly, *Studies in Rural Capitalism in West Africa* (Cambridge: Cambridge University Press, 1970).

——, *Migrant Cocoa-Farmers of Southern Ghana: A Study in Rural Capitalism*, 2nd edn (Oxford: James Currey, 1997).

Hopkins, A. G., *An Economic History of West Africa* (New York: Columbia University Press, 1973).

——, 'Innovation in a Colonial Context: African Origins of the Nigerian Cocoa-Farming Industry, 1880–1920', in Clive Dewey and A. G. Hopkins (eds), *The Imperial Impact: Studies in the Economic History of Africa and India* (London: Athlone Press, 1978), pp. 83–96.

——, 'Property Rights and Empire Building: Britain's Annexation of Lagos, 1861', *Journal of Economic History*, 40:4 (1980), 777–98.

——, 'The "New International Economic Order" in the Nineteenth Century: Britain's First Development Plan for Africa', in Robin Law (ed.), *From Slave Trade to 'Legitimate' Commerce: The Commercial Transition in Nineteenth-Century West Africa* (Cambridge: Cambridge University Press, 1995), pp. 240–64.

———, *Capitalism in the Colonies: African Merchants in Lagos, 1851–1931* (Princeton: Princeton University Press, 2024).

Houk, Richard J., 'Recent Developments in the Portuguese Congo', *Geographical Review*, 48:2 (1958), 201–21.

Hunt, Nancy Rose, *A Nervous State: Violence, Remedies, and Reverie in Colonial Congo* (Durham: Duke University Press, 2016).

Hyde, David, '"Paying for the Emergency by Displacing the Settlers": Global Coffee and Rural Restructuring in Late Colonial Kenya', *JGH*, 4:1 (2009), 81–103.

Isaacman, Allen F., *Cotton is the Mother of Poverty: Peasants, Work, and Rural Struggle in Colonial Mozambique, 1938–1961* (Cape Town: Heinemann, 1996).

Jacks, David S., 'From Boom to Bust: A Typology of Real Commodity Prices in the Long Run', *Cliometrica*, 13:2 (2019), 202–20.

Jerónimo, Miguel Bandeira, *The 'Civilising Mission' of Portuguese Colonialism, 1870–1930* (Basingstoke: Palgrave Macmillan, 2015).

———, 'Repressive Developmentalism: Idioms, Repertoires, and Trajectories in Late Colonialism', in Martin Thomas and Andrew S. Thompson (eds), *The Oxford Handbook of the Ends of Empire* (Oxford: Oxford University Press, 2018), pp. 537–54.

———, 'A Robust Operation: Resettling, Security, and Development in Late Colonial Angola (1960s–1970s)', *Itinerario*, 44:1 (2020), 55–79.

———, and José Pedro Monteiro, 'Colonial Labour Internationalized: Portugal and the Decolonization Momentum (1945–1975)', *International History Review*, 42:3 (2020), 485–504.

Jha, Shalene, Christopher M. Bacon, Stacy M. Philpott, V. Ernesto Méndez, Peter Läderach, and Robert A. Rice, 'Shade Coffee: Update on a Disappearing Refuge for Biodiversity', *Bioscience*, 64:5 (2014), 416–28.

Jiménez, Michael F., '"From Plantation to Cup": Coffee and Capitalism in the United States, 1830–1930', in William Roseberry, Lowell Gudmundson, and Mario Samper Kutschenbach (eds), *Coffee, Society, and Power in Latin America* (Baltimore: Johns Hopkins University Press, 1995), pp. 38–64.

Joyce, Pedro Avelino, *O café nas nossas colonias* (Lisbon: Ilustração Portugueza, 1915).

Juif, Dácil, and Ewout Frankema, 'From Coercion to Compensation: Institutional Responses to Labour Scarcity in the Central African Copperbelt', *Journal of Institutional Economics*, 14:2 (2018), 313–43.

Kale, Madhavi, *Fragments of Empire: Capital, Slavery, and Indian Indentured Labor Migration in the British Caribbean* (Philadelphia: University of Pennsylvania Press, 1998).

Keese, Alexander, *Living with Ambiguity: Integrating an African Elite in French and Portuguese Africa, 1930–61* (Stuttgart: Franz Steiner Verlag, 2007).

———, 'The Constraints of Late Colonial Reform Policy: Forced Labour Scandals in the Portuguese Congo (Angola) and the Limits of Reform under Authoritarian Colonial Rule, 1955–61', *Portuguese Studies*, 28:2 (2012), 186–200.

———, 'Searching for the Reluctant Hands: Obsession, Ambivalence and the Practice of Organising Involuntary Labour in Colonial Cuanza-Sul and Malange Districts, Angola, 1926–1945', *Journal of Imperial and Commonwealth History*, 41:2 (2013), 238–58.

Kelly, Alexandra Celia, *Consuming Ivory: Mercantile Legacies of East Africa and New England* (Seattle: University of Washington Press, 2021).

Klein, Herbert S., *African Slavery in Latin America and the Caribbean* (Oxford: Oxford University Press, 1986).

——, and Francisco Vidal Luna, *Slavery in Brazil* (Cambridge: Cambridge University Press, 2010).

Krug, C., and R. A. De Poerck, *World Coffee Survey* (Rome: FAO, 1968).

Law, Robin (ed.), *From Slave Trade to 'Legitimate' Commerce: The Commercial Transition in Nineteenth-Century West Africa* (Cambridge: Cambridge University Press, 1995).

——, *Ouidah: The Social History of a West African Slaving 'Port', 1727–1892* (Athens: Ohio University Press, 2004).

——, Suzanne Schwarz, and Silke Strickrodt (eds), *Commercial Agriculture, the Slave Trade and Slavery in Atlantic Africa* (Woodbridge: James Currey, 2013).

Likaka, Osumaka, *Rural Society and Cotton in Colonial Zaire* (Madison: University of Wisconsin Press, 1997).

Lima, Tania Andrade, 'Keeping a Tight Lid: The Architecture and Landscape Design of Coffee Plantations in Nineteenth-Century Rio de Janeiro, Brazil', *Review (Fernand Braudel Center)*, 34: 1/2 (2011): 193–215.

Link, Stefan, and Noam Maggor, 'The United States as a Developing Nation: Revisiting the Peculiarities of American History', *Past and Present*, 246 (2020), 269–306.

Lofkrantz, Jennifer, and Olatunji Ojo, 'Slavery, Freedom, and Failed Ransom Negotiations in West Africa, 1730–1900', *JAH*, 53:1 (2012), 25–44.

Lourenço, Fausto Martins, 'História do café robusta em Angola', *Revista de Ciências Agrárias*, 15:3 (1992), 57–117; 15:4 (1992), 85–119; 16:4 (1993), 35–80.

Lovejoy, Paul E., and David Richardson, 'The Business of Slaving: Pawnship in Western Africa, c. 1600–1810', *JAH*, 42:1 (2001), 67–89.

Lu, Sidney Xu, 'A Great Convergence: The American Frontier and the Origins of Japanese Migration to Brazil', *JGH*, 17:1 (2022), 109–27.

Lucassen, Jan, *The Story of Work: A New History of Humankind* (New Haven: Yale University Press, 2021).

Luttinger, Nina, and Gregory Dictum, *The Coffee Book: Anatomy of an Industry from Crop to the Last Drop*, rev. edn (New York: New Press, 2006).

Lynn, Martin, *Commerce and Economic Change in West Africa: The Palm Oil Trade in the Nineteenth Century* (Cambridge: Cambridge University Press, 1997).

Machado, Pedro, *Ocean of Trade: South Asian Merchants, Africa and the Indian Ocean, c.1750–1850* (Cambridge: Cambridge University Press, 2014).

McClellan, Charles W., 'Land, Labor, and Coffee: The South's Role in Ethiopian Self-Reliance, 1889–1935', *AEH*, 9 (1980), 69–83.

Manjapra, Kris, 'Plantation Dispossessions: The Global Travel of Agricultural Racial Capitalism', in Sven Beckert and Christine Desan (eds), *American Capitalism: New Histories* (New York: Columbia University Press, 2018), pp. 361–88.

——, *Colonialism in Global Perspective* (Cambridge: Cambridge University Press, 2020).

Mann, Kristin, *Slavery and the Birth of an African City: Lagos, 1760–1900* (Bloomington: Indiana University Press, 2007).

Marques, João Pedro, *Os sons do silêncio: O Portugal de Oitocentos e a abolição do tráfico de escravos* (Lisbon: Imprensa de Ciência Sociais, 1999).

———, 'Arsénio Pompílio Pompeu de Carpo: Um percurso negreiro no século XIX', *Análise Social*, 36:160 (2001), 609–38.

———, *Sá da Bandeira e o fim da escravidão: Vitória da moral, desforra do interesse* (Lisbon: Imprense de Ciências Sociais, 2008).

Marquese, Rafael de Bivar, 'African Diaspora, Slavery, and the Paraiba Valley Coffee Plantation Landscape: Nineteenth-Century Brazil', *Review (Fernand Braudel Center)*, 31:2 (2008), 195–216.

Martin, Phyllis M., *Leisure and Society in Colonial Brazzaville* (Cambridge: Cambridge University Press, 1995).

Martino, Henrique, '"Panya": Economies of Deception and the Discontinuities of Indentured Labour Recruitment and the Slave Trade, Nigeria and Fernando Pó, 1890s–1940s', *AEH*, 44:1 (2016), 91–129.

———, '*Dash*-Peonage: The Contradictions of Debt Bondage in the Colonial Plantations of Fernando Pó', *Africa*, 87:1 (2017), 53–78.

Martins, Conceição Andrade, 'Trabalho e condições de vida em Porugal (1850–1913)', *Análise Social*, 32:142 (1997), 483–535.

Mata, Maria Eugénia, Leonor Fernandes Ferreira, and João Pereira Dos Santos, 'Success and Failure in Portuguese Colonial Africa: The Case of the Cazengo Agricultural Company (1900–1945)', *Entreprises et histoire*, 3:88 (2017), 53–73.

Maul, Daniel Roger, 'The International Labour Organization and the Struggle against Forced Labour from 1919 to the Present', *Labor History*, 48:4 (2007), 477–500.

McCann, James C., *Green Land, Brown Land, Black Land: An Environmental History of Africa, 1800–1990* (Oxford: James Currey, 1999).

McCook, Stuart, *Coffee Is Not Forever: A Global History of the Coffee Leaf Rust* (Athens: Ohio University Press, 2019).

McCreery, David, 'Wage Labor, Free Labor, and Vagrancy Laws: The Transition to Capitalism in Guatemala, 1920–1945', in William Roseberry, Lowell Gudmundson, and Mario Samper Kutschenbach (eds), *Coffee, Society, and Power in Latin America* (Baltimore: Johns Hopkins University Press, 1995), pp. 206–31.

———, 'Coffee and Indigenous Labor in Guatemala, 1871–1980', in William Gervase Clarence-Smith and Steven Topik (eds), *The Global Coffee Economy in Africa, Asia, and Latin America, 1500–1989* (Cambridge: Cambridge University Press, 2003), pp. 191–208.

Mendes, Afonso, 'A promoção das massas rurais indigenas', *Estudos Ultramarinos*, 7 (1957–8), 9–29.

Meylan, Louise, Christian Gary, Clémentine Allinne, Jorge Ortiz, Louise Jackson, and Bruno Rapidel, 'Evaluating the Effect of Shade Trees on Provision of Ecosystem Services in Intensively Managed Coffee Plantations', *Agriculture, Ecosystems & Environment*, 245 (2017), 32–42.

Miers, Suzanne, *Slavery in the Twentieth Century: The Evolution of a Global Problem* (Walnut Creek: AltaMira Press, 2003).

Miller, Joseph C., *Way of Death: Merchant Capitalism and the Angolan Slave Trade, 1730–1830* (Madison: University of Wisconsin Press, 1988).

Monteiro, José Pedro, *Portugal e a questão do trabalho forçado: Um império sob escrutínio (1944–1962)* (Lisbon: Edições 70, 2018).

Morris, Jonathan, *Coffee: A Global History* (London: Reaktion Books, 2019).

Mosley, Paul, *The Settler Economies: Studies in the Economic History of Kenya and Southern Rhodesia 1900–1963* (Cambridge: Cambridge University Press, 1983).

Moya, José C., 'Modernization, Modernity, and the Trans/formation of the Atlantic World in the Nineteenth Century' in Jorge Canizares-Esguerra and Erik R. Seeman (eds), *The Atlantic in Global History, 1500–2000*, 2nd edn (New York: Routledge, 2018), pp. 187–207.

Munro, J. Forbes, *Africa and the International Economy, 1800–1960* (London: J. M. Dent, 1976).

Murray, David R., *Odious Commerce: Britain, Spain and the Abolition of the Cuban Slave Trade* (Cambridge: Cambridge University Press, 1981).

Neto, Maria da Conceição, 'De Escravos a "Serviçais", de "Serviçais" a "Contratados": Omissões, perceções e equívocos na história do trabalho africano na Angola colonial', *Cadernos de Estudos Africanos*, 33 (2017), 107–29.

Northrup, David, 'The Compatibility of the Slave and Palm Oil Trades in the Bight of Biafra', *JAH*, 17:3 (1976), 353–64.

——, *Indentured Labor in the Age of Imperialism, 1834–1922* (Cambridge: Cambridge University Press, 1995).

Nwabughuogu, Anthony I., 'From Wealthy Entrepreneurs to Petty Traders: The Decline of African Middlemen in Eastern Nigeria, 1900–1950', *JAH*, 23:3 (1982), 365–79.

Oliveira, Mário António de, 'Para a história de trabalho em Angola', *Trabalho*, 2 (Luanda, 1963), offprint.

Oliveira, Vanessa, *Slave Trade and Abolition: Gender, Commerce, and Economic Transition in Luanda* (Madison: University of Wisconsin Press, 2021).

Olukoju, Ayodeji, 'Accumulation and Conspicuous Consumption: The Poverty of Entrepreneurship in Western Nigeria, ca. 1850–1930', in Emmanuel Akyeampong, Robert H. Bates, Nathan Nunn, and James A. Robinson (eds), *Africa's Development in Historical Perspective* (Cambridge: Cambridge University Press, 2014), pp. 208–30.

Paquette, Gabriel, *Imperial Portugal in the Age of Revolutions: The Luso-Brazilian World, c. 1770–1850* (Cambridge: Cambridge University Press, 2013).

Paige, Jeffery M., *Agrarian Revolution: Social Movements and Export Agriculture in the Underdeveloped World* (New York: Free Press, 1975).

Palacios, Marco, *Coffee in Colombia: An Economic, Social and Political History* (Cambridge: Cambridge University Press, 1980).

Pélissier, René, *La colonie du minotaure: Nationalismes et révoltes en Angola (1926–1961)* (Orgeval: Pélissier, 1978).

——, *História das campanhas de Angola: Resistência e revoltas 1845–1941* (Lisbon: Editorial Estampa, 1997).

Pendergrast, Mark, *Uncommon Grounds: The History of Coffee and How It Transformed Our World* (New York: Basic Books, 2010).

Pereira, Joana Dias, 'Colonialism and Customary Land Tenure in Africa: Portuguese Representations and Policies during the 19th and 20th Centuries', *African Studies*, 82:3–4 (2023), 332–47.

Picão, José da Silva, *Através dos campos: Usos e costumes agrícolo-alentejanos* (Lisbon: Etnográfica Press, 1983).

Picó, Fernando, 'Coffee and the Rise of Commercial Agriculture in Puerto Rico's Highlands: The Occupation and Loss of Land in Guaonico and Roncador (Utuado), 1833–1900', in William Roseberry, Lowell Gudmundson, and Mario Samper Kutschenbach (eds), *Coffee, Society, and Power in Latin America* (Baltimore: Johns Hopkins University Press, 1995), pp. 94–111.

Pimenta, Fernando Tavares, 'White Settler Politics and Euro-African Nationalism in Angola, 1945–1975', in Edward Cavanagh and Lorenzo Veracini (eds), *The Routledge Handbook of the History of Settler Colonialism* (Abingdon: Routledge, 2017), pp. 277–89.

Pinto, Françoise Latour de Veiga, *Le Portugal et le Congo au XIXe siècle* (Paris: Presses Universitaires de France, 1972).

Pitcher, Anne, 'Sowing the Seeds of Failure: Early Portuguese Cotton Cultivation in Angola and Mozambique, 1820–1926', *JAH*, 17:1 (1991), 43–70.

Prestholdt, Jeremy, *Domesticating the World: African Consumerism and the Genealogies of Globalization* (Berkeley: University of California Press, 2008).

——, 'Africa and the Global Lives of Things', in Frank Trentmann (ed.), *Oxford Handbook of the History of Consumption* (Oxford: Oxford University Press, 2012), pp. 85–108.

Proença, Maria Cândida, 'A questão colonial', in Fernando Rosas e Maria Fernanda Rollo (eds), *História da Primeira República Portuguesa* (Lisbon: Tinta-da-china, 2009), pp. 205–28.

Purseglove, John William, *Tropical Crops: Dicotyledons* (2 vols, London: Longmans, 1968).

Radetzki, Marian, 'The Anatomy of Three Commodity Booms', *Resources Policy*, 31:1 (2006), 56–64.

Rapley, John, *Ivoirien Capitalism: African Entrepreneurs in Côte d'Ivoire* (Boulder: Lynne Rienner, 1993).

Richards, John F., 'Toward a Global System of Property Rights in Land', in Edmund Burke III and Kenneth Pomeranz (eds), *The Environment and World History* (Berkeley: University of California Press, 2009), pp. 54–78.

Richards, Paul, *Indigenous Agricultural Revolution: Ecology and Food Production in West Africa* (London: Hutchinson, 1985).

Richardson, David, and Filipa Ribeiro da Silva (eds), *Networks and Trans-Cultural Exchange: Slave Trading in the South Atlantic, 1590–1867* (Leiden: Brill, 2015).

Rimmer, Douglas, *Staying Poor: Ghana's Political Economy, 1950–1990* (Oxford: Pergamon Press, 1992).

Rodney, Walter, *How Europe Underdeveloped Africa* (London: Verso, 2018).

Rood, Daniel, *The Reinvention of Atlantic Slavery: Technology, Labor, Race, and Capitalism in the Greater Caribbean* (New York: Oxford University Press, 2017).

Roseberry, William 'Introduction', in William Roseberry, Lowell Gudmundson, and Mario Samper Kutschbach (eds), *Coffee, Society, and Power in Latin America* (Baltimore: Johns Hopkins University Press, 1995), pp. 1–37.

——, Lowell Gudmundson, and Mario Samper Kutschbach (eds), *Coffee, Society, and Power in Latin America* (Baltimore: Johns Hopkins University Press, 1995).

Rosenfeld, Gavriel D., 'Whither "What If" History?', *History and Theory*, 53 (2014), 451–67.

Ross, Corey, 'The Plantation Paradigm: Colonial Agronomy, African Farmers, and the Global Cocoa Boom, 1870s–1940s', *JGH*, 9:1 (2014), 49–71.

Ross, Robert, *Things Change: Black Material Culture and the Development of a Consumer Society in South Africa, 1800–2020* (Leiden: Brill, 2023).

Rowe, J. W. F., *The World's Coffee* (London: Her Majesty's Stationery Office, 1963).

Salojärvi, Jarkko, Aditi Rambani, Zhe Yu *et al.*, 'The Genome and Population Genomics of Allopolyploid *Coffea arabica* Reveal the Diversification History of Modern Coffee Cultivars', *Nature Genetics*, 56 (2024), 721–31.

Rus, Jan, 'Coffee and the Recolonization of Highland Chiapas, Mexico: Indian Communities and Plantation Labor, 1892–1912', in William Gervase Clarence-Smith and Steven Topik (eds), *The Global Coffee Economy in Africa, Asia, and Latin America, 1500–1989* (Cambridge: Cambridge University Press), pp. 257–85.

Samper, Mario, and Radin Fernando, 'Appendix: Historical Statistics of Coffee Production and Trade from 1700 to 1960', in William Gervase Clarence-Smith and Steven Topik (eds), *The Global Coffee Economy in Africa, Asia, and Latin America, 1500–1989* (Cambridge: Cambridge University Press), pp. 411–62.

Santos, José de Almeida, 'João Guilherme Pereira Barboza – O Grande Pioneiro do Cazengo', *Boletim Cultural da Câmara Municipal de Luanda*, 36 (1972), 27–32.

Santos, Oliveira, 'O problema das terras em Angola', *Estudos ultramarinos*, 7 (1957–8), 61–81.

Scanlan, Padraic X., 'The Colonial Rebirth of British Anti-Slavery: The Liberated African Villages of Sierra Leone, 1815–1824', *American Historical Review*, 121:4 (2016), 1760–1900.

Schwarz, Suzanne, 'A Just and Honourable Commerce: Abolitionist Experimentation in Sierra Leone in the Late Eighteenth and Early Nineteenth Centuries', *AEH*, 45:1 (2017), 1–45.

Scott, James C., *Seeing Like a State: How Certain Schemes to Improve the Human Condition Have Failed* (London: Yale University Press, 2020).

Sedgewick, Augustine, *Coffeeland: A History* (Dublin: Penguin Books, 2020).

Seibert, Julia, 'More Continuity than Change? New Forms of Unfree Labour in the Belgian Congo, 1908–1960', in Marcel van der Linden (ed.), *Humanitarian Intervention and Changing Labor Relations: The Long-Term Consequences of the Abolition of the Slave Trade* (Leiden: Brill, 2011), pp. 369–86.

Seixas, Margarida, 'O trabalho escravo e o trabalho forçado na colonização portuguesa oitocentista: Uma análise histórico-jurídica', *Revista Portuguesa de História*, 46 (2015), 217–36.

Seleti, Yonah, 'Finance Capital and the Coffee Industry of Angola, 1865–1895', *Transafrican Journal of History*, 16 (1987), 63–77.

Silva, Fernando Diogo da, *O Huambo: Mão-de-obra rural no mercado de trabalho de Angola* (Luanda: Fundo de Acção Social no Trabalho em Angola, 1968).

Silva, Daniel B. Domingues da, *The Atlantic Slave Trade from West Central Africa, 1780–1867* (Cambridge: Cambridge University Press, 2017).

Soumonni, Elisée, 'The Compatibility of the Slave and Palm Oil Trades in Dahomey, 1818–1858', in Robin Law (ed.), *From Slave Trade to 'Legitimate' Commerce: The*

Commercial Transition in Nineteenth-Century West Africa (Cambridge: Cambridge University Press, 1995), pp. 78–92.

Sousa, Alfredo de, *Ensaio de análise económica do café* (Lisbon: Junta de Investigação do Ultramar, 1958).

Stanley, Amy Dru, *From Bondage to Contract: Wage Labor, Marriage, and the Market in the Age of Slave Emancipation* (Cambridge: Cambridge University Press, 1998).

Stanziani, Alessandro, 'Introduction: Labour Institutions in a Global Perspective, from the Seventeenth to the Twentieth Century', *International Review of Social History*, 54 (2009), 351–8.

——, 'Serfs, Slaves, or Wage Earners? The Legal Status of Labour in Russia from a Comparative Perspective, from the Sixteenth to the Nineteenth Century', *JGH*, 3:2 (2008), 183–202.

Steinfeld, Robert J., *Coercion, Contract, and Free Labor in the Nineteenth Century* (Cambridge: Cambridge University Press, 2001).

Stolcke, Verena, 'The Labors of Coffee in Latin America: The Hidden Charm of Family Labor and Self-Provisioning', in William Roseberry, Lowell Gudmundson, and Mario Samper Kutschbach (eds), *Coffee, Society, and Power in Latin America* (Baltimore: Johns Hopkins University Press, 1995), pp. 65–93.

Strickrodt, Silke, *Afro-European Trade in the Atlantic World: The Western Slave Coast, c.1550–c.1885* (Woodbridge: James Currey, 2015).

Talbot, John M., *Grounds for Agreement: The Political Economy of the Coffee Commodity Chain* (Lanham: Rowman & Littlefield Publishers, 2004).

Throup, David W., 'The Origins of Mau Mau', *African Affairs*, 84:336 (1985), 399–433.

Tilley, Helen, *Africa as a Living Laboratory: Empire, Development, and the Problem of Scientific Knowledge, 1870–1950* (Chicago: University of Chicago Press, 2011).

Tilly, Charles, *Roads from Past to Future* (Lanham: Rowman & Littlefield, 1997).

Topik, Steven C., 'Coffee', in Steven C. Topik and Allen Wells (eds), *The Second Conquest of Latin America: Coffee, Henequen, and Oil during the Export Boom, 1850–1930* (Austin: University of Texas Press, 1998), pp. 37–84.

——, 'The Integration of the World Coffee market', in William Gervase Clarence-Smith and Steven Topik (eds), *The Global Coffee Economy in Africa, Asia, and Latin America, 1500–1989* (Cambridge: Cambridge University Press, 2003), pp. 21–49.

——, and William Gervase Clarence-Smith, 'Conclusion: New Propositions and a Research Agenda', in William Gervase Clarence-Smith and Steven Topik (eds), *The Global Coffee Economy in Africa, Asia, and Latin America, 1500–1989* (Cambridge: Cambridge University Press, 2003), pp. 385–410.

——, and Allen Wells, 'Commodity Chains in a Global Economy', in Emily Rosenberg (ed.), *A World Connecting, 1760–1900* (Cambridge: Belknap Press of Harvard University Press, 2012), pp. 591–812.

Tosh, John, 'The Cash-Crop Revolution in Tropical Africa: An Agricultural Reappraisal', *African Affairs*, 79:314 (1980), 79–94.

Trentmann, Frank, 'Introduction', in Frank Trentmann (ed.), *The Oxford Handbook of the History of Consumption* (Oxford: Oxford University Press, 2012), pp. 1–19.

Ukers, William H., *All about Coffee* (New York: Tea and Coffee Trade Journal Company, 1922).

Van der Linden, Marcel, 'Dissecting Coerced Labor', in Marcel van der Linden and Magaly Rodriguez Garcia (eds), *On Coerced Labor: Work and Compulsion after Chattel Slavery* (Leiden: Brill, 2016), pp. 293–322.

Van Dongen, Irene S., 'Coffee Trade, Coffee Regions, and Coffee Ports in Angola', *Economic Geography*, 37:4 (1961), 320–46.

Van Melkebeke, Sven, *Dissimilar Coffee Frontiers: Mobilizing Labor and Land in the Lake Kivu Region, Congo and Rwanda (1760–1900/62)* (Leiden: Brill, 2020).

Van Norman, Jr, William C., *Shade-Grown Slavery: The Lives of Slaves on Coffee Plantations in Cuba* (Nashville: Vanderbilt University Press, 2013).

Vellut, Jean-Luc, 'Diversification de l'économie de cueilllette: Miel et cire dans les sociétés de la forêt claire d'Afrique centrale (c.1750–1950)', *AEH*, 7 (1979), 93–112.

Veracini, Lorenzo, *Settler Colonialism: A Theoretical Overview* (Basingstoke: Palgrave Macmillan, 2010).

——, 'Introduction: Settler Colonialism as a Distinct Mode of Domination', in Edward Cavanagh and Lorenzo Veracini (eds), *The Routledge Handbook of the History of Settler Colonialism* (Abingdon: Routledge, 2017), pp. 1–8.

Vicente, Fernando Paula, *Angola, Colonização, Descolonização: António Cordeiro de Oliveira, pioneiro do Norte, fundador do Songo* (Lisbon: edição do autor, 2014).

Viehover, Arno, and H. A. Lepper, 'Robusta Coffee', *Journal of the Association of Official Agricultural Chemists* 5:2 (1921), 274–88.

Vinale, Adriano, '(Hi)story-Telling: An Introduction to Italian Alternate and Counterfactual History', *History*, 108:382 (2023), 355–64.

Vos, Jelmer, '"Without the Slave Trade, No Recruitment": From Slave Trading to "Migrant Recruitment" in the Lower Congo, 1830–1890', in Benjamin N. Lawrance and Richard L. Roberts (eds), *Trafficking in Slavery's Wake: Law and the Experiences of Women and Children in Africa* (Athens: Ohio University Press, 2012), pp. 45–64.

——, *Kongo in the Age of Empire, 1860–1913: The Breakdown of a Moral Order* (Madison: University of Wisconsin Press, 2015).

——, 'What Angolans Got for Their Coffee: Connecting Histories of Labour and Consumption in Colonial Africa, c.1860–1960', in Devyani Gupta and Purba Hossain (eds), *Across Colonial Lines: Commodities, Networks and Empire Building* (London: Bloomsbury Academic: London, 2023), pp. 157–77.

——, 'Family and Labour in an Angolan Cash-Crop Economy, 1910', *History of the Family*, 29:2 (2024), 280–98.

——, and Paulo Teodoro de Matos, 'The Demography of Slavery in the Coffee Districts of Angola, c. 1800–70', *JAH*, 62: 2 (2021), 213–34.

Wheeler, Douglas L., 'The Forced Labour "System" in Angola, 1760–1900: Reassessing Origins and Persistence in the Context of Colonial Consolidation, Economic Growth and Reform Failures', in Centro de Estudos Africanos da Universidade do Porto (ed.), *Trabalho forçado africano: Experiências coloniais comparadas* (Porto: Campo das Letras, 2006), pp. 367–93.

——, 'The Galvão Report on Forced Labor (1947) in Historical Context and Perspective: The Trouble-Shooter Who was "Trouble"', *Portuguese Studies Review*, 16:1 (2008), 115–52.

Wickizer, Vernon Dale, *The World Coffee Economy, with Special Reference to Control Schemes* (Stanford: Food Research Institute, 1943).

Wolfe, Patrick, 'Settler Colonialism and the Elimination of the Native', *Journal of Genocide Research*, 8:4 (2006), 387–409.

Wrigley, Gordon, *Coffee* (Harlow: Longman, 1988).

Youé, Christopher, 'Black Squatters on White Farms: Segregation and Agrarian Change in Kenya, South Africa, and Rhodesia, 1902–1963', *International History Review*, 24:3 (2002), 558–602.

Zamparoni, Valdemir, 'Da escravatura ao trabalho forçado: Teorias e práticas', *Africana Studia*, 7 (2004), 299–325.

Unpublished dissertations

Amaral, Miguel Rebordão, 'Angola: Concessões de terra e direitos tradicionais (1760–1900): Análise de legislação' (Unpublished MA dissertation, University of Lisbon, 2017), <http://hdl.handle.net/10400.5/13879>.

Figueiredo, João de Castro Maia Veiga de, 'Política, escravatura e feitiçaria em Angola (séculos XVIII e XIX)' (Unpublished PhD dissertation, University of Coimbra, 2016), <http://hdl.handle.net/10316/29906>.

Mendes, Afonso, 'O trabalho assalariado em Angola' (Unpublished PhD dissertation, Instituto Superior de Ciências Sociais e Política Ultramarina, 1966).

Neto, Maria da Conceição, 'In Town and Out of Town: A Social History of Huambo (Angola), 1902–1961' (Unpublished PhD dissertation, University of London, 2012), <http://eprints.soas.ac.uk/13822>.

Salas, Esteban, 'Making Portuguese Colonial Governance: Slavery, Forced Labor, and Racial Ideology in the Interior from Benguela, 1760–1860' (Unpublished PhD dissertation, University of Notre Dame, 2021).

Seleti, Yonah Ngalaba, 'Portuguese Colonialism, Capitalism and the Angolan Coffee Industry: 1850–1950' (Unpublished PhD dissertation, Dalhousie University, 1987).

Silva, Maria do Mar de Mello Gago da, 'Robusta Empire: Coffee, Scientists and the Making of Colonial Angola (1760–1900)' (Unpublished PhD dissertation, University of Lisbon, 2018), <http://hdl.handle.net/10451/32678>.

Souza, Alan de Carvalho, 'Do Brasil para África: O café na viragem do império português (1760–1900)' (Unpublished PhD dissertation, University of Lisbon, 2020), <http://hdl.handle.net/10451/45282>.

Web-based sources

Antweiler, Werner, 'Foreign Currency Units per 1 British Pound, 1950–2023' (2024) <https://fx.sauder.ubc.ca/etc/GBPpages.pdf>.

Edvinsson, Rodney, 'Historical Currency Converter (test version 1.0)' (2016) <https://www.historicalstatistics.org/Currencyconverter.html>.

Lewin, Bryan, Daniele Giovannucci, and Panos Varangis, 'Coffee Markets: New Paradigms in Global Supply and Demand', World Bank Agriculture and Rural Development Discussion Paper No. 3 (2004), <http://dx.doi.org/10.2139/ssrn.996111>.

May, Peter H., Gilbert C. C. Mascarenhas, and Jason Potts, 'Sustainable Coffee Trade: The Role of Coffee Contracts' (2004), International Institute for Sustainable Development, <https://www.iisd.org/publications/report/sustainable-coffee-trade-role-coffee-contracts>.

Meneses, Maria Paula G., 'O "indígena" africano e o colono "europeu": A construção da diferença por processos legais', *e-cadernos CES*, 7 (2010) <http://journals.openedition.org/eces/403>.

Seixas, Margarida, 'Escravos e libertos no Boletim Oficial de Angola (1760–1900), II parte', *E-Revista de Estudos Interculturais do CEI-ISCAP*, 3 (2015), <https://doi.org/10.34630/erei.vi3.3917>.

SlaveVoyages (2019) <https://slavevoyages.org>.

United Nations General Assembly, 'Document A/6000/REV.1: Report of the Special Committee on the Situation with Regard to the Implementation of the Declaration on the Granting of Independence to Colonial Countries and Peoples' (New York, 1965), <https://digitallibrary.un.org/record/732453?ln=en>.

Van der Eng, Pierre, 'Food Supply in Java during War and Decolonisation, 1940–1950' (2008), MPRA Paper No. 8852, <https://mpra.ub.uni-muenchen.de/8852/>.

Van der Graaf, Andries Pieter, 'My Years in Angola, 1950–1970' (2012), typescript manuscript published online at <https://www.asclibrary.nl/docs/341217840.pdf> (Africa Studies Centre Library, University of Leiden).

Index

www.ingramcontent.com/pod-product-compliance
Lightning Source LLC
Jackson TN
JSHW010954040625
85590JS00002B/10
* 9 7 8 1 8 4 7 0 1 3 5 6 9 *